# Wiring Prometheus

# Wiring Prometheus

## Globalisation, History and Technology

Edited by Peter Lyth
and Helmuth Trischler

Aarhus University Press

*Wiring Prometheus*
© The authors and Aarhus University Press 2004
Cover design: Jørgen Sparre
Graphic design: Brandpunkt a|s, Viby J
Printed in Denmark by Scanprint a/s, Viby J


ISBN 87 7288 947 0


Published with financial support from
the Deutsches Museum, Munich


AARHUS UNIVERSITY PRESS
Langelandsgade 177
DK-8200 Aarhus N
Fax (+45) 8942 5380
www.unipress.dk

73 Lime Walk
Headington, Oxford OX3 7AD
United Kingdom
Fax (+44) 1865 750 079

Box 511
Oakville, CT 06779
USA
Fax (+1) 860 945 9468

# Contents

# Globalisation, History and Technology

## An Introduction

*Peter Lyth and Helmuth Trischler*

*"Only connect ... "*[1]

If one had to select a single word to symbolise the last decade of the 20th century it would have to be *globalisation*. The adjective *global* is now used to describe such a large number of phenomena sharing a transnational or world-encompassing character, that it has become truly ubiquitous. We have the global economy and the global trade and capital markets which support it. We have the global environment and the global pollution that is destroying it, we have global communications and the global culture that it seems to encourage, we have global tourism endangered by global terrorism and a global climate threatened by global warming. We have a global community of corporate executives buying and selling global enterprises, we have global scientists discussing their work at global conferences, and, as a result, we have global technology, one of the chief stimuli of the global economy. Thus the process of globalisation is universal. It should not surprise us, therefore, that its impact on everything from financial markets to local culture has been analysed and debated not only in the public arena by journalists and politicians but also, and more exhaustively, in a wide range of disciplines, by academics.

The idea of globalisation raises seminal questions. Is globalisation an historical process? Is it an inevitable, perhaps the final, stage of capitalism? It also confronts us with new challenges. Does globalisation mean the end of the nation state? And if so, how will governments protect and provide for the world's citizens in the future? Could that responsibility be assumed by transnational corporations, some of which already have a turnover in excess of the Gross National Product of many sovereign states?

This book does not aspire to provide any definitive answers to these questions, but aims instead to place globalisation in its *historical* context and to focus in particular on the role of *technology* in the globalisation process.[2] The evolution of technological systems over the last two hundred years undoubtedly ranks as one of the most absorbing subjects for the student of modern history. The line of argument followed in this work is that there is also an unmistakeable thread connecting that evolution with the unfolding pattern of globalisation, indeed in the final analysis, and at a broad, interdisciplinary level, "connection" may well be what globalisation is all about.

## Globalisation

Firstly, however, *what is globalisation*? It has been an influential concept in the social sciences since the beginning of the 1990s, and both sociologists and economists have discussed and debated its meaning. At a general level we can agree with
Martin Albrow that globalisation "refers to all those processes by which peoples of
the world are incorporated into a single world society."[3] However this does not get
us very far. Globalisation tends to mean different things to different people. For sociologists it has acquired a paradigmatic quality, superceding the debate on modernity and postmodernity in the understanding of social and cultural change. For
Anthony Giddens, for example, globalisation *is* modernity or, put another way,
modernity is inherently globalising as it "introduces new forms of world interdependence."[4] However Giddens also places *connection* at the centre of the globalisation process and describes "the intensification of worldwide social relations
which link distant localities in such a way that local happenings are shaped by
events occurring many miles away and vice versa."[5]

For economists, globalisation signifies a rapidly increasing level of world trade
and capital movements, made possible by falling transport costs and new information technology – indeed everyone seems to agree that the revolution in communications technology has been vital to globalisation. Capital markets are even more
globalised than product markets because money, like information, flows more easily than people and products.[6] Globalisation has also meant the global transfer of
technology, production and marketing facilities, and, to a more limited extent, the
global movement of labour. Thanks to strategic alliances, joint ventures, acquisi-
tions and mergers, firms are emerging for whom the transnational *network* is more
important than a centralised national bureaucracy.[7] The chief concern of economists and political scientists here would seem to be that the institutions of capitalism may not be adequate to the global tasks which now face them.[8] Since capital
and technology have become so mobile, Third World countries have the potential
to produce goods as efficiently as the developed countries yet at a fraction of the
cost. In this way globalisation can be a "job-killer" in the West and governments are
understandably concerned. Some scholars have focused on the growing impotence
of national governments in the formation of economic policy and the way globalisation encourages transnational concerns to "bypass" national politics.[9] The
chief agent in this erosion of national power is the transnational corporation
(TNC). Richard Barnet and John Cavanagh believe that because of globalisation and
the increasing tendency of companies to "roam the world," the nation state is not
only losing its authority but is threatened in one of its basic functions, namely the
ability to transform economic progress into increased welfare for its citizens.[10] As
"the first human institution with both the ideology and the technology to operate

on a global scale," TNCs also head the cast of actors in the process of globalisation; they are no less than "the revolutionary force of our time."[11] These global concerns, both now and in their earlier incarnation as multinational companies, have crossed many borders since the beginning of the 20th century and through their strategic alliances with one another, have been the main channel of technology transfer between nations. Today they are the key players in the global generation of technology and probably account for as much as 75% of industrial R&D in the advanced economies.[12] Their activity has had a profound effect on the economies of host nations, but it has not always been beneficial to national technology policies. When TNCs manufacture and sell their products in many different countries they promote a global standardisation of technology and this often conflicts with the aims of individual governments trying to preserve traditions and institutions of technological innovation as a source of national strength – "techno-nationalism" as it is known.[13]

The social scientists have helped us identify the characteristics of globalisation, but they are clearly divided as to its meaning. Beyond a general recognition that there is a greater degree of global inter*connectedness*, there is little agreement as to how globalisation should be conceptualised, how it works and where, if anywhere, it is leading us. Amongst economists and political scientists there is dispute between those who believe that globalisation is inevitable and we are all subject to the dictates of a global market economy, those who see globalisation as a myth which hides a world still divided up into developed and undeveloped regions, and those who believe that globalisation is not only new but also presents us with some worrying challenges for the future.[14]

We do not intend to directly engage the "meaning" debate on globalisation, instead we will concentrate on what we consider to be its chief characteristic. We argue that over the last two centuries, a technology-driven process has steadily raised the level of *connectedness* between different parts of the world; and globalisation is the result. Barnet and Cavanagh have identified four critical global networks – *connectedness* in its most modern form. These are global financial networks, global cultural networks (from TV to theme parks), global marketing networks, and global production networks (manufacturing everything from cigarettes to airliners).[15] What these four networks have in common is global communications technology, but technology not only connects, it also deconstructs existing networks and concentrations of power. A recently-proposed phenomenological approach to globalisation, which sees it as "new change" comparable to the Industrial Revolution of the early 19th century, has yielded a number of ideas which can be fitted into an explanatory framework for globalisation built around technology. Amongst the ideas in this approach the notions of boundary erosion, the replacement of hierarchy with heterarchy, and the diminution of legitimacy are the most important.[16]

Boundary erosion, or the blurring of the boundaries, or distinctions, between "in" and "out," and "us" and "them," is clearly evident in globalisation because the boundaries that exist in business, social, cultural and even political environments are eroded by the growing intensity and volume of trans-global interactions. At the same time control and government are *de*-centralised, so that hierarchies are replaced with heterarchies. In other words, vertically-structured forms of power and organisation, typical of the national state or the Chandlerian company, are replaced with horizontally-structured ones. Meanwhile the decline of organisational authority and responsibility which accompanies this process creates a legitimacy crisis for national bodies, both economic and political. Central control, whether of the government bureaucracy or the traditionally-organised company, is giving way to decentralised control, to a series of dispersed nodes of power, connected by global webs of capital and technology.

## History and Technology

Surprisingly it is only recently that historians have become aware that globalisation affects their discipline. Certainly *world history* has a lengthy tradition and has helped widen the view of historical storytellers, but in most cases *world history* has remained linked to the concept of the nation state.[17] Globalisation, however, calls for *global history;* history which treats the planet as a single structure. It is the history, perhaps, which can only have been written since the watershed occasion in July 1969 when man stood on the moon and was able to look back at the earth and gain for the first time an instinctive understanding of its fundamentally interdependent nature.

The contribution of history and historians to the debate on globalisation must be to place it firmly within the context of time and space – to interpret it as an historical process. The phenomenon of globalisation in the last third of the 20th century is not simply something which has been triggered by path-breaking innovations like the computer. The world-encompassing technology that is driving globalisation should instead be seen as the continuation (perhaps the climax) of long-established trends. If history is an open process with undefined ends, then global history must be built upon a full appreciation of the autonomy of historical progress. It needs to be concerned with the origins of the emerging global society and how its long-term development has been shaped by geographical, economic, political, social and technological factors. In particular, as Raymond Grew has argued, global history should acknowledge the association between historical change and technology – "to understand technology in terms of its social and intellectual context."[18]

According to *The Economist*, "globalisation – the shrinking of distance and the increase in interplay and interdependence – has been a theme of the whole century and longer."[19] Historians can confidently seek its origins in the mid-19th century. The 19th century was an age when both nation states and border-crossing technologies first appeared. There were few frontiers that mattered and in many respects the world resembled a global market, with money, goods and people flowing more or less freely. At the centre of this global market was Europe, which *connected* the world with the new technologies of the telegraph, radio and the telephone, and with "communications-based systems of control," such as the Gold Standard, which had enveloped "the world in global circuits of power" by 1900.[20] Britain had led the world into an era of free trade with the repeal of the Corn Laws in 1846 and from the late 1870s it encouraged international capital mobility (through the elimination of exchange risk) with the establishment of a global financial system based on the Gold Standard.[21]

But the technological foundations of the 19th century global economy were even more momentous and lasting. They were concentrated in two areas both of which are familiar to students of 20th century globalisation: communications and transport. The telegraph grew in importance from the second quarter of the 19th century and increased the efficiency of the market by speeding up the transfer of information between financial centres. In 1851 the first successful submarine telegraph cable was laid under the English Channel, linking London's capital market to mainland Europe and in 1866 a permanent transatlantic telegraph cable was laid.[22] Moreover the Morse Code, the telegraph's "software," became the global standard for sending messages along wires, a sort of "network protocol for the world's first internet."[23] By the time of Samuel Morse's death in 1872, the world was literally *wired* with telegraph lines and submarine cables. Matching this revolution in communications were major advances in transport, forging rapid new links between producers and consumers and dramatically lowering prices. Indeed thanks to canals, railroads, steamships and refrigeration, transport costs in the period of "first globalisation" from 1840 to 1914 may even have fallen faster than in the "second globalisation" of the late 20th century.[24] These advances in transport technology prompted a convergence of world commodity prices and a new degree of connection between national markets. To quote the economists Kevin O'Rourke and Jeffrey Williamson, in a passage that should strike a familiar chord to observers of late 20th century globalisation, in 1914

> there was hardly a village or town anywhere on the globe whose prices were not influenced by distant foreign markets, whose infrastructure was not financed by foreign capital, whose engineering, manufacturing, and even business skills were not imported from abroad … not everyone was happy with the new global economy. Farmers voiced populist complaints about railroads and bankers. Rich landowners demanded protection from cheap farm products. Workers pointed to un-

fair competition from imports made with cheap foreign labor and claimed that
their jobs were being robbed by immigrants ... domestic policy makers began to
feel they were losing their ability to manage prices, interest rates and markets;
they felt increasingly vulnerable to financial panic, industrial crisis and unfavourable price shocks generated in distant corners of the globe.[25]

What stopped this "first" globalisation dead in its tracks was of course the First
World War; the unsuccessful attempts to restore prewar conditions in the 1920s
and the slide into depression and autarky in the 1930s ensuring that the second
globalisation would be delayed for another fifty years.

What has happened since 1970, at the latest 1980, is the spawning, as the political scientist John Gray puts it, of radical new technologies which have accelerated
and widened the flow of goods and information to such an extent that
globalisation has become synonymous with capitalism itself. For Gray it is the
global spread and adoption of technology, even more than the ideology of free
markets which became so fashionable in the 1980s, which is the driving force of
this new globalised capitalism.[26] Indeed it does not require a great stretch of the
imagination to see technology itself as a new ideology and, notwithstanding the
negative voices of philosophers and theologians, even a religion with the potential
to unify the globe.

Just as one might select two technologies from the 19th century, say, the telegraph and the steam engine, to symbolise and explain the first globalisation, so the
20th has two technological systems which stand out from a long list of worthy can-
didates. These are firstly, aerospace and the air transport industry, and secondly,
the communications industry embodying the globalising promise of the telephone, television, and networked computer. Aerospace is the quintessential 20th
century high-tech industry: an arena, as Ruth Schwartz Cowan sees it, "in which
technological change has been both conspicuous and celebrated."[27] It has also been
vital to the globalisation process in its present form. Because of aircraft, and in particular the jet engine, global transport is now so efficient that product parts can be
manufactured all over the world, depending on the cost of labour, and assembled
close to the final sales market. And tourism, a past-time which until the 1960s was
limited to the prosperous middle-classes, has, thanks to the jet aircraft, not only become the largest single revenue earner in history but has allowed countless millions
to travel and acquaint themselves with other parts of the world – a genuine
globalisation of human experience. Indeed the economic implications of air travel
are no less dramatic as those of the steam engine in the 19th century. Meanwhile
the communications industry has been revolutionised by recent technologies such
as satellites, lasers, microchips and fibre-optics. One example will suffice: The main
reason for the astonishing expansion of long-distance telephone capacity in the

1990s, with all its implications for fax transmissions and the internet, was the rapid development of fibre-optic cables, "the oil pipelines of the information economy."[28]

The challenge that globalisation presents to governments still wedded to techno-nationalist agendas, and to individuals worried about their prospects for employment, is mirrored by the threat it is perceived to pose for national or local *culture*: there is a widespread fear that in the train of the economic globalisation comes cultural homogenisation. The idea that technology and communication networks can homogenise culture is an intriguing one that has not surprisingly engaged a number of scholars. The impact of globalisation on culture is a good example of the boundary erosion and de-legitimisation of vertical structures, referred to above. Modern communications technology has made it harder for governments to prohibit the things which they once did: imports of capital, computer software, pornography and ideas generally, because technology has eroded the boundaries between nation states. But globalisation has meant, above all, the *democratisation* of technology; it has become faster, cheaper and more widely available than ever before, and this is in contrast to the technology-led globalisation of the 19th century. Computerisation, miniaturisation, digitalisation, satellites and fibre-optics have allowed people in previously undeveloped parts of the world to communicate, manufacture, transmit news, money, pictures and knowledge. And nations acquiring this technology can catch up fast – take, for example, India's emergence as a major player in data processing. As Kenneth Boulding noticed long ago, technology feeds on democracy and the technology of globalisation will be harder to absorb and adopt where democracy has failed to take root, where there are still "authoritarian forms of organisation and government."[29]

If there is a global culture enveloping the world in the train of global technology, then, as Samuel P. Huntington has argued, it is a culture distinguished by the ideas of freedom of expression, free trade and democracy: it is a *western* culture and therefore bound to be at odds with local particularisms in the rest of the world.[30] The columnist Thomas Friedman has described how on a visit to Egypt he noticed how the lift attendant uttered a prayer from the Koran before he operated the elevator and concluded that while Americans identify easily with modernisation and technology because they increase individul choice, "in traditonal societies, such as Egypt's, the collective or the group is much more important than the individual and empowering the individual is equated with dividing society." Globalisation means not only "being forced to eat more Big Macs," but also "changing the relationship of the individual to his state and community in a way that they feel puts their society at the risk of disintegration."[31] In a similar vein the sociologist Roland Robertson has noted that globalisation is inevitably opposed to local cultures and endangers them; the distinction being between local culture, generally seen as embodying positive (because traditional) values, and global culture, which is seen in negative terms.[32] Local culture is obviously a powerful source of identity and pride, but the perception of a threat to it posed by globalisation has to be tempered with the knowledge that local jobs may depend on global connections and networks and many traditional societies may be willing to accept a measure of globalisation to ensure economic progress. In general it seems that the non-Western world wants to be modern without being Western – but is this possible? Or is it the nature of globalising technology to be so inherently Western that the technology cannot be acquired without the culture? In the case of the internet the whole world wants to be connected to the "net" but not necessarily acquire the cultural assumptions that go with it.

## Wiring Prometheus

We have argued that globalisation is a historical process and that technology and technological change have acted as catalysts. Moreover the main technologies involved, i.e. those in transport and communications, but also manufacturing production, are only fully optimised when they work in networks. This network effect applied to the launch of the telephone at the end of the 19th century and it applies to the internet at the beginning of the 21st. Some products, it seems, are only really useful when a lot of other people have them – when *Prometheus is wired*. In the following chapters the role of networks and technology in history is examined using a multidisciplinary and contextual approach, with the object of providing elements for the historicisation of globalisation studies.

According to this historicisation, there are *two* globalisations: the 19th century one that unified nations and the 20th century one that began to unravel them. In the 19th century technical innovation was the cement which held together the emerging nation states of 19th century Europe. Railroads (and a customs union) transformed Germany from a regional grouping into an institutional nation state, as predicted by the economist Friedrich List in 1841.[33] In the United States railroads and electrification sustained white settlement of the West and led to "networks of power" which united the nation in a new web of steel and wire.[34] In the second quarter of the 20th century aircraft were the dynamic elements in a complex new transport technology which strengthened the spirit of nationalism in a nationalistic age.[35]

By the second half of the 20th century, however, the thrust of technology had changed direction. It now began to erode the nation state as technical systems became increasingly transnational. After playing a major role in shaping history, the nation state now began to seem like its victim. Information technologies, in particular, have undermined national sovereignty by eliminating geographical and social distance – by making it possible for more and more people, ideas and goods to travel faster and safer through time and space.[36]

In the opening contribution to this volume *Bruce Mazlish* looks at the ties that have bound Europeans since early modern times, dividing them into three chronological forms: patronage, connections and networks. The oldest, patronage, was a private interdependent relationship between individuals or families with a very particular set of "courtly" rules. With the Enlightenment and then the Industrial Revolution, patronage gave way to connections for a while, characterising the transition from an aristocratic to a bourgeois society. Finally connections became networks in a computer-driven world of increasing social equality. Networks, as *Mazlish* uses the term – in the sense of patronage and connections – may refer to a collection of old boys or old girls, but in the late 20th century are more likely to mean satellite television and the world wide web. In his chapter the economic historian *Rainer Fremdling* concentrates on the 19th century and the "first" globalisation. He argues that the evolving free trade regime and falling transport costs in the 19th century – particularly technological breakthroughs in the development of the steam engine – led to a high level of foreign trade between European nations which had reached the proportions of "a globalised market" by the First World War. *Stephan Lindner* takes up the theme with an study of a traditional 19th century industry: textiles. He argues that the globalisation of the spinning and weaving processes, and the loss of supremacy in textiles by European producers, was caused by the export of advanced textile machinery and the tendency of the Europeans to establish overseas production facilities. Moving to new looms needed a more intensive use of the machines to cover their capital cost, i.e. three shifts instead of one, and this intensification of labour use was only possible beyond Europe's borders. Another traditional industry is considered by *Paul Rosen*. Bicycles have now become "global" products; no matter where they are assembled, they are likely to consist of components manufactured in a large number of countries in Asia, Europe and North America. The British bicycle industry, after losing its markets to Far Eastern competitors, has sought to restructure itself and adapt to new technologies in bicycle production as well as changes in the culture of cycling. The chapter traces the interweaving of industry and culture in the mountain bike boom of the 1980s and how this global trend influenced the British industry's revival.

In his chapter *Wolf Schäfer* argues that we should no longer treat *time* as different for people around the globe at different stages of economic or social development. We can no longer treat people as "backward" (a chronometrical concept) or "behind the time." Globalisation means global time, as the factory worker in China is connected to the stock broker in New York and through him to the factory worker in Detroit; globalisation subjects us all to the same forces and constraints, and at the same time. Moreover in a society based on the exchange of information, a premium is be placed on time and the speed of interchange and transaction; distance, as Daniel Bell has observed, "becomes a function not of space but of time; and the costs of time and the rapidity of communication become the decisive variables."[37] The technologies of rapid communication and information exchange have been developing for the last century and a half. The German cultural theorist Aby Warburg predicted gloomily in 1923 that the telegram and the telephone would bring about the "destruction of distance" and lead to a "comeback of chaos."[38] Speed, for many of his generation, meant chaos, yet speed triumphed and became one of the dominant symbols of the 20th century. Two chapters on the telephone describe the early days of that instrument: a crucial artifact in the acceleration of information exchange. *Bernard Carlson* shows that American inventors and entrepreneurs like Bell and Edison promoted the new technology of the telephone not only in the United States but throughout the world, by establishing overseas operating companies and securing foreign patent rights. Both their business sense and their inventions were "global" from the outset. In his chapter *Helge Kragh* argues that it was the telephone – rather than the earlier telegraph – that represents the key technology in the establishment of the international communications network that was so critical to the globalisation of business and culture. Both *Kragh* and *Carlson* show in the case of the telephone, the importance of marrying technology to the right economic approach.

Moving forward to the late 20th century, information technology is the spearhead of the "second" globalisation. The expansion of telephone capacity through the use of fibre-optics, lasers and satellites has accelerated the rate of information and product exchange. Globalising process systems have revolutionised everything from newspaper production to banking and the travel business, and at the heart of them all, of course, is computer science. The combination of computer and telephone has brought about the on-going crusade in time-saving. Two examples are the Automated Teller Machine (ATM) which has transformed high-street banking (and threatens to make a great many bank clerks redundant), and the Computer Reservation System (CRS), now universally employed by the world's airlines. *Richard Coopey* traces the development of the ATM from its origins in the 1960s. Although the "hole-in-the-wall" has revolutionised and globalised banking and lowered the cost of transactions, the author believes that ultimately it will be seen as an ephemeral technology and replaced by a fully cashless society based on electronic fund transfer. The ATM story is a striking example of how technology can get ahead of social acceptance. Many people still expect banks to resemble marble halls laden with cash and this residual attitude will have to change before people will be entirely comfortable with the idea of conducting their financial affairs with a computer – whether in the wall of a local bank or at home on their desk. In her case study, *Nathalie Mitev* considers how a traditional transport industry – the railroad –

has been modernised in France, and looks at the troubled adoption by the French Railways of the American Airlines computer reservation system "Sabre" in the early 1990s. She shows that the difficulties experienced by the French in installing the Sabre CRS had their origins as much in human factors and cultural differences as in the nature of the technology itself. *Donald MacKenzie* also looks at computer software, without which the air transport, banking and telecommunications industries, not to mention entire national defence systems, would be unable to function. Computerisation in these fields has brought speed and flexibility, but also vulnerability to software errors. When human life or national security depend on computer systems such errors are of obvious concern, but software blunders also cost money: the London Stock Exchange lost $650 million when it was forced to abandon its automated trading system in 1993. *MacKenzie's* work prompts the question as to whether computer hardware, in the form of ever faster processors, might have got ahead of computer software – in the terminology of the historian Thomas Hughes, a "reverse salient" in the computer industry?

For those who worry that cultural standardisation follows in the train of globalising technology, the chapter by *Andre Millard* gives cause for hope. He examines the history of a classic globalising artifact – the music cassette invented by Philips in the early 1960s – to show that people are not the same throughout the world and you never know how a technology is going to be received or used. The humble cassette is a true global technology which can be found in almost every corner of the planet. However far from globalising Western music to the exclusion of all else, the cassette has actually decentralised commercial music and brought forth a wide variety of local music forms from indigenous performers. Instead of homogenising culture, this simple standard device has actually encouraged regional diversity and, as an unintended consequence, challenged the global homogenisation of music – what the author calls the "empires of sound."

As long ago as the 1930s, the philosopher Karl Jaspers spoke for many of his contemporaries when he said that "all technological and economic problems seem to have become global problems. The earth has not only become a place with a web of economic relations and possible technical solutions, but also more and more people regard it as the space in which they develop their history."[39] Jaspers was perhaps a global historian before his time; in any case the following chapters aim to show how the contemporary phenomenon of globalisation can be analysed and interpreted from a variety of standpoints and disciplines through historicisation. The idea that the earth and not the village community or nation state is space in which human beings "develop their history" is a novel and challenging one for historians, perhaps more so than for other social science disciplines, but it is an idea whose time has undoubtedly come.

## Notes

1 Epigraph to the novel of E. M. Forster, *Howards End* (Harmondsworth: Penguin Books, 1976).

2 This book arises out of an international conference entitled *Prometheus Wired: Globalisation, History and Technology,* which was held at the Deutsches Museum in Munich in October 1998.

3 Martin Albrow, "Introduction," in Martin Albrow and Edith W. King, eds., *Globalisation, Knowledge and Society. Readings from International Sociology* (London: Sage, 1990), 9.

4 Anthony Giddens, *The Consequences of Modernity* (Cambridge: Polity Press, 1990), 174-175.

5 Giddens, *Modernity,* 64.

6 Ralf Dahrendorf, "Anmerkungen zur Globalisierung," in Ulrich Beck, ed., *Perspektiven der Weltgesellschaft* (Frankfurt am Main: Suhrkamp, 1998), 41.

7 Luc Soete, "Die Herausforderung des 'Technoglobalismus': auf dem Weg zu neuen Spielregeln," in Friedrich Meyer-Krahmer, ed., *Innovationsökonomie und Technologiepolitik: Forschungsansätze und politische Konsequenzen* (Heidelberg: Physica-Verlag, 1993), 171-195, on 175.

8 See for example Barry Eichengreen, *Toward A New International Financial Architecture* (Washington DC: Institute for International Economics, 1999).

9 See Michael Geyer and Charles Bright, "A World History in a Global Age," *American Historical Review* 100 (1995), 1034-1060. The sudden desertion and sale of its British subsidiary, Rover, by the German automobile manufacturer BMW in the spring of 2000, is a striking example of the impotence of governments (in this case the British) in the pursuit of national economic policy.

10 Richard J. Barnet and John Cavanagh, *Global Dreams: Imperial Corporations and the New World Order* (New York: Simon & Schuster, 1994), 14.

11 Richard J. Barnet and John Cavanagh, "A Globalizing Economy: Some Implications and Consequences," in Bruce Mazlish and Ralph Buultjens, eds., *Conceptualizing Global History* (Boulder: Westview Press, 1993), 154.

12 OECD figures, see Daniele Archibugi and Jonathan Michie, "The Globalisation of technology: a new taxonomy," in Daniele Archibugi and Jonathan Michie, eds., *Technology, Globalisation and Economic Performance* (Cambridge: Cambridge University Press, 1997), 172-197, on 184.

13 Christopher Freeman, "The 'national system of innovation' in historical perspective," in Archibugi and Michie, eds., *Technology, Globalisation and Economic Performance,* 24-49, on 38.

14 For a full discussion of the participants in this debate, see David Held, Anthony McGrew, David Goldblatt and Jonathan Perraton, *Global Transformations: Politics, Economics and Culture* (Cambridge: Polity Press, 1999), 2-14.

15 Barnet and Cavanagh, *A Globalizing Economy,* 157.

16 Ulrich Steger, ed., *Discovering the New Pattern of Globalisation* (Ladenburg: Gottlieb Daimler- und Karl Benz Stiftung, 1998), 25-34.

17 An partial exception would be the world system theory of economic historian Immanuel Wallerstein who dates globalisation to the sixteenth century, when the rapidly expanding

flow of capital and goods created a capitalist world economy usually based on large impe-rial states and their areas of influence. See Immanuel Wallerstein, "The Rise and Future Demise of the World Capitalist System: Concepts for Comparative Analysis," in Imman-uel Wallerstein, *The Capitalist World-Economy* (Cambridge: Cambridge University Press, 1979), 19.

18  Raymond Grew, "On the Prospect of Global History," in Mazlish and Buultjens, eds., *Con-ceptualizing Global History*, 233.

19  *The Economist* (11.9.1999), 41: "A semi-integrated world, 20th century survey."

20  Geyer and Bright, *A World History*, 1047.

21  See Harold James, *Die Globalisierung der Wirtschaft* (München: dtv, 1997); Harold James, *The End of Globalization. Lessons from the Great Depression* (Cambridge, Mass.: Harvard Uni-versity Press, 2001); also Part 1 of James Foreman-Peck, ed., *Historical Foundations of Globalisation* (Cheltenham: Edward Elgar, 1998), 3-100.

22  Joel Mokyr, *The Lever of Riches: Technological Creativity and Economic Progress* (New York: Oxford University Press, 1990), 123-124; also James Foreman-Peck, *A History of the World Economy: International Economic Relations since 1850* (London: Harvester Wheatsheaf, 1989), 67-68.

23  *The Economist* (23.1.1999), SOS, RIP, 89.

24  Kevin O'Rourke and Jeffrey Williamson, *Globalisation and History: The Evolution of a Nine-teenth Century Atlantic Economy* (Cambridge, Mass.: MIT Press, 1999), 29.

25  Ibid., 2.

26  John Gray, *False Dawn* (London: Granta Books, 1998), 204.

27  Ruth Schwartz Cowan, *A Social History of American Technology* (New York: Oxford Univer-sity Press, 1997), 250.

28  Frances Cairncross, *The Death of Distance: How the Communications Revolution will Change Our Lives* (London: Orion Business Books, 1997), 30.

29  Kenneth E. Boulding, *The Image* (Ann Arbor, University of Michigan Press, 1956), 108-109.

30  Samuel P. Huntington, "The Clash of Civilisations," *Foreign Affairs* 72 (1993), 49.

31  Thomas L. Friedman, "Pushing Globalisation in the Land of Prayer-operated Elevators," *International Herald Tribune* (29-30 January 2000). Friedman's ideas on third world "back-lash" against globalisation are elaborated in his book, *The Lexus and the Olive Tree* (Lon-don: HarperCollins, 1999).

32  Roland Robertson, "Glocalisation: Time-Space and Homogeneity and Heterogeneity," in Mike Featherstone, Scott Lash and Roland Robertson, eds., *Global Modernities* (London: Sage, 1995), 25-44.

33  Friedrich List, *Das nationale System der politischen Ökonomie*, 2nd ed. (Jena: Fischer, 1910).

34  See David E. Nye, *Narratives and Space: Technology and the Construction of American Culture* (New York: Columbia University Press, 1997), 9. For the unifying effects of power net-works in America, see Thomas P. Hughes, *American Genesis: A Century of Invention and Technological Enthusiasm 1870-1970* (New York: Viking, 1989).

35  For the aircraft's role in the development of national consciousness, see David Edgerton, *England and the Aeroplane: An Essay on a Militant and Technological Nation* (Basingstoke: Macmillan, 1991).

36  James Rosenau, *Turbulence in World Politics* (Brighton: Harvester, 1990), 17.

37  Daniel Bell, *The Coming of Post-Industrial Society* (New York: Basic Books, 1999): "The Axial Age of Technology, Foreword to the 1999 edition," XLXII.

38  Ernst H. Gombrich, *Aby Warburg: Eine intellektuelle Biographie* (Frankfurt am Main: Europäische Verlags-Anstalt, 1981), 302-303.

39  Karl Jaspers, *Die geistige Situation der Zeit* (Berlin: de Gruyter, 1931), 68.

# Technology and Social Relations

## From Patronage to Networks

*Bruce Mazlish*

Man creates machines. The earliest fossils of Homo sapiens are found with flints beside them. These early tools were, as we know so well, followed by more advanced tools and then machines. In seeking to understand humanity, we cannot separate man from the tools and machines that he has created, for they are part of his "nature" and extend his senses and become part of his body, that is, he becomes "prosthetic man."

Seen in this light, machines also create man. It is fashionable today to say that what makes us human is our genes, that socio-biological determinism has displaced technological determinism. The fact is that both determinisms leave out culture, that unique result of humanity's symbolic capacities. Yet, without embracing *any* determinism, we can recognise that technology strongly shapes culture, indeed the title of this volume, *Wiring Prometheus*, reflects that insight, and we must further recognise that modern technology has been doing so increasingly and for some time.

The Industrial Revolution marked a giant step forward in the increasing effect of technology on our lives and cultures. As Thomas Carlyle observed in the 19th century: "Men are grown mechanical in head and heart, as well as in hand." In our own time, two further momentous developments have been taking place. One involves the evolution of computer intelligence and the other, partly driven by the expansion of artificial intelligence and other technological and social developments, is the process we call *globalisation*.

In the present paper, the piece of this twin development that I wish to examine more closely concerns the effect of technology on the way humans construct their social ties. Marx, of course, has been the pioneer in this effort. As he put it, laconically, the windmill brings feudalism, the steam engine capitalism. To put it another way, how we work and communicate with one another, using mechanical devices, helps determine our social structures and interactions. As we clearly see now, our relations with one another are culturally constructed. And, as I have already suggested, our culture is strongly influenced by our mechanical constructions, which form part of the culture.

Social ties, that is the ties that bind humans into a society, are myriad, and can take many forms ranging from physical embodiments – icons, scepters, edifices, for example – to social relations. The latter manifest themselves as processes – they are not tangible objects, but invisible links – made visible only in their exercise. Such processes can be reified and codified in a formal manner, with the forms changing over time.

I want to look specifically at three forms that have operated from early modern times to the present day: *patronage*, *connections*, and *networks*. These forms, while retaining continuity, have succeeded one another in impact. They reflect the role technology played in the society of the time in the way I have argued in the previous paragraph: in this case *patronage* is the dominant form, relying on simple tools more than powerful machines. With the coming of industrialised society, *connections* marks industrialised society in 19th-century Britain and it also serves as a transitional form as we move toward *networks* as a major and perhaps dominant form of social tie in our present globalised society. Studying these forms, especially in the light of the emergence of computer networks and globalisation, will help illuminate the transformation of early modern Europe from the 18th century to the beginning of the 21th century.[1] More specifically, it will shed light on the characteristics of globalisation in regard to some of the key issues of this volume: "boundary erosion" and "hierarchy."[2] Such a study will also exemplify in a very human manner the way in which machines and men, technologies and cultures, interact within given societies.

## Patronage

Patronage is an ancient and widespread form of social relation, which seems to have succeeded the feudal arrangements in early modern Europe as a dominant system. What was, and is, patronage? In early modern Europe it was a widespread social institution through which, as Mario Biagioli puts it, "socio-cultural identities and hierarchies were developed and maintained."[3] Patronage, especially, encapsulated a process by which power was exercised. As in the tango, it took two to engage in the patronage dance. A patron required a client, and a client required a patron. The power of the patron was manifested in the number of clients he had and in the number of services he could provide to the client as a "gift." The client, in turn, participated in the power of his patron – thus testifying to the existence of this power – and also bestowed gifts on the patron.

Such a system fudged the distinction between public and private. The patronage system was built on private relationships, a matter between two "persons," or entities, such as families. Yet, the outcome would have public consequences; for example, positions were not filled on the basis of merit, as it might be in an impersonal bureaucratic system, but as a matter of patronage.[4]

As a process made manifest in its exercise, that is, visible only when displayed in action, patronage required a certain amount of social mobility. Individual patrons, beholden to others above them, could rise, bringing their clients along with them.

In the process, they might displace those hitherto above them; it was a volatile and dangerous system. A Sir Walter Raleigh might flourish and fade quickly. A Duke of Buckingham might lose his head in the process.

Renaissance historians have recently taken up the theme of self-fashioning. By this they mean that individuals in the patronage system could create themselves with fresh identities, more suitable to social mobility. Thus, Stephen Greenblatt identifies Raleigh and Sir Thomas More, for example, as such self-fashioning individuals, and Biagioli instances Galileo, who he sees as rising from a low status mathematician to a high ranking philosopher, and redefining philosophy and science in the process.[5]

The setting for self-fashioning, social mobility, and the patronage system in early modern Europe was the court. In such situations, the prince was the ultimate patron. All other patronage relations existed in his reflected glory. It was a pyramidal system, repeating itself with lesser and lesser glory right down towards the bottom of society. In the baroque court there was a lack of stability, except at the very top (and occasionally even there). The baroque art, which confirmed and emblematised the power relations, was an art of fragmented balances and shifting harmonies.

Numerous handbooks and rules existed to guide one through the maze of patronage relations. Ritualised gifts and games were identified, and one ignored presenting and playing them at one's peril. One "courted" power, through patronage, often creating an erotic aura to surround the desired object, by acting in the way a courtier does in the presence of his beloved. Prudence, however, was also necessary; it was a key word, but it was courtly, not bourgeois, prudence. It meant accepting the ways of the world, which meant the ways of the court, and adhering prudently to them. It meant not allowing the aggrandisement of self to flame too high, challenging one's present patron in the process.

The patronage system can be viewed usefully as an economy of power. By constantly trading and exchanging favors, one shows its presence. Patronage can also be compared to money. In fact, of course, it is a substitute for money, for the one thing that cannot enter directly into the patronage game is payment in cash. Such a visible token of buying power is not gentlemanly; it would demean one's status. It would allow the new rich to rise in the hierarchy in too blatant a manner. The cash nexus is a tie we will encounter only in the 18th and 19th centuries.

With this caveat noted, we can return to our analogy of patronage with money. Both have their value only in circulation. Both can obtain goods and posts. Both represent power, but only by symbolising it. As for patronage itself, the relationship had been tied to the emergence of courts, and to their ambitions of absolutism. For a few centuries, patronage was a dominant form of relating persons to persons, maintaining hierarchy, allocating positions within it, and distributing power in society. Its particular embrace of science was, ironically, to be the partial cause of its downfall. To elaborate on that story, however, I want to turn directly now to the subject of "connections" itself.

## Connections

First it is necessary to hint, at least, at a long and complex story. It is the tale of how the scientific and political revolutions, when complemented by the industrial revolution starting sometime in the second half of the 18th century in England, brought into being a new society, where power was shifting steadily into the hands of the bourgeoisie. In such societies, money rather than patronage became the main means of access to power. And, as we know, technological innovation played a major role in this great transformation.

In commercial and industrial societies of the kind under scrutiny, all of the old ties and traditions seemed to have been eroded. All the connections, between Man and God, Man and Nature, and Man and Man appeared to contemporaries to have been broken. In their place, as Thomas Carlyle – and then Karl Marx – put it, only one tie was seen to remain: money, or in more dramatic phrasing, the cash nexus.

Earlier, we noticed that cash was a forbidden means of exchange in the patronage system. But after that it seemed to be the sole embodiment of such transactions. A man's "value" was defined increasingly in terms of his financial "worth" rather than his birth or status.

Or so it seemed! I want to suggest, however, that another dominant form for establishing "socio-cultural identities and hierarchies" – and for attaining and distributing power – developed, taking the place of patronage. This is what I shall call "connections." In using the very term itself I am seeking to retain the old sense of former ties; though patronage and networks are also forms of connection, it is the actual use of the term by contemporaries in the 19th century that warrants my use here. We can regard it as a transitional form, characterising the passage from an aristocratic society to a bourgeois one, and seemingly expressing itself most vividly in England, the first locus of the industrial revolution. It appears to hold sway during the late 18th century, a period of expanding commercialisation, and the 19th, with its industrialising forces.

A glance at the *Oxford English Dictionary* (OED) offers confirming evidence. "Connection," at first spelled with an "x," originally meant any binding or joining together of two things. A subsidiary meaning is given in 6.a., when the Dictionary defines connection as a relationship by family ties, such as marriage or distant consanguinity, often spelled in the plural. The first citation is 1773, Goldsmith, *She Stoops to Conquer*, followed by 1777, Sheridan, *School for Scandal*: "But pray, sir, are you acquainted with any of my connections …?"

An extension of the use of the term "connections" is given in sub-heading 7: "A body or circle of persons connected together, or with whom one is connected, by political or religious ties, or by commercial relations." The initial citation is 1767, Chesterfield, who speaks of "What is called the Rockingham Connection ..." (there is some confusion as to date, for the cited letter is 1774); and such usage persists, with another citation to Macaulay in 1848. Religious connection is exemplified by Wesley, who in 1753 spoke thus of those associated with him, a terminology repeated by many of his followers.

The dates are significant. The term "connections," as germane to my argument, surfaces according to the OED in the second half of the 18th century and persists into the late 19th. It fluctuates between the social, political, economic, and religious realms, encompassing all of them on occasion. Thus, it confirms my overall thesis that "connections" became a form of "invisible tie" during the revolutionary transformations from early modern Europe to the present, serving as an alternative to the ever-increasing power and ubiquity of money, while incorporating the latter. I shall argue that the imagined and unphysical institution of connections was therefore a holding action against the new rich and their invasion of established society.

As my text for illustrating this argument, I will take Jane Austen's novel *Pride and Prejudice* (1813). In Austen's British society, connections are the *sine qua non* for achieving position and place. They often involve patronage, as with Mr. Collins, a clerical suitor for the hand of a young woman, Elizabeth, securing his parish at the hands of Lady Catherine de Burgh. But more is involved, as when Mr. Collins recommends himself on the grounds of his "connections with the family of de Burgh." The something more becomes clearer when an aunt of Elizabeth's remarks about a suitor of her sister, Jane, "all our connections are so different."

At this point, connection has shifted from being mostly a matter of patronage to being a matter of one's circle, the people whom one knows and whose knowing defines one. Connection is a more equalitarian metaphor than patronage. Of course, it is still restricted to what is probably the top five to ten per cent of British society, composed of aristocrats and bourgeoisie. The rest of society does not really enjoy "connections."

Connections stands midway between patronage and what we shall now go on to discuss under the heading of "networks." When Lady de Burgh scorns Elizabeth as "without family, connections, or fortune," she is identifying the bases of socio-cultural being and power. Family and fortune are readily identifiable; they are visible ties. Connections is a largely invisible tie, but no less powerful for that. Its pervasive existence in early industrial Britain marks the situation, as noted, in which an aristocratic hierarchy is in the process of being replaced by a bourgeois one that, along the way, tries also to "connect" with the hierarchy.

Is it restricted to British society and not to be encountered in other societies as they embarked upon industrialisation? Do we find "connections" or its equivalent in, say, late 19th-century France or Germany? Or in early 20th-century Russia? If not what – if anything – occupies its place? Here is a research topic that awaits further work.[6] What we do know for the moment is that patronage, which flourished so strongly in early modern Europe, especially in the Mediterranean area, was supplemented in the next few centuries, especially in Britain, by a newer and less hierarchical form of invisible tie, connections.

## Networks

Biagioli refers to the "patronage networks" of early modern Europe.[7] A moment's reflection reminds us that his usage is anachronistic. No 16th-century patron or client would think of himself as being in a network. The trope is a 20th-century one.

The concept of networks marks a significant shift not only from the patronage system, but from the connections that I have just described which succeeded patron-client relations. There is an intermediate point leading to networks, for in its later phases connection itself took on the image of a web, as in the novelist George Eliot's usage, where the stress is on interconnections rather than stratifications (the notion of a web then lends itself later to development into a World Wide Web). Web was substituted for the use of chain, with its notion of hierarchical ordering, as in the Great Chain of Being, the pre-Darwinian vision of a hierarchical world in which each species and each individual was related to all the rest as either "above" or "below." The web is a biological, ecological and somewhat Darwinian metaphor. As I have remarked elsewhere, a "web is many-stranded, and represents an awareness of constant pulls and tugs, emanating from many directions, of many possible lines that hold one to others."[8]

The idea of connections, and its tendency toward web-like imagery, marked a society's movement away from an aristocratic principle and power to a bourgeois-dominated one. The idea of networks, I would argue, marks a further shift in the direction of social equality. It is the reflection of an acute leveling spirit. It is implicitly, and usually explicitly, more democratic than either the patronage system or connections. It has the potential of distributing socio-cultural identities, position, and power in a more evenly accessible fashion than either of its predecessors.[9]

In dealing with the predecessors of networks, I worked from particular texts, i.e. Biagioli or Austen. I have no such original text with regard to networks. Perhaps a Bill Gates or similar figure might serve, but I have not felt particularly inspired by any single source. Networks are simply in the air, literally and figuratively.

Resorting again to the *Oxford English Dictionary*, the term "network" refers originally to anything "arranged in the fashion of a net" – threads, wires, and especially fabrics. Citations in this vein start in 1560 and continue to the present. Definition 2.d. seems more promising when it speaks of networking, but peters out with: "a representation of interconnected events ... used in the study of work efficiency." Most relevant to our purposes is 2.h., "An interconnected group of people; an organization," and under this rubric the entries range from 1947 to 1974. Equally suggestive for us is "network" as a verb, with references to simultaneous broadcasting over a number of radio or television stations and to computer linkages, with all citations coming from 1940 onwards.

Let us focus on a number of different usages of "networks." The first indicates a set of personal connections. This usage reminds us again that we are on a continuum, as we move from patronage to connections to networks. Thus, the famous "old boy network" succeeds the Austenesque-"connections," though without the stress on marital ties. Here, a small group of persons knowing one another determine, or attempt to determine, the allocation of jobs and power. Harking back to good old fashioned patronage, such networks exist in corporations and universities rather than courts. In this sense, of course, it is more democratic than its predecessors.

Such old-boy and old-girl networks persist. Increasingly, however, they take the form of meritocracies. One forms a social network by going to the "right" schools, where entrance is increasingly on the basis of achievement (although such "achievement" can be fostered by wealth and access to culture and training). This phenomenon is most clearly evident in graduate business schools, where "contacts" are often cited as more important than curriculum by the selected students. One must work hard at making and keeping such contacts, and here the phrase "to network" as an active verb comes into its own. Where formerly one was hierarchically patronised or patronising, or was born into the proper "connections," now one "networks," semi-horizontally and semi-democratically, on the basis of achievement. Later, we will come back to this theme.

For the moment, let us look further at the meaning of "networks" in terms of a group of broadcasting stations, as in a radio or TV network. Such networks build on the earlier linking of peoples and places to be found in the invention of the telegraph, with Samuel Morse constructing a line between Washington and Baltimore in 1843, to be succeeded by the cross-Atlantic wireless telegraphy of Guglielmo Marconi at the dawn of the 20th century. In its initial stages, radio was often a modest, decentralised hobby, indulged in by amateurs. Over time, and rather quickly, it became a form of big business. As such, it lost much of its democratic organisational character, and became a top-down operation. Nevertheless its desire to appeal to large numbers of listeners, in order to secure advertising revenues, forced the radio networks towards cultural populism, if not democracy.

Television never went through the amateur stage. Its technology was too complex and expensive from the outset. Still, its trajectory was much like that of radio, which, in a sense, it incorporated by the addition of visual images. Again, the networks operated in a top-down fashion, but even more constrained than radio because of financial pressures to be responsive to the *vox populare*, expressed though the rating system. A certain skepticism is in order, however, as to whether the TV networks in fact create their own echo chambers, i.e. produce an answer from audience surveys where the audiences have already, so to speak, been pre-programmed and brainwashed. Nevertheless, certain "democratic" features remain.

Finally, "network" means the totality of the computer-linked world, the world of cyberspace. Before going further, however, it must be emphasised anew that networking is a significant verb, which cannot be said of patronaging or connecting. One *uses* patronage. The same is true for connections, with the added feature that one *lives* in its milieu. But one works in and with the networks, as the name directly tells us. Networks are primarily action-oriented rather than position-based.[10]

They are also directly linked to modern science and technology. As we noted, the telegraph was first developed in the 19th century, and was an advanced form of communication allowing messages to be sent rapidly and over long distances through the air and, with cables, under the sea. The telephone followed early in the next century and established the basic metaphor of a network of wires, linking people. Radio in the 1920s provided a limited private means of communication – the amateur radio "ham," but evolved into a "public," i.e., private, network which allows for messages radiating out but not in. It is only with the computer of the 1970s that networks and networking in its advanced and most democratic form emerges.[11]

The technology, obviously, carries with it social meanings. In the case of the computer network, what it offers is information, rather than status, and it is information open to everyone. The power which the network contains is, in principle, equally available to all persons.[12] It is (especially in terms of the Internet) an electronic democracy, a cybernetic agora. Unlike patronage and connections, networks imply a society without strict hierarchy, one in which power is widely defused.

William J. Mitchell presents the issue in architectural terms. As he puts it, "the electronic agora ... subverts, displaces, and radically redefines our notions of gathering place, community, and urban life." Traditionally, arrangements of space "pegged your peer group, your social position, and your role." Location was destiny, in the sense that where you lived determined the social interactions available to you. Or, as Mitchell says, "in the standard sort of spatial city, *where* you are frequently tells *who* you are."[13] In the electronic city, however, there are no privileged residences or sumptuary laws; all computers are, like cats, supposedly black in the dark of cyberspace.

The reality, of course, may veer greatly away from the ideal type. In fact, we know that access to and sometimes control of information is the basis for concentrated and unevenly distributed power. A struggle goes on in regard to the various forms of "networks" as to who controls distribution and how it should be paid for. Private corporations and governments compete over control, and public-interest groups anxiously ponder issues of censorship and invasion of privacy.

In the overall context of various kinds of networks, especially television, "stars" have replaced princes and gentlemen as legitimating agents for authoritative statements in what appears in my depressed moments to be a mainly *de-legitimate* society. In such a system, character no longer matters. Notoriety trumps personal rectitude, and the self disappears in the endlessly changing costumes of self-fashioning.

Such a description is admittedly hyperbolic, though catching at the hemline of truth. Other characteristics of the network society are, at least, of equal importance. For example, it is global in nature, and becoming increasingly so. Patronage might still extend over a few countries, where connections tend to be more localised, but modern computer networks literally encompass the whole earth.[14] Though intrinsically democratic, the network nevertheless can function as an hospitable climate in which a monied hierarchy can grow and expand on a global scale. Thus, a global elite, connected to one another by the network, can be expected to emerge, with developing ties to one another.

Can such an elite network ensure that power will remain in its hands? A glance at Manuel Castells' *The Rise of the Network Society* offers some idea of the complexities involved in the search for an answer. At one point, he seems to say that computer-mediated communication (CMC) starts from a cultural elite, but expands downward and outward through successive waves. However in light of its origins, for example, in universities, "it will shape *habits of communication* through the uses of its first-wave practitioners"; and I would add *habits of culture*, if not of the *heart*.[15]

Will such a guided spread of values and habits develop in a more democratic society? When Castells declares that "CMC could offer a chance to reverse traditional power games in the communication process," we seem to have the possibility of an affirmative answer. But a few pages later, this prospect is dashed when he comments that "what is common to CMC is that, according to the few existing studies on the matter, it does not substitute for other means of communication nor does it create new networks; it reinforces the preexisting social patterns."[16]

An opposite tack is taken by Howard Rheingold, who argues eloquently for the emergence of a "virtual community." By this he means a group of people linked by their active and voluntary participation in computer networks, where they share expressions of their lives and ask one another for help of all kinds – a kind of on-line Dr Spock or Dear Abby.[17] Even here, however, dark shadows hang over such friendly, democratic cyberspaces. Extremists invade these benign exchanges, with their preoccupation with sex and smut and their crazy politics. Safeguards will need to be erected, and self-policing agreed upon. In other words the problems of democracy persist in cyberspace, albeit in new form.

I mention Castells and Rheingold to illustrate something of the debate in progress. There is a haziness about the question: is the democratic nature of networks apparent or real? In principle, on the network, we are all equal – even disembodied, without the markers of our social positions. As we have seen, however, there remains a distinctly elitist flavor to the situation. That does not necessarily subvert the democratic implications of the network, with its replacement of patronage and even connection. More threatening is the attempt by government to inquire into our daily lives, to snoop into our affairs, and to gaze into our private correspondence. And along with such governmental intrusion is the attempt by capitalist enterprises to command computer networks, as they have radio and TV, for their own purposes.

It is well to remember that the "democratic" network came about by accident. In the late 1950s, the U.S. Defense Department, in order to render its communication system impervious to nuclear attack, made the network independent of command and control centers. That first network, ARPANET, "decentered" cyberspace, and thus inadvertently democratised it. The question, therefore, is whether such an unintended consequence of the Cold War can persist; whether the forces of a velvet despotism can reassert themselves or the democratic implications of the network survive? Which way the balance will tip is not yet clear.

In fact, a serious tension may exist in our emerging networked world, with the word "*networks*" taking on diffuse meanings. The computer network may foster a democratic spirit; in contrast, to return to our original line of inquiry, "networking" as an activity may be merely a high-tech version of patronage and connections. To be out of the loop, in this case of the "network," may be to exist in a powerless limbo. Both tendencies of networks, one may surmise, will probably co-exist, with a shifting balance being reached at different points of time and place.

These are a few of the features of the networked society. The system is in the process of working itself out. It constitutes a research problem still in its emergent phases. Of course much more could be said even now, but enough has been noted, I hope, to suggest the direction in which events have been moving.[18]

## Conclusion

I have argued here that patronage, connections, and networks are forms of "invisible ties" ordering the social system and distributing power and identity. Elements of all three co-exist today, but the last to emerge, networks, is clearly becoming more and more dominant. The direction of change in the systems has evidently been toward greater equality and democracy of access (leaving money or fame as the sole measure of status). We have moved from aristocratic society to a bourgeois one; and now to an amorphous, almost invisible, and increasingly global "entity," whose social relations and structure are extremely nebulous (though none the less powerful for all that). In short, while concentration of power still prevails, though in shadowy form, accessibility to it, in theory, has increased.

In sum, the three forms of invisible ties that we have studied shed light on the societies that they have held together. They instruct us in the ways power and prestige have been allocated in the modern world. They offer us insight into the minds of human beings as they have gone about, and continue to go about, constructing the societies in which they live, relating as they do to one another in various fashions. They show us, finally, that tools and machines not only participate in the construction of man, but forcefully shape the conditions in which humans strive to achieve their social and cultural identities.

## Notes

1  A related version of a paper on this subject was published in *Theory, Culture & Society* 17:2 (2000), 1-19. A good starting point for our treatment might be Adam Ferguson, *An Essay on the History of Civil Society* (1767, reprint Edinburgh: Edinburg 1966). In Ferguson's view, human nature is plastic and ever-changing in its manifestation, i.e., in what we today would call culture. Thus, a variety of ties is possible, and all are equally natural. In opposition to Rousseau, Ferguson believed that mankind must be studied in groups, not as isolated wild men; he believed the concept of a state of nature to be false and misleading. We must stick to facts, i.e., be a "natural historian" (p. 2), he declared, and we should seek to collect social laws from observable nature. The echoes of Ferguson in Emile Durkheim should be obvious.

2  See the introduction of Peter Lyth and Helmuth Trischler to this volume.

3  Mario Biagioli, *Galileo, Courtier* (Chicago: The University of Chicago Press, 1993), 15, with further references to the literature on patronage.

4  Gunnar Myrdal, *The Challenge of World Poverty* (New York: Pantheon: 1970), has lamented the presence of patronage in the "soft state" of underdeveloped societies, declaring it a handicap in any efforts to "modernize."

5  Stephen Greenblatt, *Renaissance Self-Fashioning* (Chicago: The University of Chicago Press, 1980). As anyone reading Biagioli, *Galileo, Courtier*, will see, I have leaned heavily on his account of patronage; for an extension of his ideas, see Mario Biagioli, "Etiquette, Interdependence, and Socialibilty in Seventeenth-Century Science," *Critical Inquiry* 22 (1996), 193-238.

6  One possible subject of comparison is Chinese *guanxi*. Guanxi, we are told by one author, is "a Mandarin word meaning 'connections.'" In China, and in the China sphere, guanxi is the basis of daily commerce, large and small. Further, "it is the foundation of basic trust. It means that you are somewhat more than just a friend – you are a close friend, a relative, a schoolmate"; Peter J. Boyer, "American Guanxi," *The New Yorker* (14 April 1997), 48-49. Another writer comments, "*Guanxi* is an outgrowth of a Confucian attempt to establish a scale of probable trustworthiness. Like any system, it can be abused. In China, when business people must deal with someone they don't know they often ask a *guanxi* contact to certify the trustworthiness of that person"; Frank Holan, "Lost in Translation (A Letter)," *The New Yorker* (19 May 1997) 10. The differences and similarities with my use of connections should be obvious; guanxi seems limited mainly to business transactions. A further comparison of Chinese guanxi with the Methodist connection is also in order; the shared Methodist religion in England was a valuable form of trust, allowing too for extended business dealings.

7  Biagioli, *Galileo, Courtier*.

8  Bruce Mazlish, *A New Science. The Breakdown of Connections and the Birth of Sociology* (New York: Oxford University Press, 1989), 245.

9  Without pursuing it in much detail, reflection on the thesis of Walter Benjamin, *Das Kunstwerk im Zeitalter seiner technischen Reproduzierbarkeit: Drei Studien zur Kunstsoziologie* (Frankfurt a.M.: Suhrkamp, 1963) may be pertinent here. As is well known, he believed that mechanical reproduction destroyed the "aura" surrounding a work of art. Marxist though he was, Benjamin did not think this a good thing. One might have thought that

he would: the original (often privately owned) could only be contemplated by a few; reproduction made it equally available to all. As Tony Falcone (graduate student at MIT in the STS Program) remarked in a short paper on the subject, the "audience for a painter's unique work of art was originally restricted in its viewing by the work's singular physicality. Reproduction techniques erode this exclusive form of consumption/use value, such that the primacy of artistic consumption is superceded by its use in exchange" ("The Economy of Images: The Marxian Framework in Walter Benjamin's 'The Work of Art in the Age of Mechanical Reproduction,'" n.d., 3). The computer network carries one step further the "equal access" begun by photography and forwarded, as Benjamin notes disparagingly, by films. At the point when a computer-generated, full-size reproduction of a great painting cannot be told apart (except by experts using highly technical means) from the original – a happening said by my computer friends to be "in the works" – we would seem to be confronted with another version of the Turing Test. At this point, another sort of equality enters the picture.

10  In the world of Hollywood, for example, networking via the telephone is virtually essential for show biz agents. As we are told in regard to phone calls, an agent "cruises these virtual halls, and others cruise his, maintaining the network of personal relationships from which the fabric of the entertainment industry is woven"; Ken Auletta, "The Microsoft Provacateur," *The New Yorker* (12 May 1997), 76. It would be easy, of course, for us to substitute email for the telephone.

11  One must not be misled by the mere use of the term "networks." Thus, Cohn and Marriott use the term in an article but define it as follows: "Networks in traditional Indian society are widely spread, diffuse patterns of relationships. Among Indian rural networks which serve importantly to integrate regions are networks of trades, networks of marriage, political networks, and networks of contacts formed by many kinds of religious travelers"; Bernard S. Cohn and McKim Marriott, "Networks and Centres in the Integration of Indian Civilisation," *Journal of Social Research* 94 (1958), S95-S120. They offer no Indian synonym for the term networks – one wonders how the Indians themselves viewed these forms of connection, a possible future research topic? – but again the differences with my use of the term should be apparent.

12  Once more *The New Yorker* can serve as evidence, as we learn from an article on Michael Bloomberg, whose firm provides financial information via the computer. We are told that the "combination of new technology and new services like Bloomberg's and those of his two principal competitors – Reuters and Telerate – has helped democratise Wall Street. By providing more information, they free customers from relying solely on investment advisers or banks"; Ken Auletta, "The Bloomberg Threat," *The New Yorker* (10 March 1997), 43.

13  William J. Mitchell, *City of Bits. Space, Place, and the Infobahn* (Cambridge, Mass.: MIT Press, 1995), 10 and 12. In fact, overall, Mitchell may be viewed as a latter-day, computer up-dated version of Alexis de Tocqueville. As the astute 19th-century Frenchman announced in his *Democracy in America*, "Aristocracy links everybody, from peasant to king, in one long chain [patronage, in my terms]. Democracy breaks the chain and frees each link …" (trans. George Lawrence, ed. J. P. Mayer, New York: Harper & Row, 1969, 508).

14  How far this can be carried is illustrated by a computer version of the "six degrees of separation" notion, where it is claimed that through a chain of six acquaintances, everybody

would have met or talked to everybody else. Thus, we are told, "MacroView Communications, a private company based in New York, has set up 'www.sixdegrees.com.' The process is simple: would-be networkers register with the website and tell the system about a few of their friends, business contacts or relations. The computer contacts these people and asks them to confirm these relationships. If they do, they are added to the database – and encouraged to add people they know. The idea is to make ordinary networking – the stuff of Chelsea cocktail parties, Wall Street breakfasts and Japanese business cards – more efficient"; *The Economist* (3 May 1997).

15  Manuel Castells, *The Rise of the Network Society,* vol. I of *The Information Age: Economy, Society and Culture* (Oxford: Blackwell, 1996), 360.

16  Ibid., 360 and 363.

17  Howard Rheingold, The Virtual Community: Homesteading on the Electronic Frontier (Reading, Mass.: Addison-Wesley, 1993).

18  Another way of talking about some of what I have been considering here is in terms of "social capital." This is the approach favored by sociologists and economists, who wish to introduce social relations into the rational action paradigm. As Coleman, for example, defines it, social capital "inheres in the structure of relations between actors and among actors"; James Coleman, "Social Capital in the Creation of Human Capital," *American Journal of Sociology* 94 (1988), S95-S120, at S98. The example he gives is of diamond merchants, where the "strength of these ties [social capital] makes possible transactions in which trustworthiness is taken for granted and trade can occur with ease"; ibid., S99. One is reminded here of Chinese *guanxi*. – The political scientist, Robert D. Putnam, is also much concerned with social capital. By "social capital," he means "features of social life – networks, norms, and trust – that enable participants to act together more effectively to pursue shared objectives"; Robert D. Putnam, "Tuning In, Tuning Out: The Strange Disappearance of Social Capital in America," *PS: Political Science & Politics* (December 1995), 664-665. His book, *Making Democracy Work: Civic Traditions in Modern Italy* (Princeton: Princeton University Press, 1993), is, in fact, an expanded treatment of the notion of social capital. The latter notion, in my terms, is a particular contemporary way of treating the general subject of "invisible ties." For an interesting critique and alternative to Putnam's view of social capital, see Francis Fukuyama, *Trust. The Social Virtues and the Creation of Prosperity* (New York: The Free Press, 1995).

# Historical Precedents of Global Markets

*Rainer Fremdling*

During the 19th century, European countries not only industrialised heavily but also began to trade with each other and other overseas countries to an unprecedented degree.[1] By 1913, a globalised economy had emerged, which – after the drawbacks of the two world wars and the disintegration of the world economy occurring between these wars – did not reappear before the 1960s or even 1970s.[2]

Based on the available data on foreign trade[3] and world production,[4] it seems pretty clear that roughly between 1820 and 1913 world trade augmented significantly faster than worldwide production. Whereas on average the production per capita grew at a rate of 7.3% per decade, the comparable volume of foreign trade in-

*Table 1: World Trade and its Distribution by Countries and Regions, 1820-1913, volume index and percentages.*

| Year | 1820 | 1850 | 1870 | 1880 | 1913 |
|---|---|---|---|---|---|
| Volume index 1913 = 100 | 3.1 | 10.1 | 23.8 | 33.5 | 100 |
| Great Britain | 27 | 22 | 25 | 23 | 16 |
| France | 9 | 11 | 10 | 11 | 7 |
| Germany | 11 | 8 | 10 | 10 | 12 |
| Switzerland | 2 | 2 | 2 | 2 | 2 |
| Netherlands/ Belgium | 6 | 7 | 6 | 8 | 7 |
| Scandinavia | 2 | 2 | 2 | 2 | 3 |
| Italy | 4 | 5 | 3 | 3 | 3 |
| Western Europe | 61 | 57 | 58 | 59 | 50 |
| Total Europe | 76 | 69 | 72 | 71 | 64 |
| North America | - | - | - | - | 14 |
| of which United States | 6 | 7 | 8 | 10 | 11 |
| Latin America | 8 | 8 | 6 | 5 | 8 |
| Asia | - | - | - | - | 9 |
| of which India | 3 | 4 | 4 | 4 | - |
| Africa | - | | - | - | 4 |
| Various[a] | 8 | 11 | 11 | 11 | 2 |

a) mainly British colonies

Source: Based on the compilation of W.W. Rostow, *The World Economy*, Austin 1978, 71f.

creased at the same time by 33%. During the same period in the 19th century, the world's output per capita multiplied by 2.2% whereas the world's foreign trade volume per capita grew 25-fold. This enormous increase in volume can only partly be explained by expanded trade among overseas regions. Rather, it was first and foremost the advanced countries that traded with each other. The regional distribution of world trade reveals a clear European domination during the 19th and early 20th century. World trade comprised mainly the intra-European exchange of goods crossing borders and European trade with overseas countries of European settlement.[5] This European domination lasted until the First World War, although North American shares increased whereas Great Britain's position deteriorated. Around 1913, two thirds of world trade still involved Europe.

From Table 1 it becomes patent that Great Britain remained the leader in foreign trade for most of the 19th century constituting nearly one-quarter of the worldwide foreign trade. In second and third place in Europe were France and Germany. European countries depended more and more on exports and imports and in 1910, the large European countries exported 17.5% (Great Britain), 15.3% (France) and 14.6% (Germany) of their GDP.[6]

There were two necessary preconditions for a globalised world economy to emerge already before the First World War: Firstly, the governments had to decide for a policy to enhance foreign trade.[7] Secondly, innovations or technological progress had to revolutionise the transport sector which resulted in ever-decreasing costs for transport within and between countries.

## Foreign Trade Policies

Three typical cases of foreign trade policy in Europe are outlined. These concern Great Britain, France and Germany.[8] The classical country of free trade is of course the United Kingdom. One should not forget, however, that during the crucial years of her industrial revolution, i.e. from the late 18th to the first decades of the 19th century, the UK did not adhere to a regime of free trade. This was not achieved before the 1840s. During the 18th century, the UK had a complicated system of import-, export- and transit-duties. At the end of the 18th century, France and the UK negotiated over reducing trade restrictions (1786), but instead a war between them, from 1793 onwards, drove import duties up. The import duties were the main source for financing the British state budget and hence the war. This kind of tax was not sufficient for financing the war efforts, though. Furthermore, government debt increased by three times until the defeat of Napoleon and for the first time in history, even an income tax was introduced. Before the war, import duties constituted 25% of the import value on average. After the war a level of 45% was reached and it increased to 60% in 1821/22 because the income tax ("war tax") was then abolished and the state loans ("war loans") had to be served. In 1815, the state debt amounted to three times that of GDP and two-thirds of taxes had to be used for serving the debt.[9] Although the supporters of free trade gained a great ascendancy, fiscal considerations limited the latitude of the government.

What were the major reasons that interest groups put forth in favour of free trade? First of all the noted arguments of classical economists as Adam Smith and David Ricardo were put forward by liberals. I refrain from elaborating on their familiar reasoning concerning specialisation and comparative advantage. Less well known is the second argument, which in retrospect was stressed by the political economist Cunningham around 1900.[10] According to him, free trade was in the self-interest of British industrialists to ensure a monopoly on the production of industrial goods as long as possible. Of course the starting point for such "free trade imperialism" was the fact that Great Britain enjoyed a natural advantage with regard to iron and hard coal, and a monopoly on mechanical production processes. Therefore, in order to maintain this position industrialisation abroad should be hindered and to achieve this goal other countries had to be open to exports of British industrial products. For their part these countries had to be allowed to sell agricultural products and raw materials to the UK in order to create enough purchasing power abroad for buying British industrial goods. The third argument for free trade concerned the price of food and the level of wages. As prices of cereals were considered to determine the wage level, industrialists and also representatives of the working class opposed the (nearly) prohibitive corn laws, which kept the price for agricultural products rather high in Britain. Opposition against free trade or reasons for keeping import duties were twofold. Firstly, landowners who held a majority in parliament profited from the corn laws. Secondly, for fiscal considerations, the government needed the revenues from tariffs on imported goods.

Until 1840, some moderate reforms towards lower and more rational tariffs were carried out. As finished products like cloth were major export products of British firms, the duty on raw wool or raw cotton had led to a negative protection. To counter this, the import duties on raw materials were then lowered or even abolished. But in 1840, still a lot of import duties existed and the state budget drew 50% of its revenues from these import duties. On average, they made up 30% of the value of imported goods.

With the government of Sir Robert Peel as Prime Minister (1841-1846) a number of liberal reforms were pursued. Concerning the tariffs the first cautious steps were taken in 1842 when the import duties on 54 goods were abolished. The remaining duties, which still served as major state revenue, were grouped according to the following principles: raw materials were taxed at a maximum of 5% of the value, intermediate goods correspondingly with 12%, and finished products bore 20% as maximum.

Very important was that Peel (re)introduced an alternative source of revenues, namely the income tax. The movement towards abolishing or lowering tariff barriers was thus accompanied by tentative steps to otherwise ensure fiscal security. For financing government expenditure state debt still prevailed, to a decreasing degree though.[11]

The corn laws, not yet repealed, were opposed heavily within parliament and the Anti-Corn Law League founded in 1839 gathered working class representatives and liberals to attack this regulation powerfully. Although the sliding scale or the threshold of duties against imports of grain was very high from the 1830s onwards, imports of cereals were more and more necessary to meet the demand of the rapidly increasing population.[12] In the first industrial nation, an ever-growing share of the population working outside agriculture had to be fed. Because of the corn laws, the prices for grain in Britain were far above world market levels, (see the prices for Berlin and London in graph 1). As British agriculture, in terms of labour productivity, had become the most efficient in Europe,[13] it needed no protection to remain competitive on the home market for food. Hence the high price levels were not at all justified. In order to repeal the corn laws in compliance with the implementation of a general free trade regime an exogenous inducement was necessary, though. In 1845, the last pre-industrial famine in western Europe hit also the UK, namely Ireland. There millions died or left the country and the extraordinary high food prices due to successive bad harvests was the final blow to the corn laws. To make it possible to draw on cheaper overseas supplies of cereals the corn laws were successively repealed between 1846-1849. In addition, all protective import duties on industrial products and raw materials disappeared. The navigation laws were also dismissed. For the sake of fiscal purposes, though, 48 luxury goods like coffee, tea, tobacco and brandy still had to bear an import duty, which was equal to the internal indirect turnover tax. Together with the income tax these indirect taxes were sufficient to generate the revenues needed for financing Britain's government expenditures.

This institutional innovation of a free trade regime in Britain served as a model for other countries where leading politicians, scholars, as well as ordinary people demanded the same trade policy Britain pursued. The most important extension of the British free trade regime was the conclusion of the Cobden-Chevalier-Treaty between France and Britain in 1860. It marked the beginning of a free trade area in Europe. Through the most-favoured-nation clause, bilateral agreements actually created a multilateral free trade area.

The UK stuck hard and fast to a free trade regime until the first world war, and less strictly so until 1932. Attempts to create an Imperial Preference Zone with protective tariffs against, for example Germany or the U.S., had no chance until 1914.

The transition of British foreign trade policy towards a free trade regime was essential for globalising and intensifying economic relations among nations. This process might have been initiated earlier than by the crucial steps actually taken in 1842 (income tax), 1846 (repeal of the corn laws) and 1860 (Cobden-Chevalier-Treaty). But an earlier introduction of free trade had been limited by fiscal considerations and had been retarded by landowners.

The French movement to free trade differs considerably from the British way.[14] Both countries, however, converged with their foreign trade policies culminating in the already mentioned Cobden-Chevalier-Treaty. Not before 1790 had France formed a customs union with all internal tariff barriers abolished. During the French war against the UK, Napoleon finally introduced the notorious continental system designed to block any foreign trade of continental Europe with the UK.[15] After the defeat of Napoleon and the opening of French borders to British goods in 1814/15, the French government reintroduced the rather liberal tariff system of 1791. This tariff regime formed a strong incentive for import substitution as it levied no – or quite low – duties on raw materials, whereas intermediate and finished goods bore increasing taxes amounting to between 5% and 15% of the value. Obviously, the isolation from Britain during the previous two decades had led French policy-makers to a misconception about the development the British industrial revolution had brought about. Immediately after the abolition of the import barriers, the highly productive and competitive British industry flooded the French domestic markets with her products, such as cotton textiles and iron products. This caused severe difficulties for – if not the collapse – of those hot-house industries which had been established in France as well as in other parts of the continent during the years of isolation from Britain and high war-time demand.

In order to defend her industry from these huge British exports France built up a completely prohibitive tariff system against British industrial products between 1816 and 1822.[16] As against that, non-prohibitive duties on colonial products and raw materials generated some revenues for the state budget. Around 1848, the average French import duty of 20% of the value seemed low, though compared with British levels in force until the early 1840s. This measurement of protection is misleading, however, when in an overwhelmingly prohibitive system most finished products are kept out and thus do not generate any revenue at all.

Of course the high tariff walls in France met with some resistance as they made the internal price level for certain goods rise far above world market levels. As a consequence, the construction of railways for example from the 1830s onwards, became highly expensive. Even when French iron mills were able to roll rails the protected price level hardly decreased.[17] As iron served as a major input to industrial goods of various kinds, duties on iron became the symbol and the very essence of industrial protection. Similarly, laws issued from 1819 to 1821 introduced a prohibitive protection for agriculture. In order to compensate exporters of goods an increasingly complicated system of rebates and export subsidies emerged. Accordingly, the producers of woollen cloth could agree on an import duty for their raw input. If those traders then traceably exported a finished product made from imported raw material which bore a duty they were granted rebates. The principle of "identity" underlying this regime of "temporary imports" was violated more and more, though. Sugar exports may serve as a prominent example for such a violation: Refining sugar from colonial sugar cane was in accordance with this principle paying a rebate. In the case of refining sugar from domestic beets, the rebates turned into an export subsidy, which in the long run created strong incentives to over-expand the domestic beet sugar industry.[18]

Since 1830, the July Monarchy put in some moderations of import duties but it was not before the authoritarian regime of Napoleon III (elected in 1848, coup d'état in 1851, emperor from 1852 on) that the French foreign trade regime changed fundamentally. During the 1850s, import duties on raw materials and intermediate goods were lowered significantly (1853/54) and the prohibition of importing machinery and tools was repealed (1855). Moreover, most of the export duties disappeared and the navigation laws were moderated. Increasing prices for foodstuffs in 1853/54 were the occasion to lower the import duties on agricultural products significantly. Furthermore, the regime of "temporary imports" and the associated rebates were used to undermine the tariff system. The principle of "identity" was changed into the principle of "equivalence." For example, the manufacturer and exporter of a sailing ship with an iron construction was given a certificate (aquit-à-caution) for the duty-free importation of the iron embodied in the ship. That is to say, iron at a lower stage of production, in the form of pig, bar or plate iron. A market for these certificates developed, where factory owners in the north of France bought certificates in order to import duty free iron from Britain or Belgium. In this way the tariff structure was undermined considerably. The conclusion of the Cobden-Chevalier-Treaty with the United Kingdom in 1860 was the climax of Napoleon's efforts to abandon the French prohibitively protectionistic tariff system. It was no sudden event, however, and in the first instance the treaty did not mean the introduction of a completely free trade in France as was the case in Britain. But for a transitional period, a regime of moderately protectionistic tariffs was installed as a step forward to move to a liberal regime.

The third example of a trade policy which converged towards a free trade regime concerns Prussia-Germany. For the trade policy pursued by the Zollverein and later by the German Empire the Prussian regime was crucial.[19] At the beginning of the 19th century, the Junker possessed the power in Prussia. The technocrats in the administration, the civil service, also came from this group of landed aristocracy. The Junker opted for free trade because they were grain exporters who wanted to export to Great Britain as well. The industrialists always advocated protection, but in the early decades of the 19th century, they hardly had the power to enforce substantial protectionistic measures. After the defeat by the armies of Napoleon, the Prussian state desperately tried to reform its constitutional and institutional framework. Part of the reforms was a new fiscal system and thus a change in the tariff regime.

With the introduction of the new trade regime in 1818, Prussia for the first time collected duties at the political frontiers rather than doing this at bridges crossing a river, at the ports of cities or on toll roads. Compared to the United Kingdom and France, the tariffs levied at that time were rather liberal: Raw material bore no duties at all, intermediate products just moderate ones and finished goods a maximum of 10% of the value. For fiscal reasons, luxury and colonial products were taxed at 30%. Right from the beginning, however, these principles were violated insofar as fiscal considerations dominated the foreign trade regime pursued.[20]

In 1818, Prussia had no clear-cut concept of a customs union with other German states. The petty and medium-sized states in the vicinity came under pressure to join, however, because their exports to Prussia were taxed by that time and high transit duties through Prussia made imports more expensive. In the 1820s, the medium-sized German states made several attempts to create an alternative customs union in the middle of Germany. But all efforts finally failed. Instead, the union between small Hesse-Darmstadt and Prussia in 1828 served as a model for the creation of the Zollverein in 1834. Most of the states in the south and the middle of Germany joined this union. In the north, Hanover and Oldenburg followed in 1854 and Mecklenburg/Lübeck in 1868. The Zollverein created an internal free-trade area with moderate protection against the first industrial nation and her exports. Thereby the tariff structure favoured or facilitated a process of import substitution of British finished products (e.g. cotton cloth, steam engines, rails).[21] As soon as 1840, the Briton Bowring reported that the Zollverein increasingly imported intermediate products (e.g. cotton yarn, pig iron) which had been produced by the superior British industry and were then worked up to finished products by German industrial enterprises.[22] The gains from intensified trade within the Zollverein helped of course to strengthen the ties among the member countries.[23] The contract among them had to be renewed every 12 years but it is quite clear that for fiscal reasons the petty and medium-sized states did not dare to leave the Zollverein. The revenues were allocated according to the size of the population in the member countries, meaning that middle and southern German states profited more from the revenues than Prussia which, because of the length of its frontier, had the highest costs in collecting duties and the lowest population density meaning that middle and southern German states profited more from the revenues than Prussia. On the other hand, in the case of conflicts among the members, Prussia prevailed. Although every member country could veto any decision the mere threat of leaving the Zollverein helped Prussia to resolutely press her case. In this way, Prussia forged ahead with her aim to move to a free trade policy. In the aftermath of the

Cobden-Chevalier-Treaty of 1860, Prussia concluded a similar treaty with France in 1862, which the other Zollverein states had to accept.[24] Successively until 1873, when the German Empire already had taken over the function of the Zollverein, Germany became part of the free trade area of the European core countries.[25]

The period of completely free trade in Europe seems to have been a short-lived episode, as only the United Kingdom, Denmark and the Netherlands stuck to it unswervingly until 1913. Increasingly, however, from the 1870s onwards Europe was "invaded" by cheap grain from overseas. To fight back this "invasion"[26] from across the Atlantic, in core countries such as Germany, the notorious coalition of rye and iron (1879) led to the reintroduction of industrial protection and increasingly to import duties for agricultural products. From the 1880s onwards, France in a similar way returned more and more to protective measures both for industry and agriculture.[27] In both Germany and France, import duties on wheat reached nearly 40% of the value shortly before World War I, but industrial tariffs made up just 13% or 20%.[28]

In spite of these drawbacks, until 1913 the institutional arrangements in international trade, money, finance and migration remained favourable for the emergence of a globalised world economy. The gold standard with the pound sterling as key currency provided stable exchange rates for the core countries, investment capital could freely cross borders all over the world, migration of people within Europe was far less restricted than it is today and migration from Europe to all the overseas countries of European settlement was free. Furthermore, decisive for globalisation was the reduction of national and international transportation costs. This dramatic decline of "natural" protection was in itself a major cause for several European countries to return to moderate "artificial" protection. The freight rate reductions, however, went far beyond a compensation for the recurrently introduced tariffs on bulky commodities such as grain.[29]

## The Development of Freight Rates and the World Market for Grain and Hard Coal

The decline of freight rates, mainly during the second part of the 19th century, had several reasons.[30] In particular, the application of the steam engine to both sea-going vessels and boats for inland navigation, the innovation of the locomotive and the coming of the railway. But there were also numerous improvements to modern and even traditional means of transport. Modern iron steamers had been in use for decades, but these were less economic than sailing vessels. Steamers lagged behind because for a long time they had to rely on steam engines which consumed a considerable amount of coal. This had two disadvantages: first, the running costs were high, and second, the coal bunkered aboard greatly limited the capacity of the shipload. Not before the 1860s did the compound engine (later the triple-expansion engine and further improvements) become the standard equipment of steamships. These fuel-saving devices reduced the consumption of coal considerably. Harley shows that in 1855 five pounds of coal were necessary to generate one horsepower for one hour and in 1890 less than two pounds sufficed to generate the same power.[31] The fuel-saving effect directly lowered the running costs and indirectly increased the freight-earning capacity, which was further enlarged through the smaller dimensions of the improved steam engines. Long distance trade over land, on inland waterways or over the oceans was no new phenomenon, to be sure. New, however, was the fact that bulky commodities, namely goods with a rather low value compared to their weight, could be traded on a worldwide scale. Here I concentrate on grain and coal which, together with raw cotton, had become the most important commodities in international trade around 1900.[32]

Table 2 gives an account of the declining rates of grain shipment between Chicago and Liverpool.[33] All three modern modes of transportation were involved for shipping grain from the American mid-west to the United Kingdom. Freight rate quotations are given for every year between 1868 to 1902. Although there are some fluctuations, the trend emerges very clearly. If we put the level of 1902 at 100, the rates for transportation from Chicago to New York declined from 360/351 in 1868 to 100. The decline was even more pronounced for the further transportation from New York to Liverpool with rates dropping from 487 to 100. In the first instance, it is remarkable that grain from America and from other remote areas reached the British market at all and thus supplied the British people with a cheap foodstuff.

The globalisation of the grain market, though, had severe repercussions for European agriculture. The grain prices in Britain as shown in Table 2 fell less dramatically than freight rates, declining from somewhat above 200 to 100 in 1902. However, only by less than one-third can this decrease be attributed to the declining freight rates. That is to say, European grain producers not only faced overseas competition due to falling freight rates, but also because productivity gains and decreasing grain prices were passed to Europe and enforced adaptations there.[34] In principle, European countries and indigenous peasants reacted in two ways: Some countries, such as France and Germany, adopted protectionistic measures to cushion overseas competition. In other countries, such as the United Kingdom, the Netherlands and Denmark, farmers switched from growing grain to breeding cattle and to dairying.[35]

The effects of increasingly overlapping markets and of the changing trade policies and transportation costs in particular, can be observed by looking at the price movement at different key locations of the world market. The Statistische Reichsamt produced several graphs on the long term grain market prices.[36] I reproduced the graphs for wheat with prices for London (the world market), Berlin, Chicago

Table 2: The Influence of Freight Rates on Grain Prices.

| | Average Price of Wheat per quarter (=12.7 kg) | | | | Freight Rates | | | | | |
| | British Wheat (according to official quotations) | | From Atlantic ports imported wheat from the United States (declared value) | | From Chicago to New York | | | | From New York to Liverpool | |
| | | | | | On water and rail per quarter | | On rail alone per quarter | | With the steamship per quarter | |
| Year | s | d | s | d | s | d | s | d | s | d |
|------|---|---|---|---|---|---|---|---|---|---|
| 1868 | 63 | 9 | 57 | 11 | 6 | 11 | 10 | 2 | 4 | 7½ |
| 1869 | 48 | 2 | 43 | 8 | 6 | 3 | 8 | 9½ | 4 | 5½ |
| 1870 | 46 | 11 | 44 | 4 | 6 | 4½ | 9 | 8 | 3 | 11 |
| 1871 | 56 | 8 | 51 | 7[a] | 7 | 5½ | 9 | 3 | 5 | 6 |
| 1872 | 57 | 0 | 55 | 10[a] | 8 | 3½ | 9 | 11 | 5 | 2 |
| 1873 | 58 | 8 | 56 | 0[a] | 7 | 10½ | 9 | 8½ | 7 | 0½ |
| 1874 | 55 | 9 | 52 | 9[a] | 5 | 1 | 8 | 7 | 5 | 10½ |
| 1875 | 45 | 2 | 45 | 5[a] | 4 | 3 | 7 | 0 | 5 | 7½ |
| 1876 | 46 | 2 | 44 | 4 | 3 | 6½ | 4 | 11 | 5 | 4 |
| 1877 | 56 | 9 | 53 | 5 | 5 | 0½ | 6 | 5½ | 4 | 8 |
| 1878 | 46 | 5 | 47 | 10 | 3 | 9 | 5 | 10 | 5 | 1 |
| 1879 | 43 | 10 | 45 | 8 | 4 | 5 | 5 | 9 | 4 | 1½ |
| 1880 | 44 | 4 | 47 | 4 | 5 | 3 | 6 | 7½ | 3 | 10½ |
| 1881 | 45 | 4 | 47 | 6 | 3 | 5½ | 4 | 9½ | 2 | 9 |
| 1882 | 45 | 1 | 46 | 0 | 3 | 7½ | 4 | 10½ | 2 | 7½ |
| 1883 | 41 | 7 | 43 | 5 | 3 | 10 | 5 | 6 | 2 | 10½ |
| 1884 | 35 | 8 | 37 | 1 | 3 | 4 | 4 | 4½ | 2 | 4 |
| 1885 | 32 | 10 | 35 | 0 | 3 | 0 | 4 | 8 | 2 | 1½ |
| 1886 | 31 | 0 | 33 | 3 | 4 | 0 | 5 | 6 | 2 | 2½ |
| 1887 | 32 | 6 | 33 | 3 | 4 | 0 | 5 | 3 | 1 | 8 |
| 1888 | 31 | 10 | 33 | 2 | 3 | 8 | 4 | 10 | 1 | 9 |
| 1889 | 29 | 9 | 32 | 9 | 2 | 11 | 5 | 0 | 2 | 7½ |
| 1890 | 31 | 11 | 34 | 4 | 2 | 10 | 4 | 9 | 1 | 7½ |
| 1891 | 37 | 0 | 39 | 1 | 2 | 10 | 5 | 0 | 2 | 1 |
| 1892 | 30 | 3 | 33 | 1 | 2 | 6 | 4 | 9 | 1 | 9 |
| 1893 | 26 | 4 | 27 | 10 | 2 | 10 | 4 | 11 | 1 | 7 |
| 1894 | 22 | 10 | 23 | 8 | 2 | 4 | 4 | 3½ | 1 | 3½ |
| 1895 | 23 | 1 | 24 | 5 | 2 | 4 | 4 | 0½ | 1 | 8½ |
| 1896 | 26 | 2 | 27 | 2 | 2 | 5½ | 4 | 0 | 1 | 11½ |
| 1897 | 30 | 2 | 33 | 0 | 2 | 5½ | 4 | 1½ | 2 | 0½ |
| 1898 | 34 | 0 | 34 | 7 | 3 | 2 | 3 | 10 | 2 | 3½ |
| 1899 | 25 | 8 | 29 | 4 | 2 | 2½ | 3 | 8½ | 1 | 7½ |
| 1900 | 26 | 11 | 29 | 9 | 1 | 8 | 3 | 0½ | 2 | 3 |
| 1901 | 26 | 9 | 28 | 6 | 1 | 10½ | 3 | 0 | 0 | 10 |
| 1902 | 28 | 1 | 28 | 5 | 1 | 11 | 2 | 11 | 0 | 11½ |

a) Including ports of the pacific

Source: L. Brentano, Die deutschen Getreidezölle, 2e edition, Stuttgart 1911, 84-85.

*Table 3: Freight Rates for Coal Shipments from Britain,[1] 1850-1913, in shillings per ton.*

| Year | to Hamburg/ Le Havre | to Danzig | to Bordeaux | to Genoa | to South- America |
|------|------|------|------|------|------|
| 1850/54 | 9.7 | 10.3 | 11.8 | 19.4 | - |
| 1855/59 | 10.0 | 11.7 | 14.7 | 26.6 | 52.0 |
| 1860/64 | 9.2 | 10.3 | 14.0 | 23.6 | 36.8 |
| 1865/69 | 8.3 | 9.3 | 12.6 | 19.5 | 32.6 |
| 1870/74 | 8.7 | 9.2 | 10.5 | 17.2 | 30.0 |
| 1875/79 | 7.3 | 9.1 | 9.3 | 13.9 | 23.4 |
| 1880/84 | 6.3 | 8.3 | 7.8 | 12.8 | 23.3 |
| 1885/89 | 4.8 | 5.9 | 6.4 | 10.3 | 22.4 |
| 1890/94 | 4.7 | 4.8 | 4.8 | 7.5 | 16.8 |
| 1895/99 | 4.4 | 4.4 | 4.6 | 8.0 | 13.8 |
| 1900/04 | 4.3 | 4.8 | 4.3 | 7.0 | 11.8 |
| 1905/09 | 3.8 | 4.4 | 4.1 | 6.5 | 11.2 |
| 1910/13 | 4.3 | 5.4 | 5.3 | 8.8 | 17.1 |

[1] Various ports

Source: Calculated from Harley 1989, 334-336.

and Buenos Aires. During the British war with France, prices in London were considerably higher than in Berlin (forming the centre of a grain exporting country). The fact that they remained higher even in peace time was due to the corn laws. The repeal of these in laws in the 1840s, brought the prices in London much closer to the still lower quotations in Berlin. With the entrance of America's mid-west into the world market for grain, the Chicago price and the decreasing freight rates forced the price of wheat in London down dramatically until around 1900. After 1879, when Germany introduced import duties on grain, the Berlin wheat price rose even above the price in London. After 1900, Argentina also entered the world market with prices close to the Chicago ones.

The second important bulky commodity to be increasingly traded internationally was hard coal and I shall deal with this subject here by putting it into the British perspective. Furthermore, my examination is restricted to the period from 1853 to 1913 for which I compiled detailed statistics on British coal exports. During this period, import or export duties on coal played a minor role. Closely associated with the technologies of the first round of industrialisation, the demand for hard coal augmented.

*Table 4: Freight Rates for Coal Shipments from Cardiff to Various Ports, 1872-1909/11, in shillings per ton and per 100 kilometres.*

| Ports of Destination | 1872 | 1873 | 1875 | 1888 | 1890 |
|---|---|---|---|---|---|
| Group 1: Mediterranean and European Atlantic | 0.58 | 0.67 | 0.55 | 0.39 | 0.36 |
| Group 2: Baltic and North Sea | 0.57 | 0.69 | 0.62 | 0.42 | 0.43 |
| Group 3: East African | 0.33 | 0.38 | 0.30 | 0.26 | 0.19 |
| Group 4: West African | 0.36 | 0.44 | 0.37 | 0.25 | 0.17 |
| Group 5: South African | 0.19 | 0.27 | 0.21 | 0.31 | 0.12 |
| Group 6: Continental Indian | 0.23 | 0.27 | 0.19 | 0.19 | 0.13 |
| Group 7: Asian Far Eastern | 0.20 | 0.21 | 0.17 | 0.16 | 0.13 |
| Group 8: South American Atlantic | 0.27 | 0.35 | 0.23 | 0.32 | 0.26 |
| Group 9: West Indian | 0.25 | 0.26 | 0.17 | 0.20 | 0.14 |
| Group 10: American Pacific | 0.18 | 0.19 | 0.12 | | |
| Total Average | 0.53 | 0.62 | 0.53 | 0.38 | 0.34 |

Sources and notes on Table A1: 1872-1902, Thomas 1903, 505ff.; 1905/07, Jevons 1909, 13; 1909/11, Jevons 1915, 685f.

The freight rates are standardized per 100 kilometre. For each group there are unweighted averages given, and the total average is weighted by the shipped quantities in 1902. For the quantities see Thomas, Growth, p. 510.

Name of the ports (Distance from Cardiff in nautical miles):

Group 1: Alexandria (2,943), Barcelona (1,664), Bilbao (560), Bordeaux (542), Cape de Verdes (2,408), Dieppe (417), Genoa (2,020), Gibraltar (1,153), Havre (382), Lisbon (882), Malta (2,133), Marseilles (1,844), Odessa (3,272), Piraeus (2,616), Port Said (3,072), Rouen (420), Trieste (2,806), Venice (2,800).

Group 2: Antwerp (558), Cronstadt (1,776), Hamburg (821), Stockholm (1,498).

Group 3: Aden (4,489).

Group 4: Sierra Leone (2,885).

Group 5: Cape Town (5,998).

Group 6: Bombay (6,154).

Group 7: Colombo (6,606), Hong Kong (9,716), Shanghai (10,466), Singapore (8,186), Yokohama (11,094).

Group 8: Buenos Ayres (6,249), Monte Video (6,139), Rio Janeiro (5,027).

Group 9: Havanna (4,025), Jamaica (4,034), St. Thomas (3,525).

Group 10: Iquique - via Cape Horn (9,623), Iquique - via Isthmus (6,830), San Francisco – via Cape Horn (13,606), San Francisco – via Isthmus (8,175), Valparaiso – via Cape Horn (8,869), Valparaiso – via Isthmus (7,588).

| 1892 | 1893 | 1898 | 1900 | 1901 | 1902 | 1905/07 | 1909/11 |
|------|------|------|------|------|------|---------|---------|
| 0.33 | 0.28 | 0.36 | 0.40 | 0.28 | 0.25 | 0.24 | 0.26 |
| 0.27 | 0.23 | 0.39 | 0.40 | 0.28 | 0.26 | 0.25 | 0.22 |
| 0.13 | 0.12 | 0.15 | 0.23 | 0.15 | 0.12 | 0.11 | 0.10 |
| 0.25 | 0.33 | 0.36 | 0.16 | | | | |
| 0.20 | 0.25 | 0.18 | 0.14 | 0.11 | | | |
| 0.09 | 0.08 | 0.12 | 0.18 | 0.11 | 0.09 | 0.09 | 0.08 |
| 0.09 | 0.08 | 0.13 | 0.16 | 0.11 | 0.08 | 0.08 | 0.06 |
| 0.13 | 0.10 | 0.15 | 0.16 | 0.12 | 0.10 | 0.12 | 0.13 |
| 0.10 | 0.10 | 0.13 | 0.19 | 0.11 | 0.11 | 0.12 | 0.11 |
| | | | 0.08 | 0.08 | 0.06 | 0.11 | 0.09 |
| 0.27 | 0.23 | 0.34 | 0.37 | 0.26 | 0.23 | 0.22 | 0.22 |

During the 19th century, Britain's coal exports[37] grew at a faster rate then her coal output. According to the estimate by Church, British output increased from 63.5 million tons[38] in 1850 to 292.1 million tons in 1913.[39] During the same years, exports first comprised little more than 4 million tons and finally nearly 100 million tons.[40] Whereas in 1855 exports (7.5%) had clearly stayed behind the two most important indigenous consumers of coal, namely the iron and steel industry (24.9%) and domestic fuel (20.9%), in 1913, exports outstripped both of them, holding 34.1% as against 11.6% and 12.2% respectively.[41] Coal exports also contributed overproportionally to the growth of the entire British foreign trade. In the total domestic export value, coal had comprised just 1.8% in 1850, but increased to 10.2% in 1913.[42] A major cause for the enormous growth of British coal exports lay in the decreasing ocean freight rates. Many British coal districts were located along the coast or were at least connected with ports through short distance railways.[43]

Harley systematically compiled freight rates for the shipment of coal over a longer period. Some of his data are shown in Table 3. In addition, I computed freight rates from figures collected by Thomas and Jevons (Table 4). Starting before the technically far-reaching changes in ocean shipping gained momentum, Harley's data thus include the decisive transition from the wooden sailing vessel to the iron steamer. He registers no falling trend in the overall level of freight rates for coal before the 1860s. Thereafter, the rates declined dramatically until the early 1890s, in subsequent years they fell rather moderately and shortly before World

*Table 5: British Exports of Coal, 1853-1913, five years averages in per cent.*

| Country/Region | 1853-57 | 1858-62 | 1863-67 | 1868-72 | 1873-77 | 1878-82 |
|---|---|---|---|---|---|---|
| Russia | 3.1 | 5.0 | 5.6 | 6.5 | 6.3 | 7.5 |
| Sweden/Norway | 4.2 | 4.4 | 4.5 | 5.2 | 7.1 | 7.0 |
| Denmark | 7.9 | 6.5 | 5.8 | 5.6 | 5.0 | 4.9 |
| Germany | 15.5 | 15.7 | 14.5 | 15.2 | 14.3 | 12.0 |
| Netherlands | 3.9 | 3.9 | 2.6 | 3.3 | 3.2 | 2.5 |
| Belgium | 0.4 | 0.7 | 0.7 | 1.0 | 2.0 | 1.4 |
| France | 19.7 | 19.3 | 18.3 | 17.8 | 19.1 | 19.6 |
| Portugal/Azores/Madeira | 1.8 | 1.5 | 1.7 | 1.6 | 1.8 | 1.8 |
| Spain/Canary Islands | 3.6 | 5.2 | 4.9 | 4.0 | 4.0 | 4.3 |
| Italy | 2.4 | 4.2 | 5.8 | 6.0 | 6.9 | 8.2 |
| Austria | 1.4 | 1.3 | 0.7 | 0.3 | 0.5 | 0.3 |
| Rest of Europe | 6.3 | 4.6 | 4.3 | 3.3 | 4.0 | 5.6 |
| Europe | 70.2 | 72.5 | 69.6 | 69.7 | 74.3 | 75.0 |
| Egypt | 1.2 | 1.4 | 3.4 | 3.6 | 3.9 | 3.8 |
| Rest of Africa | 1.1 | 0.8 | 1.5 | 0.1 | 0.6 | 2.1 |
| Turkey | 5.1 | 2.6 | 2.1 | 2.3 | 1.8 | 1.6 |
| India | 3.2 | 3.0 | 4.5 | 3.9 | 4.8 | 5.1 |
| Rest of Asia | 1.7 | 2.1 | 2.6 | 1.1 | 1.7 | 1.7 |
| USA | 3.8 | 4.2 | 2.1 | 1.0 | 0.9 | 1.2 |
| Canada | 1.9 | 2.0 | 2.0 | 1.8 | 1.2 | 0.9 |
| Central America | 4.4 | 4.2 | 5.1 | 3.6 | 3.1 | 2.8 |
| Chili | 1.0 | 0.8 | 1.1 | 1.0 | 1.3 | 1.0 |
| Brasil | 1.8 | 2.0 | 2.2 | 2.5 | 2.5 | 2.0 |
| La Plata-Region | 0.0 | 0.6 | 1.2 | 1.8 | 1.2 | 1.3 |
| Rest of South America | 0.3 | 0.2 | 0.6 | 0.8 | 0.8 | 0.8 |
| America | 13.2 | 14.1 | 14.3 | 12.5 | 11.1 | 10.0 |
| Australia,New Zealand, Pacific Islands | 0.9 | 0.5 | 0.3 | 0.0 | 0.0 | 0.0 |
| Other Countries | 3.5 | 3.0 | 1.8 | 6.8 | 1.7 | 0.7 |
| Total (metric tons) | 5032045 | 7261365 | 9177838 | 11553735 | 14226455 | 17818577 |

Source: Computed from yearly data in the British foreign trade statistics, see *Parliamentary Papers* 1854/55ff.

War I, they increased again.[44] In Table 4 the freight rates are taken up only during their downward trend and since then they support Harley's findings.[45] The development of coal freight rates during the 19th century differs from North's statement that general ocean freight rates already showed a downward trend in the first half of the 19th century.[46]

As mentioned before, the steep fall in ocean freight rates from the 1860s was due to innovations which improved the economic performance of steamers.[47] The

| 1883-87 | 1888-92 | 1893-97 | 1898-02 | 1903-07 | 1908-12/13 |
|---|---|---|---|---|---|
| 6.1 | 5.3 | 5.5 | 6.4 | 5.2 | 6.0 |
| 7.4 | 8.0 | 9.1 | 10.0 | 9.4 | 9.5 |
| 5.0 | 4.8 | 5.0 | 5.0 | 4.8 | 4.5 |
| 11.6 | 12.5 | 13.2 | 13.3 | 14.7 | 14.0 |
| 1.5 | 1.7 | 1.8 | 2.8 | 3.8 | 3.3 |
| 1.3 | 1.5 | 1.0 | 1.7 | 1.9 | 2.6 |
| 18.5 | 16.5 | 15.8 | 17.3 | 15.7 | 16.3 |
| 1.8 | 2.0 | 1.9 | 1.9 | 1.9 | 1.8 |
| 4.8 | 5.6 | 5.8 | 5.2 | 4.8 | 4.6 |
| 11.1 | 12.2 | 13.0 | 12.7 | 13.6 | 14.0 |
| 0.3 | 0.3 | 0.6 | 0.5 | 1.2 | 1.5 |
| 5.9 | 5.2 | 4.3 | 3.5 | 3.0 | 3.0 |
| 75.3 | 75.8 | 76.9 | 80.4 | 80.0 | 81.0 |
| 4.9 | 5.4 | 5.1 | 4.8 | 4.7 | 4.3 |
| 2.1 | 2.7 | 3.2 | 3.7 | 3.1 | 2.7 |
| 1.5 | 1.5 | 1.5 | 1.0 | 0.9 | 0.7 |
| 5.4 | 4.3 | 3.2 | 1.5 | 1.1 | 0.8 |
| 1.4 | 1.2 | 1.1 | 1.0 | 1.1 | 0.5 |
| 1.0 | 0.6 | 0.5 | 0.6 | 0.6 | .0 |
| 0.5 | 0.3 | 0.3 | 0.2 | 0.2 | 0.1 |
| 1.9 | 1.2 | 1.0 | 0.4 | 0.5 | 0.2 |
| 0.6 | 0.8 | 0.9 | 0.7 | 0.9 | 1.0 |
| 2.0 | 2.4 | 2.6 | 2.1 | 2.1 | 2.4 |
| 2.3 | 3.0 | 3.4 | 3.3 | 4.6 | 6.0 |
| 0.5 | 0.3 | 0.2 | 0.1 | 0.1 | .0 |
| 8.9 | 8.7 | 8.9 | 7.4 | 8.9 | 9.8 |
| 0.0 | .0 | .0 | .0 | .0 | .0 |
| 0.6 | 0.4 | 0.1 | .0 | 0.2 | 0.2 |
| 22780126 | 28534745 | 32428068 | 41731913 | 52404256 | 66258503 |

steamship itself was decisive in increasing British coal exports. Through forward linkage effects, i.e. decreasing freight rates (caused by the very steamship), the sale of British coal was promoted on foreign markets. To reach these markets powerful backward linkage effects were induced, as this means of transportation itself consumed coal. In 1905, about 17 million tons of coal were bunkered in British ports. And a contemporary maintained before the Coal Supply Commission that in the same year at least 5 million tons of coal were shipped to foreign bunker stations.[48]

This means that nearly one-third of the coal leaving Great Britain on sea was used for running sea shipment.[49] In any case it may be stated that the tendency towards downward – and finally low – freight rates made British coal more and more competitive on foreign markets. This particularly applied since (disregarding cyclical fluctuations) British coal prices at the pit mouth had rather stagnated from the 1850s to the 1880s and even increased[50] thereafter.

How were the British coal exports distributed among the receiving countries or regions? To my knowledge, the secondary literature deals with this subject in a rather crude manner.[51] Therefore basic data had to be compiled making fundamental use of the British foreign trade statistics. I assembled yearly data on the British coal export for each destination, disregarding both the figures on patent fuel and on bunkers for foreign vessels in Britain. The regional distribution of exports is determined by the receiving port. Table 5 shows the already mentioned dominance of European customers. Between 1853 and 1913, this preponderance even increased: Initially the European share made up about 70%. During the 1870s and around 1900, it took two further upward batches of 5 percentage points. Finally Europe got about 80% of all British coal exports. Outside of Europe, large amounts were sent to Egypt, which was due to the opening of the Suez Canal in 1869. This canal helped to diffuse the innovation of steamships to the Far East.[52] It seems likely that coal exports to the rest of Africa mainly served to supply bunker stations. Initially, i.e. in 1853/57, Turkey was an important customer, but the then decreasing export shares seem to indicate an economic stagnation in this area. India took a high level until the 1880s, but like the rest of Africa, it received rather modest shares in the following decades. The local demand was increasingly met by supplies of newly explored coal mines in the regions themselves. The same applies to South Africa and Australia.[53] Until the 1860s, the shares of North America are surprisingly high, but through improved transportation systems the wealthy indigenous coal resources there could soon be better distributed to other North American regions. As in Latin America, rich coal basins had not been explored or exploited before World War I so British coal was in a position, therefore, to gain important sales in spite of high transportation costs.[54]

The significance of particular countries in Europe and the shifting export ratios over time actually require a differentiated analysis. One might expect that countries poorly endowed with coal resources but blessed with a long coast line to have offered an ideal sales market for British coal. Denmark, with her constantly high shares, lends strong support to this. But the shares of Sweden/Norway, and above all Italy, jumped too high to be fully explained by this hypothesis. The demand for coal depended on the stage of development, i.e. the timing of entering into industrialisation, which mainly was characterised by applying coal consuming techniques. Hence the shares of British coal exports to the various European countries shifted considerably.[55] France was the most important customer for British coal exports. The vicinity of channel and other Atlantic ports offered cheap transport. This explains why large regions in France preferred British coal to coal from the north of France or Belgium. In the Netherlands the market shares of coal imports were mainly determined by the changing costs of the different modes of transportation. The high Russian and the huge German shares point to a further factor of influence. Both Russia and Germany possessed enormous indigenous coal resources. But for a long time it was cheaper for locations near the coast to import British coal than to rely on domestic supplies. So these British sales were protected against domestic competition by high costs for overland transportation. Until World War I, British coal remained competitive in coastal markets in spite of the then decreasing railway freight rates.[56]

## Conclusion

These historical precedents to global markets for grain and coal cannot be attributed simply and solely to technological improvements. But the technical breakthrough in transportation was indeed essential for lowering transport costs. Only then could bulky commodities be shipped to the distant – and overlapping – markets of the various competing suppliers of these goods. Equally important, however, were political decisions to abolish, or at least reduce the existing artificial trade barriers. Otherwise it would be difficult to explain why the world economy had in fact deglobalised during the 20th century.

## Notes

1   On Europe's international trade before 1800, see Kevin H. O'Rourke and Jeffrey G. Williamson, "After Columbus: Explaining Europe's Overseas Trade Boom, 1500-1800," *Journal of Economic History* 62 (2002), 417-456. Furthermore see Knut Borchardt, *Globalisierung in historischer Perspektive* (München: Verlag der Bayerischen Akadamie der Wissenschaften, 2001).

2   James A. Foreman-Peck, *A History of the World Economy* (New York: Harvester Wheatsheaf, 1995), 116; see also Harold James, *The End of Globalization. Lessons from the Great Depression* (Cambridge, Mass.: Harvard University Press, 2001); James Foreman-Peck, ed., *Historical Foundations of Globalisation* (Cheltenham: Edward Elgar, 1998), 3-100.

3   See Table 1. Walt W. Rostow and others derived their data for the period before 1913 directly or indirectly from the estimates by Michael G. Mulhall, *The Dictionary of Statistics* (London: G. Routledge and Sons, 1899, reprint Detroit: Gale Research Co., 1969, fourth ed.), and Franz Xaver von Neumann-Spallart, *Übersichten der Weltwirtschaft* (Brünn: Irrgang, 1878ff.).

4   See the most recent compilation by Angus Maddison, *Monitoring the World Economy 1820-1992* (Paris: Development Centre of the Organisation for Economic Co-operation and Development, 1995).

5   The available figures, however, may be biased towards Europe and underestimate trade among East-Asian countries.

6   Paul Bairoch, *Commerce extérieur et développement économique de l'Europe au XIXe siècle* (Paris: Mouton, 1976), 79.

7   This was accompanied by governments' decisions to gradually let people and capital also move freely; see Richard H. Tilly, *Globalisierung aus historischer Sicht und das Lernen aus der Geschichte* (Köln: Förderkreis des Forschungsinstituts für Sozial- und Wirtschaftsgeschichte an der Universität zu Köln, 1999), 23-28.

8   For an extended version see Rainer Fremdling, "The French Iron Industry, 1820-1860. The Change from Charcoal to Mineral-Fuel based Technology," in Michèle Merger and Dominique Barjot, eds., *Les entreprises et leur réseaux: hommes, capitaux, techniques et pouvoirs XIXe-XXe siècles* (Paris: Presses de l'Université de Paris-Sorbonne, 1998), 711-724; for details see also Adolph Wagner, *Finanzwissenschaft*, parts 3-4.2 (Leipzig: Winter, 1889-1910) Forrest Capie, *Tariffs and Growth, Some Insights from the World Economy, 1850-1940* (Manchester: Manchester University Press, 1994); Donald M. McCloskey, "Magnanimous Albion: Free Trade and British National Income, 1841-1891," *Explorations in Economic History* 17 (1980), 303-320, Charles K. Harley and Donald N. McCloskey, "Foreign Trade: Competition and the Expanding International Economy," in Roderick Floud and Donald McCloskey, eds., *The Economic History of Britain since 1700*, vol. 2 (Cambridge: Cambridge University Press, 1981), 50-69; Charles K. Harley, "Foreign Trade: Comparative Advantage and Performance," in ibid., 300-331.

9   This is a statement of Patrick O'Brien pointed out at the International Economic History Congress in August 1998 at Madrid. This increase in debt was not solely a result of the war against France, but also of 18 successful wars, above all against the economic rival, Holland.

10 William Cunningham, *The Rise and Decline of the Free Trade Movement,* 2nd ed. (Cambridge: Cambridge University Press, 1905), 38-66.

11 In this respect McCloskey's interpretation misses the point; see Donald M. McCloskey, "Magnanimous Albion: Free Trade and British National Income, 1841-1891," *Explorations in Economic History* 17 (1980), 303-320.

12 The threshold allowing imports depended on a moving average of domestic price quotations, see Donald Grove Barnes, *A History of the English Corn Laws from 1660-1846* (reprint New York: Kelley, 1965), and Susan Fairlie, "The Nineteenth-Century Corn Laws Reconsidered," *Economic History Review* 18 (1965), 562-575.

13 See the overview by J. L. van Zanden, "The First Green Revolution: the Growth and Productivity in European Agriculture, 1870-1914," *Economic History Review* 44 (1991), 215-239. Only Denmark had surpassed Great Britain.

14 For details see Léon Amé, *Etude sur les tarifs de douanes et sur les traités de commerce,* 2 vol. (Paris: Imprimerie nationale, 1876), and Émile Levasseur, *Historie du Commerce de la France,* part 2 (Paris: Rousseau, 1912).

15 Technically, the system was not perfect because it was counteracted by smuggling and roundabout traffic. Even more importantly, after 1810, the French government granted special licences to traders with Britain. This was of course merely done in order to increase revenues which had dropped dramatically with the continental system between 1806 and 1809. See Eli F. Heckscher, *The Continental System. An Economic Interpretation* (Oxford: Clarendon Press, 1922), 213ff.

16 The set-up of specific import duties was very simple and straight forward: The price of British bar iron in a French port at the channel was compared with a comparable quality of French iron at the same location. The difference – plus a small additional amount – was levied on British bar iron (120%) as import duty; see Rainer Fremdling, *Technologischer Wandel und internationaler Handel im 18. und 19. Jahrhundert. Die Eisenindustrien in Großbritannien, Belgien, Frankreich und Deutschland* (Berlin: Duncker & Humblot, 1986), 52-59.

17 Ibid., 265-307.

18 At the end of the 19th century, this policy, not pursued by France alone, had led to a distortion on world markets comparable to the export policy of the European Economic Community in the 1970s and 1980s. The Brussel's convention of 1902 stopped the subsidies on sugar exports. See Hermann Paasche, "Zuckerindustrie und Zuckersteuer," in Johann Conrad, ed., *Handwörterbuch der Staatswissenschaften,* vol. 8 (Jena: Fischer, 1911), 1065-1084, in particular 1077.

19 For an overview, see Hans-Werner Hahn, *Geschichte des Deutschen Zollvereins* (Göttingen: Vandenhoeck & Ruprecht, 1984).

20 This principle was also violated insofar as – for the sake of simplicity – the *ad valorem* duty was fixed for a certain weight of the taxed good. With declining prices of industrial products in the long run, the actual *ad valorem* level increased. See Takeo Onishi, *Zolltarifpolitik Preußens bis zur Gründung des deutschen Zollvereins* (Göttingen: Vandenhoeck & Ruprecht, 1973).

21 See Fremdling, *Technologischer Wandel,* 307ff.

22  John Bowring, "Report on the Prussian Commercial Union," in *Parliamentary Papers* 1840, XXI, X., 1840, 435.

23  Rolf H. Dumke, *The Political Economy of German Economic Unification: Tariffs, Trade and Politics of the Zollverein Era*, Diss. (Madison: University of Wisconsin, 1977).

24  Helmut Böhme, *Deutschlands Weg zur Großmacht* (Köln: Kiepenheuer & Witsch, 1966), 91ff.

25  The Cobden-Chevalier-area was joined by Belgium (1862), Prussia/Zollverein (1862), Italy (1863), Switzerland (1864), Sweden (1865), Norway (1865), Spain (1865), and the Netherlands (1865).

26  Kevin H. O'Rourke, "The European Grain Invasion," *Journal of Economic History* 57 (1997), 775-801.

27  See the details in Fremdling, "The French Iron Industry."

28  O'Rourke, "The European Grain Invasion," 783, and Sidney Pollard, *Peaceful Conquest, The Industrialization of Europe 1760-1970* (Oxford: Oxford University Press, 1981), 259.

29  As against the late 1860s, it cost 55 cents less to ship a bushel of wheat from Chicago to Liverpool shortly before World War I. For the same quantity of wheat, in 1907, Germany and France levied 35.6 cents and 38.6 cents, respectively, as import duties; see Charles K. Harley, "Transportation, the World Wheat Trade, and the Kuznets Cycle, 1850-1913," *Explorations in Economic History* 17 (1980), 218-250, on 222.

30  See also Kevin H. O'Rourke and Jeffrey F. Williamson, "When did globalisation begin?" *European Review of Economic History* 6 (2002), 35ff.

31  Charles K. Harley, "The Shift from Sailing Ships to Steamships, 1850-1890: A Study in Technological Change and its Diffusion," in Donald N. McCloskey, ed., *Essays on a Mature Economy: Britain after 1840* (Princeton, NJ: Princeton University Press, 1971), 22, and Charles K. Harley, "Ocean Freight Rates and Productivity, 1740-1913: The Primacy of Mechanical Invention Reaffirmed," *Journal of Economic History* 48 (1988), 851-876.

32  Paul Lamartime Yates, *Forty Years of Foreign Trade* (London: Allen & Unwin, 1959), 150.

33  O'Rourke and Williamson, "Globalisation," 37ff.

34  O'Rourke and Williamson also put forth that "declining transport costs on their own would have led to a decline in British wheat prices of between 15 and 25%." According to them, the larger price decline reflects "not only market integration but also agricultural supply shifts in the U.S. and elsewhere." A specific explanation is unfortunately not given; O'Rourke, "The European Grain Invasion," 784f., and O'Rourke and Williamson, "Late Nineteenth-Century."

35  Van Zanden, "The First Green Revolution." By turning to protection, the agricultural population both in Germany and France were kept high in the long run. This partly explains the agricultural policy of the European Economic Community in the 1960s.

36  "Die Getreidepreise in Deutschland seit dem Ausgang des 18. Jahrhunderts," *Vierteljahrshefte zur Statistik des Deutschen Reichs*, 1935, I., 273-321; see also O'Rourke, "The European Grain Invasion," 782, and Harley, "Transportation," 219.

37  As far as I know there is no monograph on this subject. Besides small chapters within books on British coal mining in general, see the articles by Sarah Palmer, "The British Coal Export Trade, 1850-1913," in David Alexander and Rosemary Ommer, eds., *Voyages and Trade Routes in the North Atlantic* (Newfoundland 1970), 333-354; Harley, "Coal Exports"; and the older studies by D. A. Thomas, "The Growth and Direction of our Foreign Trade in

Coal during the Last Half Century," in *Journal of the Royal Statistical Society* 96 (1903), 439-522; Herbert Stanley Jevons, *Foreign Trade in Coal* (London: P. S. King & son, 1909); Erich Zimmermann, "Die britische Kohlenausfuhr, ihre Geschichte, Organisation und Bedeutung," *Glückauf* 47 (1911), 1142-1152, 1181-1191, 1219-1228, 1257-1264 and 1292-1298.

38  If not mentioned otherwise, I use metric measures.

39  These and the following figures are taken from Roy Church, *The History of the British Coal Industry*, vol. 3 (Oxford: Clarendon Press, 1986), 9, 32 and 86.

40  Coke and patent fuel are converted into coal equivalents and are included here. Bunker coal for foreign vessels in Britain and bunker coal for British vessels at foreign bunker stations are also counted as exports.

41  Slightly different figures but with the same tendency as given by Church, *The History*, are to be found in Brian R. Mitchell, *Economic Development of the British Coal Industry 1800-1914* (Cambridge: Cambridge University Press, 1984), 12.

42  Based on the figures in Brian R. Mitchell and Phyllis Deane, *Abstract of British Historical Statistics* (Cambridge: Cambridge University Press, 1962), 283f., 303 and 305. Bunker coal for foreign vessels in British ports is not included. In 1913 this comprised 25% of the remaining exports of coal after all.

43  See the map in Church, *The History*, XXI.

44  Charles K. Harley, "Coal Exports and British Shipping, 1850-1913," *Explorations in Economic History* 26 (1989), 311-338.

45  See also Herbert Stanley Jevons, *The British Coal Trade* (1915, reprint: New York: Kelley, 1969), 692f., who compiled data for eight ports from 1863/65 up to 1913 (yearly data without gaps from 1886 onwards). They also reveal the described trend.

46  See also Charles K. Harley, "Ocean Freight Rates and Productivity, 1740-1913: The Primacy of Mechanical Invention Reaffirmed," *Journal of Economic History* 48 (1988), 851-876, and Douglass C. North, "Sources of Productivity Change in Ocean Shipping," in Robert W. Fogel and Stanley L. Engerman, eds., *The Reinterpretation of American Economic History* (New York: Harper & Row, 1971), 163-174.

47  Only a few aspects of technological improvements are sketched here. For more information see Harold James. Dyos and Derek Howard. Aldcroft, *British Transport. An Economic Survey from the Seventeenth Century to the Twentieth* (Leicester: Leicester University Press, 1969), 254ff.; Harley, "The Shift from Sailing Ships," 49ff.

48  Church, *The History*, 34.

49  In 1905 hard coal exports (without coke, patent fuel, bunkers) were about 48 million tons. Source: see Table 5). Thomas even estimated that this share was more than 50%. Thomas, "The Growth and Direction," 469; see also Palmer, "The British Coal Export Trade," 337ff.

50  See the graph in Church, *The History*, 53. A similar tendency occurred in Ruhr coal mining, see Carl-Ludwig Holtfrerich, *Quantitative Wirtschaftsgeschichte des Ruhrkohlenbergbaus im 19. Jahrhundert* (Dortmund: Gesellschaft für Westfälische Wirtschaftsgeschichte, 1973), 20.

51  See, however, Harley, "Coal Exports and British Shipping." He compiled yearly data between 1850 and 1993, broken down to only seven destinations, i.e. the major shipping routes.

52 See Douglas A. Farnie, *East and West of Suez. The Suez Canal in History 1854-1956* (Oxford: Clarendon Press, 1969); Harley, "The Shift from Sailing Ships," 223ff.

53 See Jevons, *The British Coal Trade*, 783ff.; Theodor Hassel, *Der internationale Steinkohlenhandel insbesondere seine wirtschafts-statistische Gestaltung* (Essen: Baedeker 1905), 175ff.; Zimmermann, "Die britische Kohlenausfuhr," 1150; Palmer, "The British Coal Export Trade," 339.

54 Jevons, *The British Coal Trade*, 782f.; Hassel, *Der internationale Steinkohlenhandel*, 36ff.

55 Alternative domestic sources of energy should also be considered, e.g. the richness in wood in the case of Sweden; see Hassel, *Der internationale Steinkohlenhandel*, 122ff.

56 France, the Netherlands and Germany are dealt with in detail in Rainer Fremdling, "Anglo-German Rivalry on Coal Markets in France, the Netherlands and Germany 1850-1913," *Journal of European Economic History* 25 (1996), 599-646.

# Technology and Textiles Globalisation

*Stephan H. Lindner*

A 1953 study by the United Nations called the recession of 1951 and 1952 a "decisive turning-point for the textile industry" in Western Europe. After some prosperous years, "to make good the depletions of wartime," the prewar contraction of textile exports seemed to reassert itself: "In short, textiles must again be regarded as a declining industry." The future main competitor of Europe's textile industry would not be the U.S., but Japan. And the "unfavourable comparison of European and American costs with those of Japan" was not "transitory," but reflected "the abiding fact that relatively underdeveloped countries with low wages and surplus labour have the greatest comparative advantage in producing relatively simple products with a high labour content." For a while, quota or tariff restrictions could help check the loss of markets, but in the long run such a policy "would, in a direct sense, be a struggle against a strong and permanent tide." Even modernising the European textile industry in order to gain American standards of capital intensity could "provide no lasting defence against Japanese competition."[1]

About twenty years later a report of the French Comité sectoriel de l'industrie textile pour le Commissariat Général du Plan argued, however, that the textile industry in industrial countries like France was "far from being a declining industry" – given rapid technological development, strongly increasing productivity, and overall growth of international markets and trade.[2] Indeed, in the decades following World War II innovations and developments in textile technology and man-made fibres were impressive – as was the growth of worldwide consumption and production of textiles. Yet, in spite of high productivity, innovativeness, and a worldwide growing market, the textile industry in France stagnated and declined since the early 1970s and has done so since. This occurred elsewhere as well. The MIT Commission on Industrial Productivity noted in the late 1980s that "despite high rates of productivity," large parts of the U.S. textile industry were "gravely threatened by international competition." This led the Commission to ask: "How can we account for this paradox: high rates of industrial productivity but decreasing international competitiveness?"[3] Or, to put it differently: Why was there no "industrial revival through technology," as suggested by an OECD study even as late as 1988?[4]

## Prelude: The End of Lancashire's Dominance in the Interwar Years

In 1937 an economic adviser of the International Labor Office wrote: "In general, the post-war period, in so far as the textile industry is concerned, has been a period during which the industrial revolution leaped across old regional boundaries, and spread to new and distant countries."[5] While worldwide production of the manufacturing industry doubled in the period between 1911/13 and 1936/38, the textile industry grew by less than 40%. And growth was mainly due to Japan and some non-industrial countries like British-India.[6] Old European textile countries, on the other hand, suffered stagnation or even decline.[7] The cotton industry was particularly hurt – and it was by far the most important branch with 85% of total textile production at the beginning and still 75% at the end of the interwar years.[8] Rather low capital and skill requirements made it usually the easiest industry for a peasant country to develop, and the relative insignificance of transport costs made it a "footloose" industry.[9]

World War I had closed down the contact between Europe, its raw material providers and its markets. Many European textile capacities shut down. This situation gave Japan a good chance to build up textile capacities and start competing in markets formerly monopolised by England. It was also a chance for countries like British-India to build up a national textile industry, primarily in order to supply their home markets.[10] After the war, in order to reach self-supply, to protect the infant industry or to build up a national industry, many countries protected their textile industry by contingents or tariff barriers, some even by boycotts. Therefore, even though worldwide consumption of cotton goods rose (index 1913=100; 1937=136), the volume of worldwide cotton trade declined substantially (index 1913=100; 1937=62).[11]

For England's cotton industry the 1920s and 1930s were "decades of almost unmitigated disaster."[12] While the Lancashire had ruled global trade in cotton fabrics before World War I, exports declined between 1913 and 1938 by 80% in volume, though value fell by only 50%, because the textile industry moved into higher quality products. The "emancipation" of Asia from England's cotton exports was the main reason for the depression in the Lancashire, particularly Japanese competition and the loss of the important British Indian market.[13]

Stagnation or decline of the Western European cotton industry happened on the dual level of capacities and production, with the latter declining even stronger. The growth of the Asian textile industry owed quite a lot to regular two-shift or three-shift work on its modern machines. In 1913, the Asian cotton industry had only 7% of world spindlage, but its share of cotton consumption was already 19%. In 1932, with 13% of world spindlage the share was not less than 35%. The British cotton industry, on the other hand, had old machines and comparatively few and even reduced working hours in 1932. It still held 33% of world spindlage, but its share of cotton consumption totalled only 11% (Table 1).

In the period before World War I, the English cotton industry had stuck with the self-acting mule, which had to be attended by skilled male workers. English in-

*Table 1: Worldwide Development of Spinning Capacity and Cotton Consumption in Spinning Mills 1913-1932 (percent).*[14]

| | Spindles | | | | Consumption | | | |
|---|---|---|---|---|---|---|---|---|
| | 1913 | 1927 | 1930 | 1932 | 1913 | 1927 | 1930 | 1932 |
| Great Britain | 39 | 36 | 34 | 33 | 19 | 12 | 10 | 11 |
| Other European Countries | 30 | 28 | 30 | 31 | 34 | 28 | 32 | 28 |
| Europe | 69 | 64 | 64 | 64 | 53 | 40 | 42 | 39 |
| America | 24 | 25 | 24 | 23 | 28 | 31 | 27 | 26 |
| Asia | 7 | 11 | 12 | 13 | 19 | 29 | 31 | 35 |
| *World* | *100* | *100* | *100* | *100* | *100* | *100* | *100* | *100* |

dustrialists decided not to invest in ringspinning machines, which were more productive and could be attended by low-skilled female workers. And in the weaving mills mechanical looms continued to dominate. Only 1–2% of all installed looms were automatic looms, which had been developed at the end of the 19th century in the U.S. and become rather widespread around World War I.[15] English cotton industrialists did realise that it was mandatory to modernise their equipment, but they faced a dilemma. Investment costs were quite high for new textile machines. And the new machines had to be profitable. However, enterprises that planned investments in modern machines had to compete on massively declining markets with enterprises that worked with old machines which had earned their capital costs. The latter could thus offer their goods at prices that one could hardly match with newly bought equipment. Even though in the 1930s banks and the state succeeded in a substantial reduction of production capacities, there were still too many. The situation of the cotton industry was so bad that the few enterprises which were able to afford modernisation would not dare spending existing reserves.[16] According to an estimate of the Board of Trade in 1946, about two-thirds of the lost cotton trade were the result of growing self-supply by formerly importing countries. Only about one-third was the result of increasing competition by other exporting countries: "Thus, even if Britain had been able to reduce her costs by enough to keep up with Japan, her exports at the end of the 1930s would still have been less than 50% of her exports in 1913."[17] Given these circumstances, even William Lazonick, who usually stresses very different reasons for Lancashire's decline, came to the conclusion: "The extreme competition for a declining market at all horizontal levels of the British cotton industry was neither propitious for re-equipment by existing firms nor for the updating of plant and machinery by the entry of new firms."[18]

In the Japanese textile industry production costs were, on the one hand, lower than in England due to low wages for mostly low skilled workers.[19] On the other hand, the Japanese used most modern and highly productive machines. Having started primarily with "secondhand textile machinery" bought in the U.S. or in England, since the mid-1920s they used machines "of the latest design," mostly "high draft ring spindles and the high-speed Toyodo loom."[20] Although in the mid-1930s only 10% of the installed looms were automatic, the mechanical looms in Japan had some extras which made them faster and more productive than the English looms. And the machines were generally used very efficiently: About 80% of the labour force were cheap, highly productive 14-18 year old girls; they worked on machines that ran faster than in England, and the girls attended a very high number of ringspindles. With regard to the performance per worker and machine, including wages, production costs per kilo yarn (average) on English selfacting mules were, according to a contemporary Swiss study, almost three times as high as on the Japanese ringspinning machines. Also weaving was about 2.5 times more expensive in England than in Japan. Japan's comparative advantage was thus not only due to low wages, but also to regular shiftwork, few holidays and the use of most modern equipment – the comparison of costs was in fact based on 2,400 working hours per year in England and on 6,180 working hours in Japan.[21]

Yet, Japan also suffered from widespread protectionism and striving for autarchy. British-India did not only try to stop English, but also Japanese imports. France and other colonial powers tried to stop Japan from selling textiles to their colonies in order to monopolise these markets themselves. The U.S. finally forced Japan in the 1930s to sign a "Gentlemen's Agreement" to "voluntarily" limit its exports.[22] As a result, already by the late 1920s spindles in Japan were idle.[23] Nevertheless, competitors often regarded the Japanese textile industry as the "source of all the trouble in the textile industry" – and the Japanese textile industrialist was declared to be the "most hated business man in the world today."[24]

In spite of the decline of the British and the problems of other European textile industries, in 1937 a study of the International Labor Office concluded that the centre of the textile industry still remained in Western and Central Europe, even though there was an obvious tendency for a shift to the Far East and other industrialising regions.[25] After World War II, this tendency turned into a new predominance.

## Growth and Internationalisation of Textile Production 1945-1990

Production and consumption of textiles grew massively from the 1950s on. Worldwide consumption of major textile fibres almost quadrupled between 1950 and the end of the 1980s – from about 10 to about 38 million tons.[26] A major reason for this

*Table 2: Textile Fibre Consumption per capita (end-use) (kilograms per capita).[27]*

| Year | World | Industrial Countries | Developing Countries | Soviet Union/ Eastern Europe |
|------|-------|----------------------|----------------------|------------------------------|
| 1950 | 3.90  | --    | --   | --    |
| 1955 | 4.60  | --    | --   | --    |
| 1960 | 5.02  | 12.17 | 1.90 | 8.54  |
| 1965 | 5.45  | 13.93 | 2.24 | 10.85 |
| 1970 | 5.88  | 15.24 | 2.58 | 12.08 |
| 1973 | 6.63  | 18.61 | 2.87 | 12.32 |
| 1975 | 6.06  | 15.45 | 2.92 | 12.87 |
| 1980 | 6.65  | 17.21 | 3.40 | 13.81 |
| 1985 | 6.76  | 17.98 | 3.61 | 13.84 |
| 1990 | 7.16  | 21.18 | 3.78 | 13.52 |

was the growing world population – from about 2.5 billion persons in 1950 to more than 5 billion in 1990. According to the International Cotton Advisory Committee, however, only about 40% of the growth in the period 1960-1990 could be attributed to population growth, the remaining 60% were "the result of faster economic growth, textile prices below inflation and increased competition among fibers which generated better knowledge about consumer preferences."[28] Per capita consumption thus rose primarily in the wealthy industrial countries. Globally, per capita consumption rose from 1950 to 1990 from about 4 to about 7 kg. In the industrial countries it rose from 12.17 in 1960 to 21.18 kg in 1990. With the economic depression of the 1970s, however, per capita consumption stagnated until the mid-1980s. In the developing countries per capita consumption doubled, but from 1.90 in 1960 to only 3.78 kg in 1990. Due to the massive population growth in many of these countries their share for the overall growth of the global textile industry was nevertheless important (Table 2).

However, even though global textile consumption rose at an impressive pace, it gradually decelerated. The average annual rate of growth of textile consumption was 3.7% during the 1960s. In the 1970s, with economic growth slowing down, it was still 3%. Finally, in the 1980s, global textile consumption increased at an annual average rate of only 2.7%. Thus, globally textiles remained a growth industry, but with the economic depression of the 1970s in the industrial countries consumption declined and stagnated until the mid 1980s.[29]

Decelerating worldwide growth coincided with a growing internationalisation of production. Worldwide the number of spindles increased between 1960 and 1989 from 126 to 165.6 million. The largest expansion of capacity occurred in the

Table 3: Geographical Distribution of World Spinning and Weaving Capacities
1963-1981 (percentages).[30]

|  | Spinning | | | Weaving | | |
|---|---|---|---|---|---|---|
|  | 1963 | 1973 | 1981 | 1963 | 1973 | 1981 |
| Developed countries | 46.8 | 34.2 | 23.7 | 44.6 | 33.1 | 24.4 |
| United States | 15.1 | 13.2 | 10.4 | 10.9 | 11.4 | 8.7 |
| Japan | 10.4 | 8.3 | 5.4 | 14.0 | 11.5 | 9.5 |
| EC (9) | 18.3 | 10.6 | 6.1 | 17.4 | 8.7 | 5.0 |
| Developing countries | 29.6 | 36.5 | 42.6 | 28.4 | 34.2 | 41.2 |
| Southern Europe | 4.5 | 4.8 | 5.9 | 4.9 | 4.9 | 4.5 |
| Asia | 16.8 | 21.6 | 25.0 | 13.8 | 16.9 | 22.3 |
| Latin America | 6.7 | 7.5 | 7.9 | 8.3 | 9.5 | 10.3 |
| Africa | 1.5 | 2.6 | 3.8 | 1.4 | 2.9 | 4.0 |
| Eastern trading area | 23.7 | 29.3 | 33.6 | 27.0 | 32.7 | 34.3 |

Table 4: Average Running Time of Machines in the Textile Industry in 1988.[31]

| Country | Days per year | Hours per year |
|---|---|---|
| Sweden | 225 | 5,100 |
| France | 222 | 5,321 |
| West Germany | 246 | 5,480 |
| Japan | 274 | 5,854 |
| Italy | 291 | 6,712 |
| U.S. | 305 | 7,320 |
| China | 306 | 6,885 |
| South Korea | 306 | 7,338 |
| Hong Kong | 330 | 7,930 |
| Taiwan | 354 | 8,496 |

new industrial and the developing countries in Asia and in Eastern Europe. Centres
of growth were China, South Korea, Taiwan, India, Indonesia and Pakistan. The
number of spindles declined in the U.S., in Western Europe and in Japan, where capacities had still been built up in the 1950s. Also weaving capacities increased –
from 1960 to 1974 the number of looms rose from 2.6 to 2.86 million. The number
declined until 1980 to about 1.9 million, to then grow again – in 1987 there were
2.76 million looms. As with spinning, expansion occurred in Asia and Eastern Eur-

*Table 5: Textile Fibre Consumption (end-use) (1,000 Metric Tons).[32]*

|  | World | Eastern Europa and USSR | Industrial Countries | Developing Countries – All | Developing Countries in Asia |
|---|---|---|---|---|---|
| 1960 | 15,152.8 | 2,645.6 | 7,440.6 | 5,066.6 | 3,124.1 |
| 1965 | 18,182.4 | 3,587.2 | 9,051.0 | 5,544.1 | 3,089.9 |
| 1970 | 21,741.3 | 4,216.4 | 10,497.0 | 7,027.9 | 4,174.0 |
| 1975 | 24,716.7 | 4,153.7 | 12,570.7 | 7,992.3 | 4,734.3 |
| 1980 | 29,575.5 | 5,291.9 | 12,769.0 | 11,514.6 | 6,978.9 |
| 1985 | 32,807.4 | 5,524.2 | 13,741.1 | 13,542.0 | 8,913.6 |
| 1990 | 37,889.3 | 5,395.3 | 16,645.6 | 15,848.5 | 11,140.3 |

ope, while there was a substantial decline in the U.S., Western Europe and Canada.[33] Spinning and weaving capacities thus moved strongly from 1960 to 1980 to the developing countries and the Eastern trading area, the latter including the Soviet Union, Eastern Europe and Red China (Table 3).

Again, not only capacities moved, but due to shift-work and the longer working hours in Asian countries, textile production moved to an even stronger degree towards Asia. The average running time in the world textile industry is shown for the late 1980s in Table 4.

In the Soviet Union and Eastern Europe, textile fibre consumption more than doubled between 1960 and 1985, while in the developing countries it more than trebled. The largest expansion occurred in Asia's new industrial and developing countries. Unfortunately, Table 5 groups all the industrial countries together. Since Japan and, probably even South Korea or Taiwan by the 1980s, are referred to as "industrial countries," we cannot see the real growth of the Asian textile industry, but only the growth of the Asian developing countries.

The strong shift of global textile production towards Asia can be seen on Table 6. It shows only capacities; nevertheless it illustrates well the substantial decline of the

*Table 6: Global Spinning and Weaving Capacity at the End of the 1980s (percent).[34]*

|  | Spinning Capacity (1989) | Weaving Capacity (1987) |
|---|---|---|
| Asia | 50.8 | 49.5 |
| Western Europe | 8.7 | 11.3 |
| North America | 9.4 | 11.0 |
| South America | 5.1 | 5.6 |
| Africa | 5.1 | 4.8 |
| Eastern Europe | 19.4 | 13.5 |
| All Others | 1.5 | 4.0 |

Western European textile industry and the new supremacy of Asia – particularly if you compare the numbers of the 1980s with the numbers of the 1930s, as shown in Table 1. Yet, capacities do not tell us anything about productivity and the de facto use of them – for this we need to refer to Table 4 and to Table 5 with the reservations mentioned above.

## Textiles Technology 1945-1990

There was not only a remarkable shift of capacities and production in the global textile industry. While there had been some inventions for the production process in the interwar years, there had been no substantial innovations. The step from invention to innovation, the first economic use of an invention, and from there to its diffusion mostly did not occur before 1945.[35] With regard to fibres, there had been some progress with the development and growing use of cellulotic fibres. The decades after World War II, however, brought decisive changes. Already in the first postwar years, progress in textile technology was "phenomenal both in the development of new materials and in the introduction of new techniques for the manufacture of known and new fibres into finished fabrics."[36] This continued in the following decades. As a result, the textile industry was no longer a "mature" industry, but it was characterised by constant development of new materials, improvements in existing production technologies as well as development of new production technologies, steady productivity growth and increasing automation of production. The "old," labour-intensive textile industry turned into a modern, high-tech, capital-intensive industry.

After World War II man-made fibres made their way, being used for very different purposes and end-uses – like cotton in the 19th century. Consumption grew extraordinarily. By the end of the 1980s, man-made fibres were the most important raw material for textiles next to cotton. Man-made fibres could not only serve different end-uses and fulfill different needs – making fabrics waterproof, fireproof, or easy to wear. They also allowed further productivity growth, since the speed of spinning or weaving machines also depends on tensile strength.[37] Endless synthetic fibres finally "substituted" the process of spinning, being directly used for the manufacture of textile fabrics, woven or tufted. Man-made fibres became increasingly competitive with regard to prices, even though they were usually more expensive than cotton. But the improvement of the quality of the tissue or the specific properties of a tissue through man-made fibres allowed them to succeed (Table 7).

Reflecting the development of Nylon by Du Pont, the strong growth of synthetic fibres and the important effects on the textile industry, two American historians of technology concluded: "In little more than a quarter century, Du Pont R&D effected a revolution in textiles reminiscent of those sweeping changes in weaving

Table 7: World Consumption of Major Textile Fibres (1,000 Metric tons).[38]

| Year | Total | Cotton | Wool | Chemical Fibres – All | Non-Cellulosics | Cellulosics |
|------|-------|--------|------|------------------------|------------------|-------------|
| 1960 | 15,153 | 10,356 | 1,495 | 3,302 | 702 | 2,600 |
| 1962 | 15,339 | 9,902 | 1,501 | 3,936 | 1,080 | 2,856 |
| 1964 | 17,256 | 10,830 | 1,460 | 4,966 | 1,687 | 3,279 |
| 1966 | 18,796 | 11,539 | 1,545 | 5,712 | 2,371 | 3,341 |
| 1968 | 20,434 | 11,763 | 1,565 | 7,106 | 3,578 | 3,528 |
| 1970 | 21,741 | 12,105 | 1,500 | 8,136 | 4,700 | 3,436 |
| 1972 | 24,417 | 12,903 | 1,578 | 9,936 | 6,377 | 3,559 |
| 1974 | 25,267 | 12,986 | 1,262 | 11,019 | 7,487 | 3,532 |
| 1976 | 26,537 | 13,211 | 1,515 | 11,811 | 8,601 | 3,210 |
| 1978 | 28,246 | 13,415 | 1,481 | 13,350 | 10,032 | 3,318 |
| 1980 | 29,576 | 14,291 | 1,567 | 13,718 | 10,476 | 3,242 |
| 1982 | 28,890 | 14,243 | 1,556 | 13,091 | 10,145 | 2,946 |
| 1984 | 31,253 | 14,831 | 1,621 | 14,800 | 11,804 | 2,996 |
| 1986 | 34,956 | 17,461 | 1,708 | 15,786 | 12,927 | 2,859 |
| 1988 | 37,359 | 18,234 | 1,803 | 17,313 | 14,417 | 2,896 |
| 1990 | 37,907 | 18,714 | 1,522 | 17,671 | 14,913 | 2,757 |

and spinning techniques associated with the Industrial Revolution in eigh-teenth-century England. But this was a revolution in fibers – in the creation of wholly synthetic fibers to supplement and sometimes even supplant the natural ones that had been used throughout human history."[39] The new fibres and mix-tures did not only result in product innovations like medical textiles or geotextiles, they were also at the origin of a good number of innovations in the production process.

The rise of man-made fibres and many labour saving innovations for the production process altered the face of the textile industry. In the 1950s modern American machines arrived in Western Europe – automatic looms and new spinning machines, as well as the Swiss Sulzer rapier projectile loom. The 1960s brought improved carding machinery. The 1970s witnessed the dissemination of open-end spinning machines, the perfection of ring-spinning, important improvements of the projectile and rapier looms, and the advent of the water-jet and air-jet loom. The 1980s, finally, saw the perfection of open-end spinning and air-jet weaving. The new machines increasingly automatised the production process, with productivity growing, even multiplying. The quality of products spun or woven on the new machines remained high or even improved. With increasing automation and ever higher productivity, there was less and less need for labour. Automation, the use of micro-electronics and robots "emptied" the mills. Only some workers, both un- skilled and skilled, and some highly qualified technicians and engineers remained. As a result, labour costs declined, while capital and energy costs rose substantially. In order to demonstrate the growing capital-intensity, a representative of the "In- ternational Textile Manufacturers Federation" published some comparative data in the mid-1980s:

> In the most modern *ring spinning mill* available in 1950 capital intensity per workplace amounted to SFrs. [1]61,000. In 1981 it had risen to SFrs. 809,000 a more than fivefold increase over the inflation adjusted cost level of 1950.
>
> Comparing a shuttle-less *loom installation* of 1982 with a 1960 mill equipped with fly-shuttle looms we arrive at a nearly 3.5 fold rise in capital intensity from an inflation adjusted SFrs. 250,000 to SFrs. 845,000.
>
> It is in the area of *rotor spinning* technology that the most spectacular develop- ment has taken place. From an inflation-adjusted DM 1,535,000 in 1971, capital intensity per workplace in a mill equipped with the most modern and fully auto- matic machinery and spinning a yarn Nm28 has jumped to DM 5.5 million in 1983, a more than threefold increase in only 12 years."[40]

We might expect that this dramatic change in production technology, with new raw materials and high capital intensity, would lead to a "technological revit- alisation" of the old textile centres, yet the opposite was the case. Growth happened mainly in the underdeveloped countries with low wages and surplus labour.

## Modern Textile Technology and Its Effects on Old Textile Centres

The United Nation's 1953 study was not alone in considering textiles a "declining industry." Like in Lancashire in the interwar years, a major obstacle to modernising the industry, itself a prerequisite for fighting decline, was existing equipment. A 1949 report on the Western European textile industry had also considered its mod- ernisation mandatory. However, the report argued that it was "irresponsible" to in- vest too much and thereby create overcapacities. That danger seemed realistic, if one looked at the modernisation plans in some of the countries: "These plans are based on the expectation that the whole textile export from Western-European countries will be 40% higher in 1953 than they were in 1938. This expectation may be called not less than absurd."[41] And a 1957 study of the OEEC on the Western European cotton industry wrote of overcapacities due to the loss of former markets. The cotton industry had to modernise, the study insisted, but the problem was that there were still too many old machines in place, having a long life to go and working with a high profitability. Many machines needed to be scrapped, before modernisation was possible. According to the study, Western Europe's cotton industry could again be internationally competitive with about half of the actual capacity working on a two-shift or three-shift basis.[42]

In 1965, an OECD study elaborated the double-edged results of technological developments and progress. The problem for the old textile countries was, according to this study, the rather slow growth of its markets. If the cotton industry was changing into a capital-intensive industry, it was "obliged not only to keep its plant fully employed but even to cut down production capacity considerably because of the lack of rapidly expanding markets." The strong improvements in productivity doubled or even trebled production per man-hour between 1945 and 1964. This made a bad situation for the old textile centres even worse – due to the loss of former markets. If a textile enterprise wanted to modernise its equipment, it had to take into account that "the net profit which can now be earned in Europe in a modern mill is only marginal when compared with a mill of the 1945-1950 type." There was a major difference according to this study: The old mill was sooner or later "doomed to extinction," while the modern one had a chance to survive. The problem for the Western European textile industry was, however, that the modern mill would possibly not survive the end of the old one: "[T]he margin between fixed costs in a modern mill and variable costs, mainly composed of labour costs, in an old mill is not yet such that the old mills automatically disappear." Therefore, textile entrepreneurs remained reserved towards modernisation: "In theory, the replacement of an old mill by a modern one is justified when the savings in variable costs as a result of new investments are sufficient to provide an adequate income on invested capital. In practice, the risk entailed in investment in modern equipment is such that the firm, with its traditional structure, is hesitant to take it, since expensively equipped mills, in view of the fixed charges they have to face, are in fact more vulnerable to a fall in demand and to market fluctuations." A further problem in many Western European countries was labour shortage, which posed a problem for shift work or led modernised textile firms to keep an economically unreasonable over-abundance of workers for the very fear of labour shortage – in spite of attainable productivity gains. Thus, the study argued, the cotton industry could be a capital-intensive industry, but it was not sure that the textile industry was "actually making the investments needed to keep up with technological progress since the low level of profits it has attained for many years as a result of disorganised competition often renders such operations impossible, and this is one of the main causes of its present difficulties."[43]

Like in Lancashire in the interwar years, it was not "irrational" to keep the old machines running. The problem, highlighted by the 1965 OECD study, was illustrated by a comparison of costs for manufacturing cotton fabrics with a mechanical

*Table 8: The Structure of Production Costs for 50,000 tons Cotton Yarn Nm 60 in 1965
with Modern and Old Production Technology (1,000 German Marks).*[44]

| | Using Modern Production Technology | | | Using Old Production Technology |
|---|---|---|---|---|
| | One shift | Two shift | Three shift | |
| Labour Costs | 16,634.6 (17.32%) | 16,842.5 (25.17%) | 17,882.2 (30.74%) | 35,009.1 (54.8%) |
| Energy Costs | 16,201.9 (16.87%) | 16,201.9 (24.22%) | 16,201.9 (27.86%) | 13,630.9 (21.3%) |
| Maintenance Costs | 4,516.9 (4.70%) | 4,516.9 (6.75%) | 4,516.9 (7.77%) | 9,518.2 (14.9%) |
| Costs for Space | 5,050.2 (5.26%) | 2,525.1 (3.78%) | 1,683.4 (2.89%) | 5,721.6 (9.0%) |
| Capital Costs for Machines | 53,638.0 (55.85%) | 26,819.0 (40.08%) | 17,879.2 (30.74%) | - - - |
| Production Costs Total | 96,041.6 (100%) | 66,905.4 (100%) | 58,163.6 (100%) | 63,879.8 (100%) |

loom, an automatic loom and a Sulzer rapier projectile loom in a West German weaving mill around 1960. It showed that even non-automated mills were able to compete as long as the salaries in West Germany allowed them. Labour shortage and rising labour costs would, however, in the long run force textile enterprises to modernise.[45] Furthermore, in order to earn its capital costs, new equipment had to run at full capacity, whenever possible three shifts per day and seven days a week. Yet, as already mentioned, in many Western European states this was hampered, if not made impossible by the problem of labour shortage, by legal restrictions or by very high extra renumerations for shift work. Textile industrialists could not operate their mills lucratively if they were unable to deploy new machines on a three shift basis, as Table 8 on the production in a West German spinning mill in 1965 shows – at least as long as labour costs did not rise substantially.[46]

The dual problem of profitably running old equipment and a strongly rising productivity through modern equipment and complementary investments can be well illustrated by the example of West Germany. There, investments in new textile machines between 1950 and 1962 did not only lead to a compensation of scrapped material, but enlarged overall capacity by not less than 90%.[47] Before the late 1950s most looms in Germany had been mechanical looms. Investing in automatic looms in the 1950s and early 1960s, standard in the U.S. since around the end of World War I, led to a massive increase of weaving capacity and resulted in overcapacities. This then stopped investments in the even much more productive and labour-saving "shuttleless" looms, which were available since the late 1950s. The problem was that the market for textile products did not grow to the same extent as did productivity through "technological progress," a problem highlighted by the OECD study of 1965. Since the rationalisation and modernisation in the 1950s and early 1960s had already led to overcapacities, many West German textile industrialists refrained from investing in the more modern technology in the following years – also since profits in the textile industry were quite high all through the 1950s and 1960s without new major investments. There was more talk about having to invest than a true necessity to do so.[48]

The situation in the old textile centres was complicated by the fact that the large majority of innovations in the textile industry did not originate within the textile industry, but in the chemical and textile machine industry.[49] The textile industry was therefore never able to control the innovation process. The innovations – in general being designed for exports – were always accessible to all competitors and rival nations. First British, then American machines dominated the worldwide textile industry – until around the 1960s. Since then European – Swiss, German, Czechoslovak – and Japanese textile machines dominated the industry. The textile machine industries of these countries exported their machines to all countries that would buy them, and they thus created or helped competitors of their own national textile industry. Textile machines were "footloose", too – disseminating the latest technology all over the world.[50]

In some cases this was even supported by the respective nation state. After World War II, the U.S. assisted the Western European textile industries to recast their textile machinery and gain higher productivity with the so-called "missions": Americans analysed the situation of the Western European textile mills and Western European industrialists visited American mills in order to rationalise production through the introduction of technological and organisational developments in the U.S. As a result, many Western European textile industrialists bought new machines, like automatic looms, in the U.S.[51] And from the early 1950s on, the West German government supported capital good industries, even at the expense of consumer good industries. It was not only favourable to exporting the products of the textile machine industry, which exported about 90% of its production in the late 1970s. The West German Government also subsidised investments in textile plants abroad. And in 1978, before an international economic conference in West Germany, the federal government even advertised in newspapers that "Mrs. Müller buys a shirt made in Sri Lanka." That might cost jobs in the West German textile industry. Yet, as the ad assured its readers, it saved the jobs in the West German textile machine industry, where Mrs. Müller's husband was working.[52]

Thus, capital-intensity did not necessarily lead to a comparative advantage for industrial countries, as was claimed by many economists, politicians and textile industrialists in the 1960s and 1970s. The more capital-intensive an industry was, the more uninterruptedly its machines needed to run in order to earn their capital costs – and the market for its products needed to grow respectively. However, the textile market, particularly the market for staple products, grew primarily in Asia, not in Western Europe. The labour-intensive apparel industry, the most important client of the textile industry, moved to the Asian new industrial and developing countries – contributing to the spectacular growth of the Asian textile industry. Furthermore, the "Pax Americana" of the postwar decades demanded relatively free trade – the Western Europeans had to open their markets. Not all of them did it voluntarily and many still tried to hamper imports. But inspite of protectionist measures through bilateral and international agreements such as the various Multifibre Agreements since 1973, the Western European textile industry could not compete with its cheaper and often more technologically advanced competitors in Asia.[53]

In the 1970s and 1980s, the textile market in the industrial countries stagnated – and these countries had to fight growing imports from Asia, given the liberalisation of trade in textiles. Western European countries like West Germany and France faced a problem comparable to the one that Peter Temin described and analysed when writing on the relative decline of the British steel industry in the late 19th century. According to Temin the relative decline of the British steel industry was a "natural" result: Investments made to extend production are lacking in stagnating markets. As a result, the average age of installed equipment tends to rise. The equipment will necessarily then be older than the equipment in dynamically expanding markets, where new machines are regularly installed to meet the growing demands of the market. After a while the equipment in the stagnating markets will be much older than in the dynamically growing markets. This then further deteriorates the competitive capacity of industries in stagnating markets, given the modernity of the machines and the other comparative advantages of the newcomers.[54]

This scenario describes well the situation and problems of the Western European textile industry in the past decades and explains the reluctance of the textile industrialists to invest in the latest equipment in the decisive 1960s and 1970s. The demand for textiles in the industrial countries at that time did not grow considerably, in the 1970s it even stagnated or declined – as a result necessary investments at that time were hardly made. The textile industry already suffered overcapacity and it simply did not pay to buy the latest, highly productive, labour-saving technology. This situation stopped modernisation for many years and only with labour shortage, rising labour costs and the strongly increasing competition in the 1970s and 1980s, did textiles become a capital-intensive industry in Western Europe.

Yet, since the capital-intensive, high-tech textile machinery was "footloose," that is, it was available to all competitors and also not too difficult to install, it was more lucrative to build up mills, particularly for bulk production, in countries offering cheap labour, few rights for labour, and long working hours – like in Asia. And even there, the comparative advantage led to the closing of the cotton mills in Shanghai in the 1990s – due to high labour costs.[55]

## From Internationalisation to Globalisation:
## A New Putting-Out System in Textiles

The textiles industry was, if not the first, surely the foremost global industry. A major reason for this was its "footloose" nature in a dual sense – first with regard to raw material and transportion costs and second with regard to the fact that the machinery industry and the chemical industry supplied most of its innovations. Thus, the textile industry was never able to control the innovations. However, textile industrialists, too, went abroad, built up factories that then competed with the textile industry at home. From the 1970s on, "outsourcing" became a main feature of the textile industry in old textile countries – in order to save costs, circumvent tariff barriers and conquer new markets.[56]

In 1956, a French geographical study concluded that the loss of European supremacy in textiles was to a large degree due to European initiatives, since Europeans built factories abroad or sold textile machines – "to put it briefly, in one way or the other the old industrial countries delivered the secret of their power like Samson."[57] So the argument of this article is not new. The article stresses rather the fact that innovations *per se* do not necessarily solve problems of an industry. Innovations have to be contextualised not only politically, socially and culturally, but also economically in order to understand their possible effects. To neglect this will lead to many interesting, but in the end unsatisfying answers for the decline of a highly innovative industry.

The scenario left few alternatives for the textile industrialists in the old textile centres. The 1953 study of the United Nations suggested that the Western European countries avoid looking for remedy in a technical solution, that is, to strive for capital-intensity as in the U.S. The European textile industry should not compete on price grounds, but excel in "efficient selling, and producing what consumers like, or can be induced to like."[58] Some firms went into specialties and high quality goods and were quite successful. A good example for this was Wolford, a highly successful firm in Bregenz (Vorarlberg, Austria) that specialised in high-priced stockings, bodies and bathing suits.[59] Yet, newcomers would soon try and in many cases successfully compete on these segments of the textile market, too. Until the early 1990s, the just-in-time market seemed to offer an alternative for local textile industrialists to keep some bulk production at home, but given the increasingly cheaper communication services and the ever lower costs for air transportation, textile mills in Indonesia or Turkey took over that market segment, too.

With transportation costs decreasing and the progress in information technology accelerating, a new form of "putting out system" has developed in the last two decades: Western European textile firms limit themselves to design work in their local "factory," with all the work done on personal computers. The design information is then sent to Pakistan, India, Indonesia or Turkey via e-mail, where the information is transferred to high-tech looms, which manufacture the product accordingly. Planes promptly ship the finished fabric to Europe with the label "designed by" or "manufactured for" a well-known European firm. The former textile manufacturer has thus become a merchant – reversing the 18th and 19th century relationship, when merchants went into manufacturing. Dierig in Augsburg is a fine example. In the 1980s and early 1990s, it used to have parts of its production made by partners in Indonesia. Today Dierig confines itself to designing, purchasing and selling textile products, using its know-how and its long-established relations. The mills of Dierig, until the 1980s one of the largest textile firms in West Germany and one of the most important enterprises and employers in the industrial city of Augsburg, closed in the mid-1990s.[60]

Another and still rather successful alternative has been specialisation in industrial textiles, a know-how intensive branch in which innovations originate to a large degree in the textile firms themselves. Thus, the firms maintain proprietary control over the innovation process, in some cases even service these textiles, which gives them even more control over these innovations. But again, this small, though highly lucrative segment of the textiles market is not a "protected species." Its products can also be imitated and eventually even improved by others.[61] Therefore, inspite of the innovations and the high capital-intensity, no "technological revitalisation" for the old textile centers has occurred. Given the situation described and analysed above, even with the greatest endeavor and though there will be some successful firms, the industry as a whole will continue to decline.

## Notes

1 United Nations. Department of Economic Affairs, *Economic Survey of Europe Since the War. A Reappraisal of Problems and Prospects* (Geneva, 1953), 182-196. This article was first published in *History and Technology* 2002, Vol. 18 (1), 1-22. The author is very grateful to the publisher, Taylor & Francis Group, http://www.tandf.co.uk, for kindly granting permission to reprint it in this volume.

2 Commissariat Général du Plan. Préparation du 6e Plan. Commission de l'Industrie, *Rapport du Comité. Industrie textile* (Paris: La documentation français, 1971), 13.

3 MIT Commission on Industrial Productivity, *The US Textile Industry: Challenges and Opportunies (Working Paper)* (Cambridge, Mass., 1989), 14, 16.

4 OECD, *Industrial Revival Through Technology* (Paris 1988), 7-13, on textiles 96-124.

5 Lewis Lorwin, *The World Textile Conference* (New York: Nat. Peace Conference, 1937), 25.

6 GATT, *A Study on Cotton Textiles* (Geneva 1966), 9.

7 Heinz Grünbaum, *Die Welttextilkrise. Zur Umschichtung der internationalen Industriestruktur* (Berlin: Hobbing, 1931), 10.

8 See Willem Titus Kroese, "The Past, Present and Future of the Cotton Industry (1904-1954)," in IFCATI, ed., *The Cotton Industry – Today and Tomorrow* (Manchester, 1954), 71-73; Henri Nozet, *Textiles chimiques. Fibres modernes* (Paris: Eyrolles, 1976), 8.

9 Lars Sandberg, *Lancashire in Decline: a Study in Entrepreneurship, Technology, and International Trade* (Columbus: Ohio State Univ. Press, 1974), 218-219, 207-211.

10 See Sandberg, *Lancashire in Decline*, 176-177; Edmond de Moreau d'Andoy, "La crise des industries du coton," in: *Banque Nationale de Belgique. Service des Etudes Economiques. Bulletin d'Information et de Documentation*, vol. 6–1, Nr. 5 (10 March 1931), 145-157.

11 J. H. Porter, "Cotton and Wool Textiles," in Neil K. Buxton and Derek H. Aldcroft, eds., *British Industry between the Wars. Instability and Industrial Development 1919-1939* (London: Scolar Press, 1979), 25-47, on 28.

12 John Singleton, *Lancashire on the Scrapheap. The Cotton Industry 1945-1970* (Oxford: Oxford Univ. Press 1991), 11.

13 William Lazonick, *Competitive Advantage on the Shopfloor* (Cambridge, Mass: Harvard Univ. Press 1990), 142-151; Sandberg, *Lancashire in Decline*, 178-195, 211-212; André Allix and André Gibert, *Géographie des Textiles* (Paris: Génin, 1956), 349; Porter, "Cotton and Wool Textiles," 28; Singleton, *Lancashire on the Scrapheap*, 11; James H. Bamberg, *The government, the banks and the Lancashire cotton industry, 1918-1939* (Diss. Cambridge University, 1984), 31; Armin Spälty, *Die Lage der englischen Baumwollindustrie, Konkurrenzverhältnisse und Sanierungsmöglichkeiten* (Diss. Zürich, 1936), 53, 66-67; Moreau d'Andoy, "La crise des industries du coton," 153.

14 Edmond de Moreau, "La crise cotonnière en 1931-1932," in *Banque Nationale de Belgique. Service des Etudes Economiques. Bulletin d'Information et de Documentation*, vol. 7–2, Nr. 10 (25 Nov. 1932), 337-355.

15 Lazonick, *Competitive Advantage*, 139; see also Irwin Feller, "The Diffusion and Location of Technological Change in American Cotton-Textile Industry, 1890-1970," *Technology and Culture* 15 (1974), 569-593.

16 Bureau International du Travail, *L'industrie textile dans le monde. Problèmes économiques et sociaux*, vol. 1 (Geneva, 1937), 344; Bamberg, *The government*, 32, 369; Spälty, *Die Lage der englischen Baumwollindustrie*, 133.

17 Sandberg, *Lancashire in Decline*, 204-205.

18 Lazonick, "Industrial Organization and Technological Change: the Decline of the British Cotton Industry," *Business History Review* 57 (1983), 195-236, on 204.

19 Werner Pascha, *Strukturanpassung in schrumpfenden Branchen. Japans Textilindustrie vor dem Hintergrund veränderter Wettbewerbsvorteile* (Berlin: Duncker & Humblot, 1986), 12.

20 Herman Edward Michl, *The Textile Industries. An Economic Analysis* (Washington, D.C.: Textile Foundation, 1938), 180-181.

21 Spälty, *Die Lage der englischen Baumwollindustrie*, 174-181, 190-191, 196-197; Bureau International du Travail, *L'industrie textile dans le monde*, 246.

22 See Sandberg, *Lancashire in Decline*, 187, 194; Georg Koopmann, *Handelspolitik und internationale Wettbewerbsfähigkeit: das Beispiel der amerikanischen Textil- und Bekleidungsindustrie* (Hamburg: Verlag Weltarchiv, 1989), 18.

23 Bureau International du Travail, *L'industrie textile dans le monde*, 182.

24 Quoted in Lorwin, *The World Textile Conference*, 46.

25 Bureau International du Travail, *L'industrie textile dans le monde*, 81.

26 Kroese, "The Past, Present and Future," 50; International Cotton Advisory Committee (ICAC), *World Textile Demand* (October 1994, Washington, D.C. 1994), 28: table 14. See also Victor Prévot, *Géographie des textiles. Etude d'un espace économique*, 2nd rev. ed. (Paris: Masson, 1986), 51: His numbers include all fibers; but most statistics only include the so-called "major fibers."

27 ICAC, (1994), 12: table 3; for 1950 and 1955: Arbeitgeberkreis Gesamttextil, *Die Textilindustrie in Europa und der Welt*, vol. 6 (1965) (Frankfurt a. M., 1966), 7: Textilfaserverbrauch pro Kopf der Bevölkerung.

28 ICAC, *World Textile Demand. Report prepared by the Secretariat for the 50th Plenary Meeting of the International Cotton Advisory Committee* (Antalya, Turkey, Sept. 1991), 11.

29 ICAC, *World Textile Demand. Report*, 11.

30 GATT, *Textiles and Clothing in the World Economy. Background Study prepared by the GATT Secretariat*, vol. 2: Appendices (Geneva, 1984), 26: Appendix Table A.25: Spinning = Short-staple, ring spindles. As for 1981, open-end rotors are first converted into ring spindle equivalent (1 rotor = 3 ring spindles), and then added to the total ring spindles installed. Weaving = Cotton-type looms; as for 1981 shuttleless looms are included without any adjustment for productivity difference.

31 Werner International, quoted in Michael Breitenacher, *Textilindustrie im Wandel* (Frankfurt am Main: Gesamttextil, 1989), 73, Table 18.

32 ICAC, *World Textile Demand. Report prepared by the Secretariat for the 52nd Plenary Meeting of the International Cotton Advisory Committee* (New Delhi, India, Oct. 1993), 6: Table 2.

33 Roy Pepper and Har Bhattacharya, "Changing Trends in Global Textile Technology and Trade," in Saha Devan Meyanathan, ed., *Managing Restructuring in the Textile and Garment Subsector. Examples from Asia* (Washington, D. C.: World Bank, 1994), 31-58, on 42-45.

34 Pepper and Bhattacharya, "Changing Trends," 43-46, particularly Figure 2.4 and Figure 2.5: On the assumption that open-end capacities are 2.5 times more productive than con-

ventional spindles, the global distribution of spinning capacities was accordingly adjusted. For weaving, the shuttle loom was taken as the common denominator. On the assumption that shuttleless looms were again 2.5 times more productive, capacities were adjusted accordingly. The spinning capacity of Asia in 1989 includes that of Oceania.

35 Gerhard Egbers, "Innovation, Know-how, Rationalization, and Investments in the German Textile Industry during the Period 1871-1935," in Hans Pohl, ed., *Innovation, KnowHow, Rationalization and Investment in the German and Japanese Economies 1868/1871-1930/1980* (Wiesbaden: Steiner, 1982), 234-256.

36 Frank Happey, ed., *Contemporary Textile Engineering* (London: Academic Press, 1982), 1 and 19.

37 Prognos, *Die Textilnachfrage und das Textilangebot in Westeuropa. Entwicklungsperspektiven der westeuropäischen Textilindustrie bis zum Jahre 2000* (Basel, 1986), 203 (that part of the study by Gerhard Egbers).

38 ICAC, (1994), 28: table 14.

39 David A. Hounshell and John Kenly Smith, *Science and Corporate Strategy. Du Pont R&D, 1902-1980* (Cambridge: Cambridge Univ. Press, 1988), 384.

40 Herwig M. Strolz, "Textile Machinery Investments, 1974-1983: A World Perspective," in The Textile Institute, ed., *World Textiles: Investment, Innovation, Invention* (Manchester, 1985), no pagination (quote at the end of the article). In the original article the number is 61,000 instead of, correctly, 161,000. But this is simply a typing mistake – telephone call with Mr. Strolz, 2 Nov. 1998.

41 U.S. National Agricultural Library, Beltsville, Maryland: Economic Institute for the Textile Industry, The Structure of the Textile Industry in Western Europe. The Danger of Over-Investment. Summary of Report, April (1949).

42 OEEC, *The Future of the European Cotton Industry. Report by a Group of Experts* (Paris, 1957), 15-21, 65-76.

43 OECD, *Modern Cotton Industry. A Capital-Intensive Industry* (Paris, 1965), on 15, 18, 100-101, 87, 124, 95-96.

44 Fabian, *Produktionstechnischer Fortschritt*, 233, Table 38: Die Struktur der Fertigungskosten für 50.000 t Baumwollgarn Nm 60 1965 bei moderner und bei alter Produktionstechnik (in 1,000 DM).

45 Eduard Terrahe, *Die Wettbewerbsfähigkeit der deutschen Baumwollrohweberei (insbesondere Nesselweberei) gegenüber Ländern mit asiatischem Lohnniveau sowie Ländern mit us-amerikanischer Produktions- und Automationsintensität – Möglichkeiten und Grenzen der Rationalisierung durch Automatisierung* (Diss. Münster 1960), 55-57 (the calculations of the Table on p. 56 are sometimes incorrect).

46 See Franz Fabian, *Produktionstechnischer Fortschritt, Mindestbetriebsgrösse und Konzentration in der Textilindustrie, untersucht am Beispiel der westdeutschen Baumwollspinnerei und -weberei* (Münster: Forschungsstelle für Allgemeine und Textile Marktwirtschaft, 1969), 233, Table 38 for spinning, and 335-377 for weaving; Terrahe, *Die Wettbewerbsfähigkeit*, 58-59, 65-67, 98-99, 296.

47 Hans-Dietrich Grosser, *Produktivität und technischer Fortschritt in der Textilindustrie* (Frankfurt am Main: Deutscher Fachverlag, 1963), 54-55.

48  See Terrahe, *Die Wettbewerbsfähigkeit*, 58-67; Fabian, *Produktionstechnischer Fortschritt*, 335-377; Michael Breitenacher, *Textilindustrie*, 2nd rev. ed. (Berlin: Duncker & Humblot, 1971), 105-106; Peter Sass, *Die Finanzierung der Investitionen in der Textilindustrie* (Münster: Forschungsstelle für Allgemeine und Textile Marktwirtschaft, 1970), 5-6.

49  OECD, *Industrial Revival Through Technology*, 101.

50  See Brian Toyne et al., *The Global Textile Industry* (London: Allen & Unwin, 1984), 43-44.

51  See Stephan H. Lindner, *Den Faden verloren. Die westdeutsche und die französische Textilindustrie auf dem Rückzug (1930/45-1990)* (Munich: Beck, 2001) 92-109.

52  Ibd., 109-120, 137-145; on the advertising of 1978 see 139.

53  See Vinod K. Aggarwal, *Liberal Protectionism: The International Politics of Organized Textile Trade* (Berkeley: Univ. of California Press, 1985); Donald B. Keesing and Martin Wolf, *Textile Quotas Against Developing Countries* (London: Trade Policy Research Centre, 1980); Jürgen Wiemann, *Selektiver Protektionismus und aktive Strukturanpassung. Handels- und industriepolitische Reaktion Europas auf die zunehmende Wettbewerbsfähigkeit de Entwicklungsländer – dargestellt am Beispiel der Textilpolitik der EG* (Berlin: Deutsches Institut für Entwicklungspolitik, 1983).

54  Peter Temin, "The Relative Decline of the British Steel Industry, 1880-1913," in Henry Rosovsky, ed., *Industrialization in Two Systems: Essays in Honor of Alexander Gerschenkron* (New York: Wiley, 1966), 140-155.

55  "China Mills Close a Chapter. Textile Workers Who Spun Revolution Lose Jobs" (by Edward Cody), *International Herald Tribune, Zürich* (6 Jan. 1997).

56  See Folker Fröbel, Jürgen Heinrichs, Otto Kreye, *Umbruch in der Weltwirtschaft. Die globale Strategie: Verbilligung der Arbeitskraft/ Flexibilisierung der Arbeit/ Neue Technologien* (Reinbek near Hamburg: Rowohlt, 1986), 103-106, 181-187.

57  Allix and Gibert, *Géographie des Textiles*, 339-340, quotation on 340: "bref que d'une manière ou de l'autre les vieux pays manufacturiers aient livré comme Samson le secret de leur force."

58  United Nations, *Economic Survey of Europe*, 192.

59  Stephan H. Lindner, "Der lange Abschied vom Textilland Vorarlberg," *Alemannia Studens* 7 (1997), 55-87, here 85.

60  Interviews with two top managers of Dierig, Augsburg: Mr. Verstynen, chairman, and Dr. Kampen, technical director, 27 and 28 June 1996.

61  Friedrich Aumann, "Auswirkungen der Osterweiterung der EU auf den Produktionsstandort Deutschland für Textilien und Bekleidung – eine empirische Analyse zu Stand und Trends," in Roland Döhrn, ed., *Osterweiterung der EU – Neue Chancen für Europa?!* (Berlin: Duncker & Humblot, 1998), 51-73.

# Production and Culture in the Global Cycle Industry

*Paul Rosen*

## Introduction

The increasing attention paid to globalisation by social theory arises largely out of a growing concern with space and spatialisation that has developed within debates around modernity and postmodernity. Discussions of globalisation within sociology have consequently followed for the most part the cultural focus of these debates.[1] However, the introduction of a spatial dimension to how we approach the shift from modernity to postmodernity offers an opportunity to broaden our understanding of how the production and consumption of goods has been changing in ways that are multidimensional – they are simultaneously social, cultural, economic, political, technological and spatial. Economic and political changes in the late 20th century have combined with innovations in communication technologies to allow firms and industries that were once more firmly rooted within their home markets to spread production across the globe in order to pursue cheap labour and reduced regulation. At the same time, commentators argue, the globalising culture of postmodernity often makes it possible to sell these global products to a "de-differentiated" world consumer market – the "global car" being the most commonly cited example of this.[2]

How accurate, though, are such accounts of global change? Are the shifts that have taken place as straightforward as is commonly portrayed? Several writers have questioned whether globalisation is truly global, in the sense of affecting all parts of the world equally. It is argued that what has actually taken place is simply a reconfiguring of international economics that follows existing patterns in albeit new and more intense forms.[3] Similar questions might be applied to "global" consumer culture. To what extent are the changes in American or British culture that so often shape sociological thinking a valid account of other parts of the developed, or even more so, the developing worlds? And however accurately a concept such as the global car represents changes in that one product, does it apply equally for other products, other industries and other markets? The history and sociology of technology tell us that the contingencies and uncertainties of change make this very unlikely. The story of any one product is shaped through the interactions of numerous factors in the product "lifecycle" – from conception and design, through production and distribution, to consumption and use. The globalisation of these processes makes the social shaping of technology far more complex than is the case in many accounts of technological change. It is worth asking, then, what form – if any – globalisation takes in particular industries and with particular products. What factors enable or prevent the more intensified internationalisation or globalisation of certain aspects of the product lifecycle? What role do the different components of change – social, cultural, technological, economic – play in bringing about this shift? And do such stories offer any lessons for mitigating the negative impacts of global change, especially for those areas of the globe which suffer the costs of globalisation but rarely see the benefits?

In this chapter I will examine these issues with regard to the changing fortunes of the British bicycle industry, taking the perspective of the social construction of technology approach within the sociology of technology. The organisation and methods of production of the bicycle industry interact not just with the nature of the goods produced but also with the culture of consumption that forms around those goods. More broadly, production changes in industry have generally over the 20th century been heavily implicated in the progression of modernity through to what is commonly regarded as postmodernity; globalisation is considered to be a central aspect of these changes, and this is clearly evident in the case of the bicycle. Before looking in more depth at this case, I will first outline the relationship between technology and production on the one hand, and modernity, postmodernity and globalisation on the other.

## Modernity and Postmodernity

Technological change is seen as integral to the intensification of modernity that took place in the 19th century. New technologies of power, travel, manufacturing and communications brought about a changing experience of the world, a shrinking of time and space, and newly globalised economic, political and social relations.[4] Marshall Berman vividly depicts the ambivalence thrown up by living in this newly modern world, which was at the same time both exciting and extremely threatening. He describes

> the highly developed, differentiated and dynamic new landscape in which modern experience takes place. This is a landscape of steam engines, automatic factories, railroads, vast new industrial zones, of teeming cities that have grown overnight, often with dreadful human consequences; of daily newspapers, telegraphs, telephones and other mass media, communicating on an ever wider scale; of increasingly strong national states and multinational aggregations of capital; of mass social movements fighting these modernisations from above with their own modes of modernisation from below; of an ever-expanding

world market embracing all, capable of the most spectacular growth, capable of appalling waste and devastation, capable of everything except solidity and stability.[5]

Similar arguments have been made for the late 20th century, notably by David Harvey, who is concerned with the emergence in recent decades of postmodernity and postmodernism.[6] He regards the transformations that have taken place since the 1960s in the organisation of the state, in modes of financial regulation, in production and capital accumulation, and in culture, to be a highly intensified recurrence of the same processes that heralded modernity and modernism. In particular, he highlights parallels between the association of Fordism with modernity in the early part of the 20th century, and an equivalent association between post-Fordism – which he terms flexible accumulation – and postmodernity.

Harvey and others have described how Fordism grew beyond being just a description of mass production, into a set of practices and principles that underpinned most Western societies. The Fordist state, Fordist regimes of capital accumulation, Fordist societalisation and Fordist mass consumption developed alongside and reinforced Fordist mass production, especially during the post-war years.[7] The collapse of this Fordist consensus since the 1960s has left national and global economic and political structures more fragmented. Mass production has been replaced by flexible specialisation, underpinned by non-specialised equipment that allows manufacturers to respond quickly to fragmented niche markets.[8] The accumulation of capital also has become more flexible, with manufacturers chasing around the globe in search of ever-cheaper labour and lower taxes. The result has been a variety of globalised production processes, including not just the notion of a global product made identically in numerous locations around the world, but also the globally dispersed production of different parts of a final product that only come together geographically at the point of assembly. Accompanying these changes in production have been developments that have reduced the role of the nation state and transferred global economic power from nation states to transnational corporations.

Underpinning these arguments about changing political, economic and cultural relations is an understanding that the temporal concerns of modernity – the assumption of a progression from the traditional to the modern and then the postmodern – need to be augmented by spatial concerns embodied in notions of globalisation.[9] Nevertheless, the associated concepts involved in modernity, postmodernity and globalisation are subject to numerous, often convincing, critiques – for example, questioning how appropriate Fordism and car production are as models for manufacturing in general, questioning the degree to which mass production has really been eclipsed by flexible specialisation, and questioning the extent to which globalisation has really involved the marginalisation of the nation state.[10]

It is not necessary to rehearse all these debates here, but a common theme worth highlighting is the argument that the processes described by theorists of flexible specialisation, postmodernity and globalisation have in fact been with us for longer than just the last few decades. As noted with Harvey, more recent developments are seen by some as an intensification of long-established processes rather than the emergence of something qualitatively new. Paul Hirst and Grahame Thompson put forward an argument in respect to globalisation that is reminiscent of Harvey's analysis of postmodernity.[11] They question whether there is any valid empirical basis behind the concept of globalisation. For them, the features of the world economy that are commonly labelled globalisation – notably the exploitation of resources and identification of new markets by Western capital at a global scale – have been present for over a century, and have even diminished in some respects. What has changed, they argue, is an *internationalisation* of the global economy, with new patternings of trading relations centred around three clusters of nations focused on the U.S., Europe and Japan.

One way of trying to understand this kind of transformation on the ground is through Gary Gereffi's concept of *global commodity chains*. This approach has the benefit of allowing an analysis of specific commodities within the context of general trends, and hence overcomes some of the problems associated with theories of globalisation. It does not assume that all industries undergo the same changes in the same timeframe. Gereffi sets out two kinds of global commodity chain: those that are producer-driven, shaped by the strategic investment decisions of transnational manufacturing firms – and akin to the mass production approach; and those that are buyer-driven, shaped by the retailers and branded merchandisers whose orders "mobilise global export networks composed of scores of overseas factories and traders" – and thus more akin to flexible specialisation.[12] Reflecting critiques of the notion of post-Fordism, Gereffi regards these two types of chain not as representing different temporal stages of industrial development. Rather, they are two different trends that are usually associated with particular industries – producer-driven chains tend to be characteristic of more established industries such as heavy engineering, whilst buyer-driven chains are evident more in newer industries including clothing and high technology.

This notion of global commodity chains captures the shifts in international economic relationships that are discussed by writers such as Hirst and Thompson. For both analyses, the degree to which these changes are truly global is less significant than the way in which they reinforce existing economic and political relations. At the same time, they underline the ways in which globalisation has involved a simultaneous strengthening of *locality*, as processes which on the surface are global, nevertheless take on specific meanings in particular local or regional contexts. The meaning of a global commodity chain varies, for example, depending on your position along the chain. These economic and cultural shifts are not, then, simply global; rather, they take the form of "global localisation" – or "glocalisation" – as global processes become integrated within specific localities.

## Sociotechnical Frames in the Social Construction of Technology

I want to explore debates about globalisation, modernity and postmodernity, and their relationship to technological change, taking the case of the bicycle industry and the culture of cycling in Britain during two key periods of transformation – firstly, the interwar years, and secondly, the period from the late 1970s through to the turn of the twentyfirst century.[13] These two periods have both involved substantial – and parallel – shifts in production methods, the organisation of the bicycle industry, bicycle design, bicycle usage and the cultural meaning of bicycles. Issues around modernity, postmodernity and globalisation are highly pertinent to these shifts, which I characterise as transitional phases that have occurred between different *sociotechnical frames* of bicycle production.

I have adapted the concept of a *sociotechnical frame* from Wiebe Bijker's *technological frames*, a concept which forms a central component of his social construction of technology (SCOT) approach developed with Trevor Pinch. SCOT was first developed as a means of challenging overly technical accounts of technological change. Pinch and Bijker identified the social dimensions of such change, centred around the competing meanings held for any artifact by a range of different *relevant social groups*. It is social processes, they argued, rather than technological ones that lead to the emergence of a single meaning for an artifact – thus the *interpretative flexibility* that characterises many technologies in their early stages is followed by *closure* of meaning, and technological *stabilisation*.[14]

Having established the notion that technological change is not simply a self-evident technical process but one which is socially constructed, Bijker and others have taken SCOT further, developing a set of concepts which account for how this process plays out in different contexts.[15] For Bijker, technologies are constituted by the interactions which take place around them. These interactions will establish a consensus among different interest groups around how "effective" or "successful" a particular design is. Bijker sees *technological frames* as the settings in which these interactions take place; innovators, industrial designers, marketing people and so on, as well as users or even non-users of the artifact might each have their own technological frame for thinking about and interacting around an artifact. The focus of the interactions that take place within a frame centres especially around the knowledges and practices of the relevant social groups involved. Technological frames provide, then, the cultural context within which those involved with an artifact – as engineers, manufacturers or consumers – engage with it and with other interested parties.

This SCOT framework has been subjected to critique from a number of directions, not always entirely fairly. The most sustained criticism has concerned the potential of this approach to address questions of power in the social relations of technology, a shortcoming which I believe results more from a lack of attention to this issue in what is still a fairly new field than anything intrinsic to the framework.[16] The conclusion to this chapter shows, I hope, that such inattention does not have to be the case.

A more significant problem is the way that the concepts of SCOT are applied within the framework to particular artifacts in the case studies used. In Bijker's account of the development of Bakelite, for example, he attaches a specific technological frame to each professional activity involved in the emerging story – there is one technological frame for celluloid chemistry, another for electrical chemistry, and a third for Bakelite itself.[17] The same is the case in Eduardo Aibar's and Bijker's recent account of a competition to redesign Barcelona in the mid-19th century; the different proposals for the city are aligned with particular approaches to urban design and urban governance.[18] Such an approach works well for the case studies which Bijker presents, since he discusses artifacts – and the social groups concerned with those artifacts – that appear to be quite discrete. In the Bakelite story, especially, the three different fields of celluloid chemistry, electrical chemistry and plastics are distinct in that they were practiced in different laboratories using different methods. Bijker's analysis only touches incidentally on the other artifacts within these laboratories – the plates, the photographic paper, the plant apparatus and so on – since these were not important to the shift he is depicting which resulted in the development of a new product. The Bakelite story as Bijker tells it – as with the stories in many other SCOT accounts – concerns only a small number of clearly distinguishable objects.

What happens, then, when the story one is trying to tell involves a variety of different artifacts, and when the relationship between these artifacts is crucial to how the story unfolds? SCOT is explicitly concerned to blur the distinction between the social and the technical, something which some take even further in their attempts to challenge the primacy that is usually given to human over non-human agency.[19] However, other boundaries tend to be left intact, notably the boundary that establishes one key technology (whether Bijker's Bakelite, Michel Callon's electric vehicles or Bruno Latour's automatic door closers) as the focus of concern. Other artifacts that interact with this key technology in the processes of design and development, production and consumption are, on the whole, forgotten about.

Paying attention to these other artifacts might, though, lead to the opening up of a whole new set of "black boxes" that would problematise this boundary.[20] This is certainly the case in the realm of production, which requires consideration of how the design of an artifact is shaped by – or influences the shaping of – the equipment used to produce it. A framework that is concerned only with discrete artifacts can present difficulties for understanding the importance of production equipment to the shaping of industrial products. A more appropriate approach might therefore be not to focus – as Bijker and Pinch do – on just the social interactions that shape the development of individual technologies, but instead to consider how *technologies, social groups and cultural factors* cohere together in particular ways to form a *sociotechnical frame* that encompasses a wider range of relationships than just those within and between relevant social groups.

This framework differs from Bijker's in a number of ways. It includes the interactions and activities of social groups that could perhaps appear less relevant from an engineering or design point of view, for example policymakers and activists concerned with particular issues. It includes cultural factors which are not explicitly part of Bijker's account, such as the discourses that underpin interactions around an artifact – for example, discourses around modernity, efficiency or particular pro-

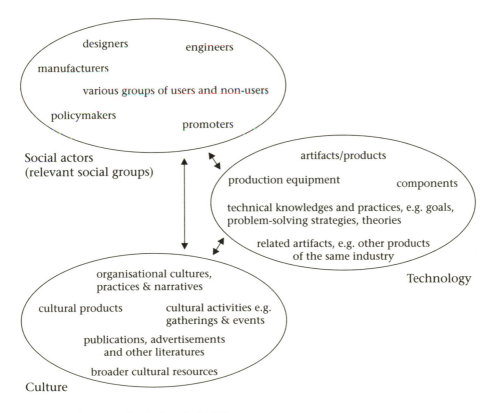

*Figure 1: Elements of a Sociotechnical Frame.*

duction values – and defining moments in the process by which a particular *sociotechnical ensemble* has become established, for example key sporting events in the history of cycling. It also includes the wider technological context of the specific artifact being studied – such as components or markets shared with other artifacts – and the wider social, political, economic and organisational contexts of the actors involved.[21]

The focus of sociotechnical frames is, then, less narrowly technical than Bijker's concept, it is not focused exclusively on accounting for single artifacts, and it is more heterogeneous in the kinds of things it includes and in whose concerns these things reflect. In short, it brings together a range of interlinked artifacts and components, discourses and practices focused around particular sociotechnical "objectives." A further important dimension to the difference between this and Bijker's concept is in terms of how sociotechnical frames relate to each other. For Bijker, several frames can initially cohere around a single artifact; over time, one is likely to become dominant (albeit undergoing changes of its own in the process) as the others fall by the wayside. This reflects his view of relevant social groups as the key agents of sociotechnical change. In contrast, change from one sociotechnical frame to another is something that results from a more thoroughgoing shift in the relations among the social, the cultural and the technical. Whilst design flexibility may be indicative of such a shift, it is only one dimension.

I will illustrate these points in the discussion that follows, which is concerned with the sociotechnical objectives of, firstly, establishing mass production methods among British cycle manufacturers during the inter-war years, and secondly the replacement of mass production with globally flexibilised methods since the 1960s. I will deal with the first of these in the following section.

## Modernity and Globalisation in the Sociotechnical Frames of the Mass Bicycle

The bicycle was the product of several decades of experimentation with self-propelled wheeled vehicles, beginning around 1817. Over the following decades, a small number of engineers across Western Europe worked on refining what was for the most part a curious plaything for the wealthy, until in the 1860s a small bicycle industry and upper class leisure cycling market became established in France, followed closely by Britain and the U.S. The French lead was curtailed by the Franco-Prussian War of 1870-1871, at which point the English Midlands became the centre of cycle innovation, and the foundation from which the British car industry was to emerge a few decades later. Following several years of rapid innovation and uncertainty over the direction of bicycle design, a period of stabilisation began in the 1890s.[22] The design that resulted formed a central component of the *sociotechnical frame of the factory bicycle* that then endured into the 20th century.[23]

As cycling became a more widespread pursuit among the upper and upper middle classes in Britain and elsewhere, the leisure-based cycling culture that resulted led to greater sales and an associated predictability of consumer tastes. At the same time, the rapid innovation of earlier decades diminished with the stabilisation of bicycle design around the low-wheeled, pneumatic-tyred, rear-driven safety bicycle. This gave British cycle manufacturers the confidence to begin investing in the up-to-date production equipment already in use in America and Germany. Nevertheless, this early sociotechnical frame was at the same time underpinned by a commitment to craft production – in contrast to the American sociotechnical frame of the bicycle which centred wholly around mass production and consumption.[24] The British industry at this time set great store by the benefits of a craft approach, matching the kind of service valued by consumers. Largely unhindered by machine tools that would later come to set many of the parameters of what was possible in product design, manufacturers at this stage took advantage of the greater scope that craft methods allowed for competitive advantage through innovation, customising, and consequently higher quality and higher priced machines. The craft basis of the industry at this time meant also that labour retained control over what Wayne Lewchuk calls the "effort bargain."[25] In terms of consumers, high prices meant that bicycles continued to be an exclusive product, percolating more fully into the middle classes only when the bicycle boom of the mid-1890s brought down prices and hence increased the bicycle's popularity.[26]

Conceptualising this constellation of bicycles, their riders, their makers and the equipment used to make them as a sociotechnical frame overcomes the difficulty that Bijker's approach would have in trying to account for what might seem less relevant social groups such as craft workers, or closely linked artifacts such as machine tools. This frame was not, though, to be long-lived. The seeds of transformation had already been sown in the 1890s as British companies sent their engineers to America to borrow ideas and to buy new automatic machine tools. Following the end of the First World War, which had enforced reduced outputs as the larger manufacturers concentrated their efforts on munitions, there was a period of some twenty years during which many key elements of the early sociotechnical frame were progressively abandoned. This period involved substantial modernisation of production, borrowing heavily from Fordist methods and from the more flexible version of mass production known as Sloanism. Process innovations and greater standardisation of design resulted in lower prices, and these were reinforced by an expansion of hire purchase. Together, such factors helped to reshape the meaning of the bicycle as a form of everyday transport for the middle and working classes, and no longer as just a toy for the rich.

At the same time, cycling culture retained its love of the pre-modern. Whilst craft methods had been abandoned in practice, they still played an important role discursively, sustaining an image of the bicycle and of cycling that has endured ever since – as a means of escape from the hectic life of the city. Images of rural cycling idylls were and still are common in magazine illustrations and cycle manufacturers' brochures, indicating a long-running theme within cycling culture of an ambivalence towards modernity.[27] Modernity was crucial to cycling culture both as the stimulus that led city dwellers into the countryside, and also as the force that provided them with affordable and well-built bicycles, as well as the metalled roads on which to ride them. This theme played a central role as a key meaning of bicycles and cycling within the *sociotechnical frame of the mass bicycle* which was beginning to be established, coexisting with the bicycle's other prominent meaning that centred around utility-based transportation, for which most bicycles were used during this period.

The mass bicycle was well-established by the late 1930s. Companies such as Raleigh had by this time completed their adoption of automatic production equipment and overhead conveyors, and standardised their product ranges. Nevertheless, the shift from one frame to another did not represent an absolute break. Whilst no longer adhering to the ethos of craft production, management across much of British industry – including the bicycle industry – differed from American counterparts such as Ford's in that they did not take control of the shopfloor. This remained in the control of labour, through a combination of factors. Labour mobilisation in Britain was stronger than in America, and in a better position to resist both the physical threats and the pay incentives used by management at Ford's to control the shopfloor.[28] British management also benefited from the existing system, in the sense that it worked for them as much as for their workforces. To adopt American management methods and hence bring about further industrial strife had no sense at a time when the market could not support the levels of production that Fordism would bring about. So whilst the technology changed, the relations of production of this later sociotechnical frame were little different to those of the earlier one – the systems of foremen and chargehands, piece rates and bonuses established in the preceding decades were retained even as production moved towards increasing automation and standardisation.[29]

A key feature of the mass sociotechnical frame as it became consolidated during the 1940s and 1950s was the centrality of the industry's export markets. This is highlighted by negotiations that took place during the mid to late 1950s between Raleigh and the British Cycle Corporation (BCC), which together owned almost all the major cycle brands of the time. Their shared dominance of the industry was enhanced with Raleigh's purchase in 1957 of the brands owned by BSA, which had been the third main industry player during the preceding decades. During the

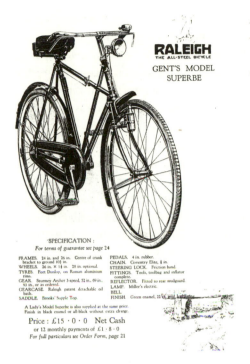

*Figure 2: Typical mass production Raleigh – the Gent's Model Superbe, from the 1929 Raleigh catalogue.*
*Copyright: Raleigh Industries.*

1950s, Raleigh and the BCC held negotiations over export markets and what might now be called "core products," in order to stem what they realised was becoming a saturated global market. In 1959, for example, Raleigh agreed to close down its South African factory in return for an interest in the BCC's operations there. A few years earlier, discussions broke down over an offer by the BCC to stop producing variable gears in return for Raleigh curtailing its production of either bicycles or steel tubing. Eventually, in 1960, the two companies merged, primarily because of a recognition that they could not continue to compete successfully in global markets that were beginning to develop their own production facilities.

The new company that resulted from the merger retained the Raleigh identity, and became responsible for some 75-80% of UK bicycle output, with around 60% of its production going for export. This new Raleigh's main overseas markets included Nigeria, Iran, and the United States. The kind of product being exported to these countries, just like those sold domestically, is clear from my earlier description of the sociotechnical frame of mass cycle production. They were for the most part fairly heavy utility or sports bicycles with three-speed gears, available in four key designs with some variation beyond that in styling (see Figure 2). The output of this frame was, then, a de-localised sociotechnology – an artifact that would look the same – however appropriate or inappropriate – wherever it was bought in the world. This blanket standardisation of bicycle design resulted from the constraints set by mass production, a point made as early as 1933 in a speech made by Raleigh's chairman, Sir Harold Bowden, to the company's agents.[30] Most importantly, it depended on high production levels at Raleigh's Nottingham plant; few overseas facilities were established before the 1950s, and these mainly focused on assembly of imported parts rather than on production.[31] This did not, therefore, bear much resemblance to the kind of global design strategy rooted in flexibility and dispersed production that has been advocated more recently in the car industry.

Whilst very different in form from those that pertain today, global economic and technological relations were central to the sociotechnical frame of the mass bicycle. In fact, the British industry's growing dependence on exports developed out of the logic of that sociotechnical frame, since the ability to significantly increase production of standardised products generated a need to create new markets. Unfortunately for Raleigh, the decline of its export markets in the 1960s and 1970s also contributed towards the collapse of this frame, and posed a serious threat to the British cycle industry.

## Global Flexibilisation, Postmodernity and Mountain Bikes

Having sketched the global relations of cycle production up until the 1960s, I want to look in more depth at developments that have followed. Just as the conquest by British manufacturers of global cycle markets during the 1940s and 1950s was closely linked to the modernisation of the UK bicycle industry, so too have changing global relations in the industry since the 1970s been linked to flexibilisation and fragmentation, not just in Britain but at a global scale. The changes that have taken place during this period can be regarded as a global flexibilisation of bicycle production, bicycle design, bicycle markets and cycling culture, resulting in a new sociotechnical frame of the bicycle. Just as happened with the shift that resulted in the mass bicycle, the sociotechnical frame of global flexibilisation again features some continuities with its predecessor alongside many discontinuities.

Most strikingly at a market level, British production no longer accounts for the bulk of domestic sales. Raleigh's production figures dropped steadily from an early 1990s peak of three quarters of a million bicycles (which was itself a significant drop from the 2.8 million produced following the 1960 merger) down to just a few hundred thousand by the end of the decade. The parallel drop in Raleigh's UK market share – from over 75% to less than 30% – has resulted from a transformation of bicycle production and cycling culture globally since the late 1970s. Central to these changes have been the emergence of new production techniques developed outside the traditional centres of production, along with associated changes in management styles, and a particular kind of bicycle – the mountain bike – that has both benefited from and further enhanced these changes. At the same time, the mountain bike has keyed into cultural developments that have served both to transform the meaning of cycling and consequently to revitalise it as an activity across much of the developed world. Mountain bikes now account for over 50% of all bicycles sold in the UK, a figure that matches other developed markets, and in many ways they have come to symbolise the global flexibilisation of the bicycle.

The decline in Britain of the sociotechnical frame of the mass bicycle involved a number of factors that were already coming into play before the emergence of new production methods and products. One important element was the decline in labour relations, as struggles in the late 1960s between management and the shop-floor resulted in the elimination of piece rates in favour of day rates. Similar developments in the British car industry are seen as crucial in moving more consistently towards Fordism.[32] At Raleigh, on the contrary, this can be seen rather as one of the factors that pushed the company away from its version of mass production, and towards more flexible approaches. This wasn't a straightforward progression, though. Labour struggles continued into the 1970s, culminating in 1977 in a strike that seriously damaged production during the crucial run-up to Christmas, when a high percentage of the industry's annual sales take place. Almost immediately following the resolution of the strike, Raleigh's parent company, TI, began to discuss ways of modernising the factory, beginning with a shift from long conveyors to short assembly tracks staffed by worker "cells." One obvious advantage to management of this shift towards cellular working was in drawing workers into seeing the company's welfare as coterminous with their own. This was extended with the adoption in the late 1980s of a version of Total Quality Management. This shift in the organisation of production at Raleigh and elsewhere in the UK facilitated the emergence of the new sociotechnical frame of globalised flexibility during the late 1980s. The fact that Raleigh came close to closure several times during the 1970s and 1980s, prior to its sale by TI to a group of cycle enthusiast financiers, indicates its likely fate had such changes not been adopted.

As well as labour relations and production methods, Raleigh has also been faced with new kinds of competition and a rapidly changing market since the end of the 1970s. Domestic production began to be challenged in the 1970s by increasing imports that ate into the home market. These came initially from Europe, but from around the mid-1970s the bulk of imports were coming from the Far East – Japan, Taiwan and elsewhere. At the same time, Raleigh's key export markets were one by one closed off – American sales were affected by the strength of the pound, Nigeria cancelled all foreign debts due to an internal economic crisis, and the Iranian revolution put an end to its foreign trade. Raleigh responded with a noteworthy transformation of its marketing strategy. It began to look to Europe as a source of potential new sales, duly sponsoring a Tour de France racing team. In 1982, Managing Director Roland Jarvis told *The Guardian* "we have given up our global ambitions."[33]

In contrast, competitors from the Far East were beginning to realise their global ambitions, based on the successful development of an innovation from California. Mountain bikes developed as a hobby among Californian hippie "bike bums" in the 1970s, who adapted old balloon-tyred Schwinn children's bikes for fast downhill racing in the dirt tracks of Mount Tamalpais in Northern California. Soon, frame-builders within this group and from the surrounding neighbourhood began to draw on the design of these old machines in building bikes of their own. The term "Mountain Bikes" comes from the name of the company set up by three central participants, Tom Ritchey, Gary Fisher and Charlie Kelly. As they and others were discovering it was possible to sell reasonable numbers of their new California-made product, another approach was being established by the bicycle accessory importer Specialized, setting the pattern for the newly emerging sociotechnical frame of the globally flexible bicycle. Specialized supplied a Japanese factory with specifications for its Stumpjumper mountain bike, which it then imported back into the United States. At the same time, mountain bikers' thirst for new components that would be able to withstand the assault that downhill racing put on the bikes brought them to the attention of the innovative Japanese component manufacturers Shimano and SunTour. In the words of Charlie Kelly, this

> was the last stage of assembling the infrastructure necessary for mass production, and from that time forward mountain bike production swung into high gear, maintaining for several years the highest growth curve in the bicycle industry. For better or worse, mountain bikes were no longer a garage industry ...[34]

The manufacturing process used for mountain bikes was not mass production, though. The boom in mountain bike sales – in the mid 1980s in America, and the late 1980s in the UK – allowed the economies of scale of mass production, but these were combined with a form of flexible specialisation involving global subcontracting and niche marketing. A mountain bike commentator and designer with the British company Muddy Fox – which epitomised this approach as one of the first companies to launch the bikes in the UK – labelled it "remote control manufacturing."[35] He described for me the process of choosing the design and specifications of a mountain bike as follows:

A. Tubing is selected, usually like the Tange series [a Japanese brand]. Many companies use no-name tubes supplied by factories, often of dubious quality.

B. Shimano supply "groupsets" [of components], through the Far East factorys [sic]. Many companies do not use the full "group" to save money, just utilising the brakes + transmission.

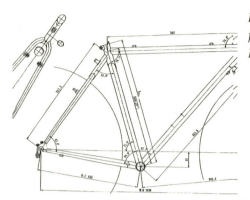

*Figure 3: Bike design specification sheet, from photocopy supplied by Hilton Holloway at Muddy Fox (1992).*

C. Frames can be selected of [sic] the shelf, though most detail their own designs.

D. So the factory will submit a drawing like this [see Figure 3]. It is pretty simple, but suffices for most manufacturers. Better companies will go into more detail.

E. Ancillary components are selected from a vast catalogue, the "Taiwanese Bicycle Guide."[36]

Design in the new sociotechnical frame of the globally flexible bicycle is thus often a case of picking and mixing pre-existing elements rather than originating new ones, reducing cycle "manufacturers" in many cases to "little more than marketing companies with just an office and a phone."[37] Design innovation has often been left to the trading companies and factories that firms like Muddy Fox deal with in the Far East.

What this means for the British bicycle industry is far more complicated than simply the notion that British manufacturers have lost market share to overseas competitors. The industry has in fact been fragmented and reshaped in quite complicated ways. A significant number of foreign manufacturers are engaged in the UK market – for example the Taiwanese company Giant and the American Trek both have UK offices and market directly in the UK. One interesting twist here was the purchase of Muddy Fox in 1992 by TI Cycles of India (Raleigh's former Indian subsidiary), which invested in Muddy Fox as a means of gaining access to the British market for its own cheaply produced bicycles – an ironic reversal of its former colonial relationship with Raleigh. In addition to these kinds of relationships, though, an increasingly large proportion of UK cycle firms have adopted the methods I have described to import from the Far East either finished or partly finished bicycles which are then badged locally by the importer. The resulting product is an outcome of complex global relationships – involving designers, framebuilders and component manufacturers that can span two or possibly three continents. This global transformation of the industry is likely to continue as cheaper labour markets open up in China, for example – a phenomenon that has already been seen with the shift from Japan to Taiwan as the production centre for mountain bikes.

Such transformations of the organisation of production have been underpinned by the appearance of new manufacturing methods, to which Raleigh's shifts of the late 1970s and 1980s were a partial response. As well as the more obvious economic benefits to flexibly specialist approaches such as short tracks and cellular working, a key feature of the global flexibilisation sociotechnical frame has been the abandoning of traditional methods of brazing together bicycle tubes in favour of a particular form of welding, TIG-welding. This method appears to have travelled to Japan and Taiwan via BMX and then mountain bikes, having originated in the Californian aerospace industry. Its significance lies in the great adaptability it allows for bicycle frame angles, compared to the rigidity of design imposed by mass production methods. It thus caters to a mountain biking culture that is characterised by a burgeoning of ever-more specialist uses that require the minutely differentiated "frame geometries" that are made easy with TIG-welding.[38] More recent developments such as laser cutting of tubes enhance this flexibility, enabling large scale manufacturers to produce high volumes without the need for standardisation.

This last point highlights a sharp contrast between this and the preceding sociotechnical frame of the bicycle. If the mass frame resulted in global standardisation – and hence de-localisation – of bicycle design, the products of global flexibility are far more complex. Mountain bikes have become ubiquitous, at least in the developed world, to a great extent replacing the utility, touring and racing styles that preceded them. However, the flexibility of production methods that now characterises the bicycle industry means that alongside the globalisation of production and distribution there is more scope for a re-localisation of the meanings of mountain bikes as they spread beyond their Californian origins. This re-localisation takes place largely in the cultural realm, and it is notable that however much the spread of mountain bikes has been helped along by developments in manufacturing techniques, by the organisation of production and by changing global economic relations among producers, the key to the success of mountain bikes has been their cultural resonance at several levels.

During the mountain bike booms in the U.S. and UK, these novel machines, whose design was based on post-war children's bikes, evoked memories of childhood cycling among the baby boomer generation. This evocative nostalgia was an important aspect of the rise of mountain bikes as a cultural product, not just in the United States – as might be expected – but in Britain also.[39] It ensured that unlike the BMX boom that had come a few years earlier, mountain bikes were identified from the start as adult bikes, and not, initially, as children's bikes at all. Mountain bikes in their early days carried clear connotations of the yuppie consumerism of the 1980s, something that manufacturers such as Muddy Fox capitalised on from the start.[40]

Their cultural resonance for baby boomers also tied them into some of the boomers' key cultural concerns at this time – health, fitness and the environment. At a time when utility cycling had seriously declined – or even disappeared in many cities in the U.S. – mountain biking revived adult leisure cycling as a route to improved health, and also as an activity that allowed people to engage with the countryside – something that refers back to the point made earlier in relation to cyclists' ambivalent relationship to modernity. This ambivalence resulted in mountain bikes becoming simultaneously associated with a growing concern for the environment, yet at the same time being seen by certain groups as a threat to it. As growing numbers of mountain bikers took to the American wilderness, environmentalists became concerned at the threat posed to natural habitats and forest ecosystems. This led to restrictions being imposed on mountain bikers on the very tracks where the sport originated. In the UK, smaller numbers of mountain bikers, and a more managed countryside landscape, have meant that there are mostly voluntary agreements in place in the national parks that are affected.

Despite environmental conflict over the use of mountain bikes in the wilderness, in urban areas the technology associated with mountain bikes has been important in boosting the role of cycling more generally as a component of growing environmental awareness, especially in relation to traffic problems such as pollution, congestion and the depletion of resources. Alongside their evocative qualities, various technical features of mountain bikes have enhanced their attractiveness to adult users, making them central to a growth in cycle sales and use. Their sturdiness and resilience have made them seem ideal for negotiating poorly maintained city streets and leisure tracks such as canal towpaths. Their upright riding position, and the rapid innovations that have appeared through the 1980s and 1990s to improve braking and gearing, mean that they are seen as ideal bikes for inexperienced riders or those who simply feel unsafe in traffic on a racing bike. There are concerns about the ecological impact of mountain bikes, especially the built-in obsolescence of many components, and their inaccessibility for amateur repairs. Nevertheless, in an urban context – and more so in Britain than the U.S. – rather than damaging the environment, mountain bikes have come paradoxically to be seen as one route to protecting it, by encouraging more people to abandon their cars for cycling.

The above discussion indicates how mountain bikes have come to be ubiquitous in a range of contexts that are often far removed from the downhill mountainside racing where they originated. To an extent, they represent a global cultural spread of the values of American baby boomers; nevertheless, it is possible to see differences in how these values are re-contextualised locally just by looking, as I have, at the British and American contexts. Research into other markets outside the West, or even the northern European settings where cycling never shifted so fully from a means of transport to a leisure activity, would provide further insights into the re-localisation of this globally flexible technology.

## Conclusion – Beyond Globalisation in the Sociotechnical Frame of the Bicycle

In this article I have described two processes of change from a British perspective. The first of these processes, involving a shift from an early, craft-based socio-technical frame to one rooted in mass production and consumption, was instrumental in establishing Britain as the dominant global supplier of bicycles, with markets and subsidiaries throughout the developed and developing worlds. Bicycle design was standardised across this global market, based on a conception of the bicycle as a sturdy, reliable and easily maintained transporter of people and – often – goods. This was matched by a home bicycle market that was rooted in utility cycling, alongside a further dimension of cycling culture, the escape from modernity that was expressed by leisure cycling in the countryside.

The subsequent disintegration of this sociotechnical frame brought about transformations that mean that the global relations of cycle production have been thoroughly destabilised and reconstituted. Distribution is no longer primarily uni-directional, as was the case when mass produced bikes were exported *en masse* from Britain to markets in its former colonies. Instead, production is fragmented across the globe, involving complex and multiple exchanges among different production centres. Distribution is also fragmented, in ways which blow apart the industry's earlier colonial relationships – in some cases, former colonies now export to Britain; in others it is hard to even state categorically whether a bicycle should be regarded as British (where it was badged) or Far Eastern (where it was designed and manufactured). Matching these changes in production and distribution is a fragmentation of cycling markets and of cycling culture. Markets in the developing world can no longer be relied on to import huge quantities of Western goods; whilst in the home markets of companies such as Raleigh, consumers will no longer support mass producing and standardising industries, preferring instead the variety of choices offered by flexible specialisation. This shift in consumer tastes (which has both helped bring about, and been shaped by, industrial change) reflects a diversification within Western cycling cultures to include a variety of different kinds of cycling (mostly leisure-based) requiring different kinds of products.

The resultant changes in both British production and the commodity chain that supplies British consumption mean that it is no longer possible to speak with any certainty of a *British* bicycle industry. Although there are British manufacturers of bicycles, bicycle components and accessories, these are all tied into a variety of global networks of relationships of manufacturers, suppliers, sub-contractors and consumers, that can best be understood in terms of the *global commodity chains* discussed earlier. It is noteworthy that the two sociotechnical frames of the mass and the globally flexible bicycle equate more-or-less to the two kinds of commodity chain Gereffi describes. The colonial-style producer-driven relations with its overseas markets that characterised the British cycle industry until the 1960s have been superseded by the more dynamic approach of newer entrants to the industry; and even the few remnants of the old approach have had to change their practices. This is evident in the way Raleigh's parent company during the late 1980s and 1990s, Derby International, also owned a trading company in Taiwan, which could source and supply parts for bikes to be assembled in Nottingham. This situation is aptly described in Gereffi's account of *triangle manufacturing*, where firms in the Newly-Industrialised Countries of the Pacific Rim act as trading company sub-contractors for Western manufacturers; for Gereffi, this an important factor in facilitating successive shifts to cheaper labour markets.[41]

Gereffi raises an important question concerning who benefits from such developments. He argues that the sub-contracted nations involved in triangle manufacturing can only benefit if they can somehow acquire the most value-added position within the commodity chain – as happened with TI Cycles of India's purchase of Muddy Fox. It is, for Gereffi, always the core firms in the chain who have most to gain. This is undoubtedly true, although the complexity of global commodity chains sometimes makes it difficult to identify quite where the core is. For the bicycle industry, certainly, it isn't entirely clear whether the core is the American and British branded mountain bike companies, or the Taiwanese trading companies and factories whose economies of scale have enabled them to take a market share that would have been incomprehensible as recently as fifteen years ago. It is similarly difficult to state categorically whether the shift from a strong global position to a weaker one has necessarily been a bad thing for British manufacturers, given the unsustainable direction the industry was moving in during the 1950s – for example, Raleigh's unquestioning sense of prosperity allowed it to open a new factory in 1957 at a cost of £5 million, which it then had to leave empty for five years as sales began to go into decline for more-or-less the first time in the company's history.

One shortcoming of an approach such as Gereffi's is that like much other discussion of globalisation – particularly as the phrase enters popular discourse – it fails to maintain an understanding of the links between economic and cultural change. In both the sociotechnical frames of the bicycle that I have discussed at length, the economic and the cultural have been interdependent. In the shift towards global flexibilisation, especially, the outcome for the British cycle industry would have been very different had it not coincided with the emergence of mountain bike culture; similarly, mountain bike culture would probably have suffered a similar fate to BMX had the industry not been so receptive to a new, and highly marketable, product innovation to accompany its new production and organisational innovations.

That said, it is important to note that the ways in which the production and consumption of bicycles have changed with global flexibilisation are not identical. Whilst changes in production and organisation make this industry something of an exemplar of globalisation, the consumption side is very different. There has been without doubt a global spread of the products of this new sociotechnical frame, but this has not been even across all markets. Rather, there has been an intensified differentiation between developed and developing world cycle markets. The mountain bikes which typify global flexibilisation have come to dominate cycle sales across much of the developed world, despite their very strong and specific cultural resonance primarily for American baby boomers. Their meaning and utility have somehow been translated and relocalised into very different contexts than the Californian mountains where they originated, in part through the multiplicity of design variations that new production methods have made possible.

In contrast, cyclists in the developing world – often in the very countries where many mountain bike parts are produced – still ride, for the most part, standard heavy roadsters which are very similar to those that Raleigh was exporting around the globe in the 1950s. The globalisation of production does not, then, represent a thorough globalisation of cycling culture, which has instead divided into two distinct cultures – one maintaining traditional uses and values for the bicycle as a mode of transport (albeit encroached upon by the gradual emergence in the developing world of a car culture); the other increasingly fragmented among different uses, primarily centred around leisure and sport. The crucial point to note is that the bicycle industry which has been globalised is the one which is geared towards the latter markets, matching the continual desire of consumers for innovation and change with its own continual search for cheaper labour costs and the least regulated production conditions. Indigenous cycle industries in Africa and Asia have not experienced anything like this amount of change. Seen in this way, globalisation does not appear to represent something that is strikingly new in the history of capitalism.[42]

What does the future hold for the bicycle, and what might be the characteristics of its *next* sociotechnical frame? There are many possibilities, and exploring these opens up questions not just about the future of technology and society, and about the relationship between transport and leisure, but also about the role of analysts of sociotechnical change in lobbying for and even trying to bring about certain kinds of sociotechnical scenarios. Is it enough simply to tell the story of a technology such as the bicycle, or should we be actively engaging in debates about technology, change and globalisation – debates which have become public and highly political in recent years, for example in the way that the work of Anthony Giddens[43] has influenced the British Labour Party, and in the conflicts over who controls world trade that have been evident in the international protests against the World Trade Organisation, the G8 and so on?

There is considerable scope to explore in far more depth the issue raised by Gereffi of net winners and losers in the development of global commodity chains. In the bicycle industry, there are implications both locally and globally arising from the shift from a monolithic British-dominated world cycle trade to one where British companies are just part of a larger chain. This raises important questions over the precise ways in which the sociotechnical frame of the bicycle might develop beyond globalised flexibility. In terms of production, the mass British manufacturers of the 1950s and 1960s might well be simply replaced by others – notably the Taiwanese trading companies and the component giant Shimano – whose activities are just as imposing as those of their predecessors for peripheral participants in the commodity chain. For this reason, many cycle activists and even some industrial players mobilise to resist the power of a company such as Shimano.[44]

In the context of consumption, it is to be hoped that the bicycle will become a more integral component of a sustainable transport system, and thus move beyond its primary position at present in the UK as a leisure object whose use is often dependent on unsustainable transportation, such as when people drive their mountain bikes out of the city in order to then ride in the countryside. Such a shift is, I believe, to be strongly encouraged, and gains support from UK policy shifts which favour the development of sustainable transport networks. The bicycle is, hopefully, only at the modest beginning now of a renaissance as a mode of transport rather than as a leisure object.[45] This could have substantial benefits for the bicycle industry, too, especially at the relatively undeveloped utility end of the market – provided the industry shifts its focus to match policies which are already some way advanced, on paper at least. Perhaps British cycle producers and consumers have something to learn here from the former colonial markets where cycle production and repair remain indigenous industries that support a transport-based bicycle culture.[46]

How important utility cycling, and an industry geared to supporting the utility market, will come to be as components of the next sociotechnical frame of the bicycle, remains to be seen. Highlighting this possible path for the sociotechnology of the bicycle shows, at the very least, the importance of addressing the social and cultural as well as the technical components of sociotechnical change. In order to increase utility cycling it is necessary to pay attention not just to the technical infrastructure of cycleways which is the most common approach of cycle campaigners, but also other factors such as: the social and cultural infrastructures of cycling, for example the constraints and opportunities for cycling afforded by people's domestic and workplace situations; bicycle accessories; the design, production, marketing and distribution of bicycles; and the global organisation of the bicycle industry. The notion of *sociotechnical frames* is a valuable tool in helping us to understand change in this way, as heterogeneous. To return to my earlier comments on Bijker's work, sociotechnical change, in his analysis, comes across as a characteristic of particular artifacts and the groups whose interactions and activities within a technological frame constitute those artifacts. What I have tried to present here is an approach that shifts the focus slightly, so that change is instead a characteristic of a process that may centre on a particular artifact or group of artifacts, but involves also a whole range of disparate elements including the relations of production, national and global economies, and the cultural meanings of these products and processes. Sociotechnical change cannot be reduced to any one of these elements, but rather is a product of their inter-relationship.

## Notes

1 Mike Featherstone and Scott Lash, "Globalization, modernity and the spatialization of social theory: an introduction," in Mike Featherstone, Scott Lash and Roland Robertson, eds., *Global Modernities* (London: Sage, 1995). Thank you to Andrew Webster for suggestions and comments whilst I was writing this paper, to Brian Rappert for reading and commenting on an earlier draft, to Colin Divall for his commentary at the *Prometheus Wired* conference, and to the anonymous reviewers for helpful suggestions.

2 Scott Lash, *Sociology of Postmodernism* (London: Routledge, 1990).

3 David M. Gordon, "The global economy: new edifice or crumbling foundations?" *New Left Review* 182 (1990), 24-64; Paul Hirst and Grahame Thompson, *Globalization in Question: The International Economy and the Possibilities of Governance* (Oxford: Polity, 1996).

4 Hirst and Thompson, *Globalization in Question*.

5 Marshall Berman, *All That is Solid Melts into Air: The Experience of Modernity* (London: Verso, 1982), 18-19.

6 David Harvey, *The Condition of Postmodernity* (Oxford: Blackwell, 1989).

7 Bob Jessop, "Post-Fordism and flexible specialisation: incommensurable, contradictory, complementary, or just plain different perspectives," in Huib Ernste and Verena Meier, eds., *Regional Development and Contemporary Industrial Response: Extending Flexible Specialisation* (London: Belhaven, 1992), 25-43.

8 Michael J. Piore and Charles F. Sabel, *The Second Industrial Divide: Possibilities for Prosperity* (New York: Basic Books, 1984).

9 Featherstone and Lash, "Globalization, modernity and the spatialization."

10 Miriam Glucksmann, "In a class of their own? Women workers in the new industries in inter-war Britain," *Feminist Review* 24 (October 1986), 7-37; Karel Williams, Tony Cutler, John Williams and Colin Haslam, "The end of mass production?" *Economy and Society* 16 (1986), 405-439.

11 Hirst and Thompson, *Globalization in Question*.

12 Gary Gereffi, "Capitalism, development and global commodity chains," in Leslie Sklair, ed., *Capitalism and Development* (London: Routledge, 1994), 211-231, on 215.

13 For a more detailed account see Paul Rosen, *Framing Production: Technology, Culture and Change in the British Bicycle Industry* (Cambridge, Mass.: MIT Press, 2002), where full citations of research material can be found.

14 Trevor J. Pinch and Wiebe E. Bijker, "The social construction of facts and artefacts: or how the sociology of science and the sociology of technology might benefit each other," *Social Studies of Science* 14 (1984), 399-441; Wiebe E. Bijker, *On Bikes, Bakelite and Bulbs: Towards a Theory of Socio-Technical Change* (Cambridge, Mass.: MIT Press, 1985).

15 Wiebe E. Bijker and John Law, eds., *Shaping Technology, Building Society: Studies in Sociotechnical Change* (Cambridge, Mass.: MIT Press, 1992).

16 Stewart Russell, "The social construction of artefacts: a response to Pinch and Bijker," *Social Studies of Science* 16 (1986), 331-346; Langdon Winner, "Social constructivism: opening the black box and finding it empty," *Science as Culture* 3 (1993), 427-452.

17 Bijker, *On Bikes, Bakelite and Bulbs*.

18 Eduardo Aibar and Wiebe E. Bijker, "Constructing a city: the Cerdà plan for the Extension of Barcelona," *Science, Technology, and Human Values* 22 (1997), 3-30.

19  Michel Callon, "The sociology of an actor-network: the case of the electric vehicle," in Michel Callon, John Law and Arie Rip, eds., *Mapping the Dynamics of Science and Technology: Sociology of Science in the Real World* (Basingstoke: Macmillan, 1986), 19-34; Bruno Latour, "Where are the missing masses? The sociology of a few mundane artefacts," in Bijker and Law, eds., *Shaping Technology,* 225-258.

20  Wiebe E. Bijker, Thomas P. Hughes and Trevor Pinch, eds., *The Social Construction of Technological Systems: New Directions in the Sociology and History of Technology* (Cambridge, Mass.: MIT Press, 1987).

21  Janice McLaughlin, Paul Rosen, David Skinner and Andrew Webster, *Valuing Technology: Organisations, Culture and Change* (London: Routledge, 1999).

22  Pinch and Bijker, "The social construction of facts and artefacts"; Bijker, *On Bikes, Bakelite and Bulbs.*

23  Rosen, *Framing Production;* see also Pryor Dodge, *The Bicycle* (Paris and New York: Flammarion, 1996).

24  Glen Norcliffe, "Popeism and Fordism: Examining the roots of mass production," *Regional Studies* 31 (1997), 267-280.

25  Wayne Lewchuk, *American Technology and the British Vehicle Industry* (Cambridge: Cambridge University Press, 1987).

26  James McGurn, *On Your Bicycle: An Illustrated History of Cycling* (London: John Murray, 1987).

27  Peter L. Berger, Brigitte Berger and Hansfried Kellner, *The Homeless Mind: Modernization and Consciousness* (Harmondsworth: Pelican, 1974); David Patton, "Technology and tradition: interwar cycling culture and design," paper presented to the Design History Society Conference on "Moving through design: the culture of transport and travel," Southampton, December 1993.

28  Huw Beynon, *Working for Ford* (Wakefield: EP Publishing, 1975).

29  Craig Littler, *The Development of The Labour Process in Capitalist Societies* (London: Heinemann, 1982); Lewchuk, *American Technology.*

30  *Motor Cycle and Cycle Trader* (10 November 1933).

31  Gregory H. Bowden, *The Story of the Raleigh Cycle* (London: WH Allen, 1975).

32  Lewchuk, *American Technology.*

33  *The Guardian* (14 April 1982).

34  Charles Kelly and Nick Crane, *Richard's Mountain Bike Book* (London: Pan., 1990), 55.

35  Interview with Hilton Holloway, Muddy Fox, 1992.

36  Letter from Hilton Holloway, 21 February 1992.

37  *Ethical Consumer* 6 (February/March 1990), 19.

38  Paul Rosen, "The social construction of mountain bikes: technology and postmodernity in the cycle industry," *Social Studies of Science* 23 (1993), 479-513.

39  Kevin Patrick, "Mountain bikes and the baby boomers," *Journal of American Culture* 2 (1988), 17-24; Allan R. Ruff and Olivia Mellors, "The mountain bike – the dream machine?" *Landscape Research* 18 (1993), 104-109.

40  Jay Rayner, "Of Lycra cycling shorts and the wheels of fashion," *Independent on Sunday* (15 March 1992), 22.

41  Gereffi, "Capitalism, development and global commodity chains," 224-225.

42  Harvey, *The Condition of Postmodernity;* Hirst and Thompson, *Globalization in Question.*

43 Anthony Giddens, *The Third Way: The Renewal of Social Democracy* (Oxford: Polity Press, 1998).

44 See Rosen, *Framing Production*.

45 Ibid.; Department of Transport, *The National Cycling Strategy* (London: DOT, 1996).

46 Marcia Lowe, *The Bicycle: Vehicle for A Small Planet* (Washington, D.C.: Worldwatch Institute, Paper 90, 1989).

# Global History and the Present Time

*Wolf Schäfer*

> *There are three times: a present time of*
> *past things; a present time of present things;*
> *and a present time of future things.*
> St. Augustine[1]

It makes sense to think that the present time is the container of past, present, and future things. Of course, the three branches of the present time are heavily intertwined. Let me illustrate this with the following story. A few journalists, their minds wrapped around present things, report the clash of some politicians who are taking opposite sides in a struggle about future things. The politicians argue from historical precedent, which was provided by historians. The historians have written about past things in a number of different ways. This gets out into the evening news and thus into the minds of people who are now beginning to discuss past, present, and future things. The people's discussion returns as feedback to the journalists, politicians, and historians, which starts the next round and adds more twists to the entangled branches of the present time. I conclude that our (hi)story has no real exit doors into "the past" or "the future" but a great many mirror windows in each human mind reflecting spectra of actual pasts and potential futures, all imagined in the present time. The complexity of the present (any given present) is such that nobody can hope to set the historical present straight for everybody. Yet this does not mean that a scientific exploration of history is impossible. History has a proven and robust scientific method. I would like to begin this chapter, therefore, with a homage to historical criticism in the Augustinian realms of the *memory* of past things, *expectation* of future things, and *perception* of present things.[2]

## The Memory of Past Things

The historical-critical method is a sharp and unforgiving tool. It produces the facts of history and the gift of unexpected discovery; it clears the fog of false intelligence about past presents and allows judicious historians to distinguish between reliable information, fraud, and fantasy. As Peter Gay put it, "the cure for the shortcomings of enlightened thought lies not in obscurantism but in further enlightenment."[3] The enlightening power of the historical-critical method combats historical obscurantism and false memories of past things. Examples for the power of historical criticism are not hard to find.

In the second century BC, Alexandrian scholars like Aristarchus of Samothrace used an early form of methodical historical enlightenment, textual criticism, to determine the "original" conclusion of the Odyssey. The historical enlightenment itself is a good example; it stands for a great idea that has lost its 18th century luster. We judge it now as a Eurocentric phase of history that claimed equal rights for "man" at the universal level but did nothing for the working man at the local level; now we see that "mankind" included men, especially white men, and left women and children out. One can feel the sting of these historical deconstructions, yet appreciate them as a welcome confirmation that historical-critical inquiry can cut through the blinkered memories of the past.

If a student of ancient history does not know that Alexander the Great (356-323 BC) died at the age of thirty-three in Babylon, probably a victim of "Macedonian drinking," we would tell him to read O'Brien.[4] But if this student would tell us that Alexander circumnavigated the Arabian Peninsula, rebuilt Necho II's canal between the Gulf of Suez and the Nile, moved the capital of his kingdom from Babylon to Alexandria, captured Carthage in 319 BC and opened the Straits of Gibraltar for commercial shipping, we would ask him to leave us alone. Yet if our student would add that he was just recounting an exercise in "what if" history by Arnold Toynbee (1969) quoted by a German classicist investigating the benefits of counterfactual history, he would be in good standing again.[5]

An Italian humanist, philosopher, and literary critic, Lorenzo Valla (1407-1457), challenged the papal claims to secular power in 1440 by analysing the content, language, and style of the donation of Constantine in a book entitled *The Falsely-Believed and Forged Donation of Constantine*. He argued that the document, which was supposedly given by the Roman emperor Constantine to Pope Sylvester I (314-335), was concocted centuries later by "some foolish petty cleric who does not know what to say or how to say it."[6] Reading Valla can still teach us a lesson about profound rhetoric and rigorous method. Jean Mabillon (1632-1707), a Benedictine monk, pioneered the study of ancient handwriting (paleography) during the scientific revolution in the 17th century. He and his colleagues developed sophisticated principles for determining the authenticity and dates of medieval manuscripts. Mabillon made his critical tools available in *De Re Diplomatica* (1681) knowing very well that the science of diplomatics[7] would help to detect the genuine sources of history amidst a large number of retouched, interpolated, and entirely forged documents in the archives of his beloved Roman Catholic Church.

The historical-critical method, developed over centuries of careful application and refinement, has enabled the students of history to separate the wheat from the chaff when considering evidence and to regard passionate human beliefs and

wishes with equanimity. The historians who applied the critical method distinguished between authentic and attributed works (was Moses the author of the five
Books of Moses?), discovered fictions and forgeries (were the Hermetic texts written
before or after the writings that they had supposedly inspired?), dispelled errors,
myths, and legends (did Christopher Columbus prove that the world was round?).[8]
Historical criticism has solved these and similar problems. When the French historian Marc Bloch (1886-1944) reviewed the history of historical criticism in his post-
humous *Apologie pour l'Histoire* (1952) he remarked that the "mythomaniac epochs"
did not shy away from inventing false memories of their pasts.

> The Middle Ages knew no other foundation for either its faith or its laws than the
> teachings of its ancestors. Romanticism wished to steep itself in the living spring
> of the primitive, as well as in that of the popular. So it was that the periods which
> were the most bound by tradition were also those which took the greatest liber-
> ties with their true heritage. It is as if … they were naturally led, by the sheer force
> of their veneration of the past, to invent it.[9]

## The Expectation of Future Things

Historians pursue historical truth not only with regard to the concoctions of back-
ward-looking times but also with respect to the expectations of futuristic epochs
like the Modern Age. We can count on history to falsify our expectations but we can
also ask: why did people have these particular expectations in the first place? We
can dismiss the utopias from Francis Bacon to H. G. Wells as "utopian" but we can
also perceive them as indicative of the forward-looking tendencies of the last five
hundred years. Our understanding of the workings of history in the present time
can only improve when we use the historical-critical method to assess past expectations retrospectively.[10]

Historical enlightenment can compare the various products of Musil's creative
"sense of possibility"[11] with actual developments. One can juxtapose factual data
with historical prophecies, predictions, and simulations. It has been shown for the
United States between 1890 and 1940 that forecasts of technological change
stretching ten or more years into the future were more often wrong than right. The
20th century did not turn into an age of electric railways, as the "electrical enthusi-
asts" predicted around the turn of the century, but into an age of mass-produced
automobiles. "Nobody imagined in the 1930s that the TV would have such a great
influence on our everyday lives. No one saw that automobile exhaust might lead to
global warming."[12] One can prove that concrete predictions of technological inventions and innovations have a higher batting average than the predicted social,
economic, and cultural effects of these novelties.[13] Thus, historical enlightenment

about the outlook of future-oriented societies can document the unintended consequences of forecasting and analyse the paradoxical interactions between historical
expectations and subsequent outcomes.

We can easily imagine different futures but not "the" future. The future is another present time and we are not in it. We often wish we could enter this dimension and explore it like a real place though we know that this is not possible. The
space of the future is a metaphor and does not exist as real estate. This means that
one can enter the intriguing space of the future only through language. We can fire
up our imagination and put ourselves in other periods of time but we are bound to
operate in the temporal spaces of the present time. So, without exit doors from the
present and forced to look into the diffracting lenses of the present time, what do
we see? Windows painted in the style of René Magritte. The window in Magritte's
painting *The Key to the Fields* is not made to be *looked* through but to be *thought*
through. The painter had this to say about his key window:

> Let us take any window. The windowpane breaks and with it the landscape that
> could be seen behind it and through it. When that really does happen one day,
> which, after all, is possible, then I would like a poet or philosopher – my friend
> Marcel Lecomte for example – to explain to me what these broken shards of real-
> ity mean.[14]

The meaning of Magritte's reality shards is no clearer to the historian than it was to
the philosophising artist. All the historian knows is that those shards are his documents and that he must take these fragments of previous world perspectives and try
to reconstruct the social constructions of the present time that once was.

The year 1989 yielded a lot of shards, and it is likely go down in history as prom-
inently as 1789. In 1989, the University of Chicago Press published a "history of the
future" by Warren Wagar, who characterised his book as "the work of a professional
historian who has applied the methods and mind-set of historians" to the task of
"unscrolling" the history of "the next two centuries." The author approached this
assignment with the venerable hypothesis of the "future demise of world capitalism, leading to proletarian socialism and finally pure communism." The year of
publication could not have been worse timed for this prognosis; but the real irony
was expressed in the title of Wagar's book – *A Short History of the Future* – because no
scroll of the future could have been any shorter than this one, which was torn up by
real and present events the very instant it appeared.[15]

What can we learn from this debacle? First, one can neither reliably predict nor
perceive the future. We must go where the present time goes and cannot run on
ahead to observe our own future because we cannot live simultaneously in two
present times, the present present time and a future present time. Second, a reliable

"history of the future" cannot be written before the future has become a past present. Third, attempts to force open the window to an expected future will merely break the painted glass, so to speak, and reveal nothing new. However, one can study the broken shards retrospectively and reconstruct the different views that generated the various landscapes of expected futures. Magritte's key window gives us only one view but the historian can recreate numerous outlooks and try to see what a given time had "in mind." Fourth, we must distinguish between forged and authentic relics of the past on the one hand and right and wrong expectations of future things on the other. Truthful historical reconstruction can work with both kinds of expectations as well as with the revelation of false memories.

## The Perception of Present Things

It may now be asked what can the historical-critical method do for the present? My answer would be: all of the above. The present time contains false and fair memories as well as false and fair expectations and thus provides the fuel for our method. But historical enlightenment about the present time goes beyond critical bookkeeping about the usage of the past and consumption of the future; it can also help to navigate the hot zones of contemporary history. Historical criticism can begin to distinguish between false and fair perceptions of present things, such as globalisation for example, perhaps the most present, contentious, and loose thing of all at this point. Like my initial story about the entangled branches of historical time, the struggle for and against globalisation excites journalists, politicians, historians, and people worldwide.

### The Field of Global History

Increasingly conscious of all its others and ecocentric, humankind has made some progress with regard to itself and its global environment. Contemporary history has become global in many ways, but more historians are still being sought for local history than for global history. To work the planetary dimensions of contemporary history into the local perspectives of American, Argentinean, German, Turkish and all other national histories is still by and large a task to be attacked, but the task has become clear.

I try to differentiate between global history with capital and lowercase letters. Lowercased global history is not limited to certain parts of the globe but involves the whole planet and transcends the local stomping grounds of every nation and tribe. Capitalised Global History is researched and written; it investigates, documents, and interprets the transgressive forces of global history. To put my perceptions of global history and the present time on the table, let me introduce a few additional distinctions.

Global History is not a globalised World History. It is neither an epic history of civilisations nor a total history of everything, but a new field of history that concentrates on history in the present time – Martin Albrow's "Global Age" if you want.[16] Global historians explore the global in the cascades of local activities. They go at the roots of current events and if these roots are old or ancient, they trace them back in time. However, the main axis of global history is lateral and runs between the nodes of actions in, and reflections of, the three present times.

Global History works with globality and "glocalisation." Globality, the product of numerous globalisations and benchmark of the present time, has replaced the old concepts of modernity and universality. "Glocalisation" or the blending of global and local was used to describe the adaptation of Japanese products to local markets; Roland Robertson developed it as a space-sensitive alternative to globalisation. The generalised sociological meaning explains the cascades of simultaneous interactions in the present time, where global fashions meet up with local mentalities, local mentalities with global institutions, global institutions with local organisms, local organisms with natural resources, natural resources with local waste, local waste with global tourists, global tourists with local products, local products with global methods, global methods with local resistance, local resistance with global strategies, global strategies with global companies, global companies with local data, local data with global machines, global machines with local interpretations, local interpretations with global diseases, and so on, in turbulent streams.[17]

Glocal actions and reflexive reactions make global history in real time. Some people say that migratory streams, flows of goods, natural, cultural, and commercial cycles were always global, and they may be right. But they are forgetting the huge difference that real time makes. Yesterday's local actors had to wait ages, sometimes literally, for the completion of a global chain reaction like the Neolithic Revolution. The Greeks and Romans, for example, could not see that the domestication of plants and animals was slowly making its way around the globe. Today's actors can think globally and act locally without losing track of the whole because all parts of the whole are wired into the interlocking networks of global communication and information.

Global History is interdisciplinary. The phenomena of global history breach not only national and geographic but also disciplinary boundaries. For that reason, contemporary global history cannot be handled by a parochial discipline. Global History has to team up with the history of science and technology to understand global technoscience or with atmospheric sciences and environmental history to grasp the impact of the exploding population of motorcars on global climate change. Global historians must work with social and cultural historians, explore the histories of race and gender, and collaborate with political scientists and economists. Other configurations can range from medicine to theology or from communications research to musicology.

Global History employs a postconventional epistemology. The linear thinking of modernity is discredited; the one-dimensional approach of modernisation theory has done more harm than good; the isolated standpoint of the external observer has been deconstructed; research has become a form of sociocultural intervention. Classical physics no longer provides the only model for scientific inquiry; the integration of what "is" with what "should be" or "should not be" has gained paradigmatic significance in genetic engineering and global ecology; the monsters of mathematics have become everyday figures; turbulence is no longer merely a disturbance but a potential source of structure. Chaos and order are no longer opposites; global and local have converged; the periphery appears in the center and the center at the periphery.

The grand narrative of Global History is about decontinentalisation. The human race of this planet migrated out of Africa into disconnected local sites on widely separated continents. Yet as humans have moved from local arts to global technoscience and thus from local cultures into a global civilisation that affects and infects their communities everywhere, a consciously shared global environment has emerged and the splitting apart of Alfred Wegener's supercontinent Pangaea has been reversed.[18] Now technoscience is defragmenting the globe with its networks, and the new global drift towards a technoscientific Pangaea Two is bringing the world into the present time.[19]

## The "Presentism" of Global History

True or false, it seems to me that all humans are put on the same temporal plane by globalisation so that the temporal regime of global history pivots around contemporaneity, the consciousness of being together in the present time which is enabled and enforced by global technoscience (especially networks of global communication, information, and transportation). Thus the temporal focus of global history is neither the past, as in mythomaniac times, nor the future, as in modern times, but the present contemporaneity of all humans. This leads Global History to critique *the ideology of non-contemporaneity*, the claim that not all contemporaries are contemporaneous.

I shall be arguing that global history privileges contemporaneity and dispels the idea of non-contemporaneity, which was built deep into the historical system of the Modern Age and has created temporal haves and have-nots among peoples and cultures since the days of Columbus. Today, the classification of fellow human beings as "non-contemporaneous others" (i.e. primitives) would appear to be a shame ethically and a mistake politically. The Taliban were not remnants from the past or simply backward others; they participated in contemporary global history with modern weapons and a debatable cultural alternative. Yet coming to terms with the complexity of the present time, which results from the massive parallelism of cultural contemporaneities, is obviously one of the great challenges of global history.[20] So, how did the new temporal order come about and what does it mean to be knowingly contemporaneous (in the present time) with everybody else on earth?

Global information and communication in real time have become a reality in the second half of the 20th century. Today, all human societies on this planet can communicate simultaneously with one another. Thus the present time is in an excellent position from a communications point of view. The spatial distance between individuals and societies no longer delays the transmission of news. The barriers of geography that have existed since time immemorial have been reduced to virtually nothing insofar as the exchange of information is concerned. Geography has lost much of its hindrance to the transport of people and goods to every corner of the planet. Images, sounds, texts, data, and software generated at one "end" of the earth can be received by people at the other "end" within seconds. That has never been the case before.

When Thomas Jefferson was President of the United States, he said to his Secretary of State one day: "Mr. Secretary, we have not heard from our Ambassador to France for two years. If he doesn't write by Christmas, we might send him a letter."[21] This historical anecdote would not have survived if such a tolerant approach towards a lackadaisical ambassador had not been as remarkable then, nearly two centuries ago, as it would be today. Of greater interest to us, however, is the implicit message about the snail's pace of long-distance communication in the past, up to the early 19th century.

Jefferson wanted to keep the United States out of the Napoleonic wars in Europe and was keen to receive news from France; he himself was once the American envoy to Paris and was involved in drafting the French *Declaration of the Rights of Man*. Yet even a less patient president would have expected news from abroad to be delayed. Moreover, it would have never even occurred to him that one might be able to communicate with Paris *contemporaneously*. At the time, the fastest means of sending a letter from Washington to Paris was by coach and sailing ship – in other words, it was several weeks in transit, and so was the reply. Communication about current events depended upon the distance from the event and, for that reason, it invariably lagged behind the events themselves. The geographical distance between various locations imposed a temporal gap in communication that increased in proportion to the distance and the difficulties of travel. There was no difference with regard to this predicament between the Egyptian Pharaohs and Jefferson: long-distance communication was only possible non-contemporaneously.

Geography mattered because long-distance communication was overwhelmingly tied to transportation. The message could not travel faster than the human or

animal messenger. Communication was either face-to-face and immediate or mes-
senger-dependent and lagging. Contemporaneity (like community) was based on
personal communication and linked to the range of the human voice. For hundreds of thousands of years, real-time communication required close physical proximity and took place exclusively within the range of the eyes and ears of the partners in communication. The dissemination of information was a function of the se-
rene pace at which the small bands of Stone Age hunters and gatherers moved
around on the face of the earth. Later, after the Neolithic Revolution, messengers
on horseback began to accelerate the transmission of news to an average maximum
speed of about 15 kilometers per hour. The speed of light was achieved occasionally
with mirrors, flags, smoke signals in daylight or fire beacons by night. Legend has it
that the news of the fall of Troy was transmitted immediately by nightly fire signals
to Clytaemnestra, 600 kilometers away.[22] But soon after Jefferson, in 1837, the long
duration of geographical constraints to communication began to break down with
Samuel Morse's electrical telegraph.[23]

Around 1830, a letter from Europe to India via the Cape route took between
five and eight months by sea. The sender had to wait about a year for the reply. But
twenty years later, in 1850, thanks to the combination of rail and ocean steamer, a
letter from London would arrive in Calcutta 30 to 45 days after it was sent. The few
telegraph dispatches, which were exchanged in the summer of 1858 between the
United States and Europe via the first transatlantic submarine cable, included the
news that a planned shipment of British troops from Canada to India was no
longer necessary due to a change in circumstances.[24] One of the many excited
friends of the new technology calculated that the money saved as a result
amounted to about half the cost of the cable. During the American Civil War,
Abraham Lincoln and his generals kept in contact with several front lines via telegraph connections. Lincoln was among the first Commanders in Chief with the
technical capability to be physically absent, yet able to take action on various
fronts almost simultaneously.[25]

James Clerk Maxwell's electromagnetic waves circle this planet a good seven
times per second and transport their cargo via fiberoptic cable and satellite to every
point on earth instantaneously. Today we can assume, therefore, that what happens on earth happens simultaneously. People have grown accustomed to the fact
that everything that takes place anywhere can be shared and discussed everywhere
else. Communication at the speed of light has become the global standard. Demonstrators in non-English-speaking countries hold up their placards in English in
front of the ubiquitous TV cameras to globalise their concerns without delay. The
first Persian Gulf War showed the world that the American President could fight a
war and play golf at the same time. Thanks to global news in real time the deception
of an opponent and the simultaneous disinformation of one's own population

have now become routinely linked, too.[26] Reinhart Koselleck has summarised the historical trend toward instant communication as follows.

> Much of our empirical data since the eighteenth century can be plotted along exponential time curves, which confirm that the process of change is accelerating. (…) Information technology has thrown a net of communications over the globe such that the transmission times between event and information about it are approaching zero, whereas in the past news would take days, weeks, months or years to travel.[27]

The zero point at the end of the explosive acceleration and globalisation of communication and information was targeted in the 20th century by telephone, transistor radio, and television; it was reached in the 1990s with the spectacular growth of e-mail and the World Wide Web. This long-awaited "annihilation of time and space" (a popular phrase since the telegraph days) marks the true arrival of two-way communication and information in real time independent of location. The known laws of nature, the state of technoscience, and the modest size and favorable features of "spaceship earth" have made it possible to pull virtually every living person into the global maelstrom of intelligence about everything, from the most minute triviality to the largest accident.[28] It is this permanent visual and acoustic contemporaneity of all people and events that distinguishes the present time from all other historical periods as far as the potential conversation of the whole human species is concerned.

Of course, the global contemporaneity of all people and events applies *only* to terrestrial distances on our comparatively small planet and not for really long-distance conversations, say, with interlocutors in outer space. Communication with an ambassador on the moon would entail a delay of about four seconds (just under two seconds for the signals each way); the two-way transmission of a conversation with an envoy on Venus, the planet closest to us, would take about five minutes; and if we attempted to e-mail our friends on the nearest stars, Alpha Centauri and Proxima Centauri, circa 4.3 light years away, we would have to wait nearly nine years for the answer. The recently conquered non-contemporaneity of long-distance communication will come back with a vengeance when one travels beyond this globe and moves from acting globally to acting galactically.

I mention these facts to highlight the favorable position of communications on earth at the present time. Instant communication independent of location is a privilege of global history that is tied to the earth. Galactic communication will be fantastically non-contemporaneous for everyone involved. However, despite the great achievement of technically optimal conditions of communication on this planet, it does not follow that equal social and cultural relations of communication have also been established. On the contrary, the political economy of global communication is still extremely unequal.[29] I would like to turn to this problem now, yet with a twist. Socioeconomic differences are well known, but the *sociotemporal* equivalents of equality and inequality, contemporaneity and non-contemporaneity, have not been perceived so clearly.

## The Ideology of Non-Contemporaneity

In 1493, on his way back from the assumed discovery of the western route to the "East Indies," which were in fact the West Indies and Bahamas, Christopher Columbus wrote to the Spanish court that the natives of these isles were not dangerous at all and knew of "neither iron nor steel." Other observers commented on the archaic level of written Amerindian culture, while still others noted that the useful applications of the wheel – as a wagon wheel, spinning wheel, milling wheel or potter's wheel – were not known in Central America. The transoceanic seafarers from Western Europe brought the news home that the Christian world shared the earth with an abundance of unknown religions, cultures, and peoples, creatures that may not have descended from Adam. The infinitely strange multireligious, multicultural, and multiethnic world with scores of different customs and practices, which unfolded in the 16th century as a fantastic reality, confronted Christendom with an intellectual challenge. All of a sudden the earth had become very hard to grasp in its totality, and eventually people began to look for geographic, theological, and anthropological explanations.[30]

In the wake of their voyages of discovery, Europeans began to compete not only with themselves and the dead cultures of ancient Greece and Rome but also with the living peoples and cultures of Central America, Africa, and Asia. The question of how to deal with the presence of so many new and unfamiliar human beings became a crucial issue for the Modern Age. Europeans were already convinced about the superiority of Christendom but the belief in their culture's instrumental predominance grew as a matter of practical proof. From the 16th century onwards, Europe's scientific, technological, and military capabilities were aggressively and repeatedly demonstrated.[31] European colonisers, theologians, philosophers, historians, sailors, merchants, soldiers, and adventurers pronounced and consolidated the occidental claim to combined religious, political, and civilising ascendancy over all "savages." They invented a temporal order of peoples and cultures that legitimised Europe's leadership role for centuries to come.

The growing complexity of the scope of humanity in the modern world appeared as a problem. The Modern Age established a solution that was simple and ingenious but also devastating for large parts of the human race: temporal cleansing through modernity. Modernity became the benchmark of the new order. It drastically reduced the rising number of "others" in the world by placing all non-Europeans on lower evolutionary levels. The contemporaneity of Europeans with ever more different others was thus made to disappear. Others became unmodern and therefore non-contemporaneous; they were still there but no longer in the present time.[32] Military and bureaucratic approaches were taken to constrain the physical existence of others (if the reduction of complexity was not accomplished by famines or diseases), but neither fate nor force could remove all others from the present. It was the temporalisation of the geoethnic space of the globe which secured the monopoly on the sociocultural present by the West from the Renaissance into Postmodernity. It accustomed the beneficiaries of this worldview to the vertical hierarchy of a temporal order of humans and things and caught even progressive thinkers in its trap. Some examples will show how the ideology of non-contemporaneity worked.

In May 1789, the German poet Friedrich Schiller (1759-1805) who was in dire need of a livelihood and had just become a history professor at the University of Jena for that reason, delivered his inaugural lecture on *What Is and To What End Does One Study Universal History?* He stepped up to the lectern, read with a strong and steady voice, criticised his colleagues and praised world history as a process culminating in himself, the "educated man of the world" and "philosophical mind."[33] Schiller preached the logic of non-contemporaneity with great aplomb. He made it known to his students that the "raw tribes" found by European seafarers "stand like children of various ages around an adult and, by their example, remind him of what he himself once was." According to Schiller, the savages know nothing about the bond of marriage, have no idea about property, always fight, and often eat the flesh of their enemies. Schiller declared that Universal History provides the answer to the question as to how the human species advanced from "contemptible" beginnings, i.e. "from the unsociable cave dweller to the brilliant thinker" of the contemporary period; he imputed a "rational purpose to the way of the world and a teleological principle to world history." Schiller's lecture made a big impression. He was honored with a serenade and given three cheers.

The hubris and arrogance of the European enlightenment, which only Voltaire in France and Samuel Johnson in England found somewhat offensive and inappropriate, is now apparent and intolerable. Schiller's World History with its stepladder of cultures and a white genius perched on the highest rung was not an exception but the rule. The enlightened ideal that "all human beings are born free and equal in dignity and rights" and should not become victims of discrimination, is only slowly becoming the global norm.[34] The fundamental equality of all human beings has still to be defended against racist and sexist manifestos and murderous acts. That much is obvious. But temporal discrimination – the modernity syndrome – has more or less escaped public attention. The modernity syndrome creates unmodern people and repudiates their right to be part of the present. Even the most progressive of bourgeois society, who could be on the Left politically, have often been blinded by their elitist cultural modernism. They would do almost anything to avoid appearing unmodern. Let me illustrate this syndrome with a few passages from the Austrian architect Adolf Loos (1870-1933), who is deserving of our admiration in many respects. In the essay "Ornament and Crime," he complained about all the temporal "stragglers" sharing his time in 1908.

> The speed of cultural development is hampered by the stragglers. I may be living in the year 1908, but my neighbor is living around 1900 and that person over there in the year 1880. (...) The peasant in Kals[35] lives in the twelfth century. And there were tribes in the anniversary parade who would have been considered backward even at the time of the great migration. Happy is the country that does not have such stragglers and marauders. Happy America! Over here, there are unmodern people even in the cities, stragglers from the eighteenth century, who are outraged by a picture with violet shadows because they are not yet able to see the violet.[36]

The Viennese functionalist proudly declared: "I preach the aristocrat." Did Loos realise that he had internalised the temporal reconstruction of the hierarchical social order of Europe's prenational court society? Not at all. Loos was an aristocratic cultural modernist with no doubts. The aesthetic details of a neighbor's clothing told him that the fellow next door was of a lower time rung (not necessarily from a lower social class), a backward fellow and straggler, or worse, a plunderer of what had survived or, worst of all, a degenerate; for "what is natural in the Papuan and in the child is a sign of degeneracy in the modern person."[37]

A man like Loos, who saw Karl Kraus as standing "on the threshold of a new age,"[38] must be judged by his choice of language, which, as Theodor W. Adorno remarked, has a ring to it that puts him in a company of which he would not have approved. Loos, anticipating Bertolt Brecht, proclaimed "Ich esse roastbeef" and then goes on in brazen tones to talk about "the pinnacle of humanity" by which he means "our level of culture." The ideologue of non-contemporaneity looks down on "uncultivated people." He peers into the richly populated depths of some 10, 20, 100, or 1.000 years and makes out "degenerates" and "marauders" at the very bottom; he designs an escalator of decreasing contemporaneity. On its cultural time steps, with the obvious exception of the top level, non-contemporaneous contemporaries are assembled on a declining scale, with increasingly unmodern people toward the bottom. Loos is ready to "tolerate" the ornaments of "the Kaffir, the Persian, the Slovakian peasant woman, the ornaments of my shoemaker" because "all these people have no other means to reach the high points of their being," but he cannot grant "these people" historical contemporaneity.[39]

The non-contemporaneity of the simultaneous is the temporal equivalent of the hierarchically graded sociopolitical order of the chief estates under the *ancien régime* (nobles, clergy, and commons). Yet whereas the order of the estates was fairly static, the temporal order of aesthetic modernism and cultural modernity is dynamic. The old order was rendered into gas when all that was solid melted into air. The odious molecules of non-contemporaneity can envelop anyone and everything. The value of people and things is not set once and for all, but fluctuates. An individual may be awarded the seal of contemporaneity for one thing and can be dismissed the next moment as non-contemporaneous for something else.

The German philosopher Ernst Bloch (1885-1977) used the topos of *contemporaneous non-contemporaneity* to come to grips with German fascism. He developed a "theory of non-contemporaneity"[40] in *Heritage of Our Times*, a collection of essays published in Zurich in late 1934,[41] which fused contemporaneity and non-contemporaneity with Marxian terms. The chapter of the book that develops Bloch's historico-philosophical theory is entitled "Non-Contemporaneity and Obligation to its Dialectic"; it dates from May 1932 and begins deceptively low-key and crystal-clear:

> Not all people exist in the same Now. They do so only externally, through the fact that they can be seen today. But they are thereby not yet living at the same time with the others.[42]

What did Bloch expect from the concept of non-contemporaneity? The answer is hinted at a few lines down: "(...) the intolerable Now seems different with Hitler, because he paints good old things for everyone."[43] Bloch wanted to beat Hitler with Hitler's own weapon, the exploitation of non-contemporaneity. But Bloch could not simply embrace non-contemporaneity. Marxism could not rival Nazism uncritically. So, unlike Schiller and Loos, Bloch had to locate something of value in the realm of the devalued remnants of the past. He found his answer in a non-linear concept of history.

> History is no entity advancing along a single line, in which capitalism for instance, as the final stage, has resolved all the previous ones; but it is a polyrhythmic and multi-spatial entity, with enough unmastered and as yet by no means revealed and resolved corners.[44]

Bloch set out to open Marxism for the promising corners of the past. He drafted "a multi-layered dialectic" of history and made "the turbulent Now broader" by adding a couple of temporal contradictions to the traditional one between capital and labor. Bloch achieved his broadening of the present by distinguishing between contemporaneous and non-contemporaneous contradictions of history in the present time. The contemporaneous contradiction was the orthodox one between capitalism and the proletariat, whereas the new and innovative non-contemporaneous contradiction was between "the falsely and the genuinely non-contemporaneous." False or subjective non-contemporaneity was defined as "non-desire for the Now" and genuine or objective non-contemporaneity as "surviving being and consciousness" of the past.[45]

Bloch tried not to ridicule Nazism as wholly non-contemporaneous because he wanted to control the fascist "explosion of the non-contemporaneous" by creating the socialist art of making the irrational "safe, indeed helpful." He thus conceived of dividing the non-contemporaneous into good and bad anachronisms in order to oppose Nazism with the genuine non-contemporaneity "of a not wholly refurbished past."

> The subjectively non-contemporaneous contradiction is accumulated rage, the objectively non-contemporaneous one unfinished past; the subjectively contemporaneous one is the free revolutionary action of the proletariat, the objectively contemporaneous one the prevented future contained in the Now, the prevented technological blessing, the prevented new society with which the old one is pregnant in its forces of production.[46]

The philosopher of contemporaneous non-contemporaneity aligned himself with the proletariat "as the historically decisive class today." He proposed to raid the "treasure vaults" of the unfinished past and turn the weapons of unreason against the forces of reaction. He offered Marxism a position with a "more genuine awareness of 'Irratio' than the Nazis and their big business partners" – in short, Bloch tried to occupy the objective part of non-contemporaneity and give it a positive spin because he theorised that it was "high time to mobilize contradictions of non-contemporaneous strata against capitalism under socialist direction."[47]

My critique of Bloch, as my preceding critique of Loos, is ignited by specific elements of Bloch's language and not by Bloch's attempt to contend with Hitler for the "non-contemporaneous strata." Bloch – like Loos – displayed very little respect for the natives of Papua New Guinea when he spoke of "false non-contemporaneity which only appears in the guise of Papua in so far as it is not up-to-date." The temporal arrogance of the modernity syndrome informed Bloch's language and choice of words.

> The employee lashes out wildly and belligerently, still wants to obey, but only as soldier, fighting, believing. The employee's desire not to be proletarian intensifies into an orgiastic desire for subordination, for a magical bureaucratic exist-

ence under a duke. The employee's ignorance, which seeks past stages of consciousness, transcendence in the past, intensifies into an orgiastic hatred of reason, into a 'chthonism' in which there are berserkers and crusade images, indeed
in which – with a non-contemporaneity which becomes extraterritoriality in
places – negro drums rumble and central Africa rises.[48]

Thus Schiller's "raw tribes" appeared in Loos' anniversary parade as "degenerates"
and overwhelmed Bloch as "employees" with "rumbling negro drums." Yet how do
we speak about other cultures, peoples, groups, individuals, institutions, identities,
lifestyles, and modes of behavior? Are we less likely than Schiller, Loos, and Bloch
to question the contemporaneity of our global neighbors? Have we gone beyond
the ideology of contemporaneous non-contemporaneity? The problematic heritage
of five centuries of temporal discrimination has given the West a powerful cultural
attitude that cannot be underestimated.

### The Postmodern Continuity

Today, the phantom of the non-contemporaneous other seems to haunt
postmodernist thinkers. They have turned the ideology of non-contemporaneity
on its head and regard it as something to be cherished, especially the non-contemporaneities of non-Western cultures. One of the initiators of this complete rever-
sion was Ernst Bloch again, who championed the emancipation of the "third
world" in the 1950s when he was teaching in Leipzig.[49]

Bloch combined the prescribed Marxist-Leninist philosophy of history with his
theory of a temporal "multiverse" of peoples and cultures.[50] He emphasised the "to-
getherness of different times" and thus gave an optimistic slant to contemporaneous non-contemporaneity to allow for the "present awakening of Africa and
Asia."[51] Bloch declared that the Western idea of progress did not imply a European,
Asian, or African avant-garde but rather a "whole better earth."[52] He celebrated the
"polyrhythmic and polyphone" processes of decolonisation and the anticipated result, the unity of the human species, not as the product of one culture but as the
convergence of all past, present, and future cultures. His hope for the world was a
unified humanity at the end of history.[53]

The positive variant of the ideology of non-contemporaneity idealised the
non-western others as potential carriers of a global liberation but still had them
standing on wildly different levels of societal development. Postmodernism and
postcolonialism have praised non-contemporaneity as a human resource. They also
made the reverse side of positive non-contemporaneity a target of their critique
against cultural hegemony and racial supremacy and thus created negative
contemporaneity. Lothar Baier expressed this view eloquently in a public forum on
"The Matter with Time" in June 1991 in Frankfurt am Main. He identified con-

temporaneity as the "secret Utopia of Western civilization" and attacked "worldwide contemporaneity" as the West's "most totalitarian project" to date. The archetypical "other" emerged in Baier's talk not as Papuan but as Hopi. Baier praised the non-contemporaneity of the Hopi people because Hopi-time is subjective and would not allow contemporaneity, yet this was no longer a shortcoming for Baier but a cultural heritage threatened by industrial progress. He deplored the loss of the wealth of non-contemporaneities as the drainage of the "old strands of time."

> Uncultivated time has become a luxury since western modernity manages time like other resources ever more rationally. The old strands of time are surveyed, aligned, fenced in, and covered with concrete. What is washed ashore cannot lie around and perhaps take root. The encounters of cultures multiply but they happen in the shock of a moment and create nothing that is new and needs time to develop. The multiculturalism of our present time relates to the processes of past creolizations, like safe instant sex is to the formerly risky, involved, protracted and occasionally grave affair of passionate love. Modern cultural contact wears a condom. Our strands of time are narrow and sterile; a Creole or Yiddish language could not develop on them. The time of Western civilization dominating now without eastern borders has the characteristic ability to expand and contract in a double movement thereby compressing the multitemporality of the world into the homogenous contemporaneity of the *quartz watch epoch.*[54]

There is no question that the asymmetry between the power of a "world market civilization" on the one hand and the weakness of subordinate groups, cultures and nations on the other, is a scandal of global history. But the continuing temporal discrimination, lately along the lines of "oh, how beautiful is your non-contemporaneity," is scandalous too.

## Conclusion

We may be nearing the final hours of the politics of non-contemporaneity. Global history has opened the doors to the present time for all people. If access to the present time was once a privilege of the few and powerful, it has now become a basic condition of globality. The sociotemporal world order is changing in favor of contemporaneity for all, and the neopaternalistic attempt to denounce contemporaneity may not please the indigenous people of our time. The sociocultural contemporaneity of those who were until recently non-contemporaneous – *poor* guest workers, *weak* women, *backward* Indians, *underdeveloped* countries, *uncivilised* nations of the Third World and all peoples *without history* – is a fact of global history.

This historical change can be underlined with a quote that indicates the end of the non-contemporaneous as well as the beginning of a contemporaneous world situation in the 1960s. In Cheikh Hamidou Kane's *Ambiguous Adventure*, a Senegalese novel from 1961 by a Muslim politician and writer, the father of Samba Diallo, a young African revolutionary, reaches out to Paul Lacroix, a French teacher and representative of the modernising colonial power.

> We have not had the same past, you and ourselves, but we shall have, strictly, the same future. The era of separate destinies has run its course. In that sense, the end of the world has indeed come for every one of us, because no one can any longer live by the simple carrying out of what he himself is.[55]

This remark is true in both a descriptive and a normative sense. The way things were *de facto* is definitely no longer the way they are, and the way things were *de jure* is certainly no longer how they should be. The sands of non-contemporaneous time have run out. Everybody lives, or is soon going to live, under conditions of global contemporaneity and has an undeniable right to be in the present time. It is no longer allowed to declare someone non-contemporaneous because of his skin color, sex, age, religion, nationality, class, income, mode of production, and kind of society or culture. The wealth of synchronic global contemporaneities has become accessible to everybody in real time. The world's old and new connections have become so widely globalised and strongly intertwined in the last fifty years that the whole world has gained a new quality. The local consequences of global warming and the worldwide audience of the Olympic Games, for example, make globality and humanity concrete. Our historical situation is clearly marked by the contemporaneity of local activities, processes and events with global reach and glocal meaning. Multicultural societies are constituted by the unprecedented collision and fusion of these contemporaneities. Astute observers of the present time have noticed that the modern emphasis on the future has been invalidated by a thickening of the present.[56]

The "present time of present things" is becoming what the past used to be for traditional societies and the future for industrial modernity. If Fernand Braudel was right to say that the present consists, to ninety percent, of the past then this is no longer true. The inhabitants of the global present have less memory of past things, more expectation of future things, and a lot of perception of present things. Synchrony is getting the edge over diachrony in terms of historical significance and now we have to learn how to deal with the new global history that has moved everybody everywhere into the present time.

## Notes

An earlier version of this paper was published in Wolf Schäfer, *Ungleichzeitigkeit als Ideologie: Beiträge zur Historischen Aufklärung* (Frankfurt am Main: Fischer, 1994), 132-155. I would like to thank Spencer Segalla for his critical and helpful reading of this chapter.

1  See St. Augustine, *Confessions*, Book 11, chapter 20: *tempora sunt tria, praesens de praeteritis, praesens de praesentibus, praesens de futuris.* Some later theorists have responded favorably to Augustine's idea or thought along the same lines, especially George Herbert Mead, "The Present as the Locus of Reality," in George H. Mead, *The Philosophy of the Present* (La Salle, Ill: The Open Court Publishing Company, 1959), 1-31.

2  St. Augustine used "memory" for the presence of past things (*praesens de praeteritis memoria*), "expectation" for the presence of future things (*praesens de futuris expectatio*), and "perception" for the presence of present things (*praesens de praesentibus contuitus*).

3  Peter Gay, *The Enlightenment: An Interpretation. The Science of Freedom* (New York and London: W. W. Norton, 1996), 567.

4  John M. O'Brien, *Alexander the Great: The Invisible Enemy. A Biography* (London and New York: Routledge, 1992).

5  Alexander Demandt, *Ungeschehene Geschichte: Ein Traktat über die Frage: Was Wäre Geschehen, Wenn ...?*, 2nd ed. 1986 (Göttingen: Vandenhoeck & Ruprecht, 1984), 69-74.

6  Olga Z. Pugliese, *Lorenzo Valla: "The Profession of the Religious" and the Principal Arguments from "The Falsely-Believed and Forged Donation of Constantine"* (Toronto: Centre for Reformation and Renaissance Studies, 1985), 70. – Carlo Ginzburg's reading of Valla has shown that Valla's approach to rhetoric followed Aristotle and not Cicero. Aristotle, Valla, and Ginzburg oppose the "current self-referential image of rhetoric" and hold that rhetoric and methodical proof are compatible because proof is "the rational core of rhetoric." Carlo Ginzburg, *History, Rhetoric, and Proof* (Hanover and London: University Press of New England, 1999), 62.

7  A medievalist who taught diplomatics in Marburg always asked in the first meeting of his class: "Who wants to learn something about political history here?" He never failed to disappoint a few students with the revelation that diplomatics was not about diplomacy; I was one of these ignoramuses.

8  Having a reliable tool and using it are two different things. Russell showed that 19th- and 20th-century writers, including historians, created the nonsense of the medieval belief in a flat earth; Jeffrey B. Russell, *Inventing the Flat Earth: Columbus and Modern Historians* (New York: Praeger, 1991).

9  Marc Bloch, *The Historian's Craft* (New York: Vintage Books, 1953), 95.

10  Lynn White, "Technology Assessment from the Stance of a Medieval Historian," *American Historical Review* 79 (1974), 1-13.

11  The Austrian writer Robert Musil wrote: "To pass freely through open doors, it is necessary to respect the fact that they have solid frames. This principle, by which the old professor had always lived, is simply a requisite of the sense of reality. But if there is a sense of reality, and no one will doubt that it has justification for existing, then there must also be something we can call a sense of possibility." Robert Musil, *The Man Without Qualities* (New York: Knopf, 1995), 10-11.

12  Sungook Hong, "Unfaithful Offspring? Technologies and Their Trajectories," *Perspectives on Science* 6 (1998), 259-287, 263.

13  See George Wise, "The Accuracy of Technological Forecasts, 1890-1940," *Futures. The Journal of Forecasting and Planning* 8 (1976), 411-419, 414; his sample of 1556 predictions broke down as follows: *"fulfilled*: 499 predictions (32%); *in progress*: 121 predictions (8%); *not proven*: 420 predictions (27%); and *refuted*: 516 predictions (33%)."

14  Quoted in René Magritte (Munich: Kunsthalle der Hypo-Kultur-Stiftung, 1987), 39 "La Clef des Champs, 1933." Magritte's comment is translated from the German translation; the catalog lists as source for this comment the film by Luc de Hensch fron 1960 ("Magritte on la leçon de choses"). – A scanned image of The Key to the Fields can be found in the Global History Gallery at cgh.stonybrook.edu/ghg/.

15  W. Warren Wagar, *A Short History of the Future*, 2nd ed. (Chicago and London: University of Chicago Press, 1992), XIV, XV and XIII. The foreword to the second edition states that substantial parts of the book have been rewritten. The original foreword appeared unchanged in the second edition, but chapters two and five, and substantial portions of other chapters, were rewritten "to take account of the new face of international politics" (IX). I wonder: is a second (or third, fourth and fifth) account in the best interest of futures studies? How can we learn from our failed expectations if we overwrite them with new guesswork?

16  Martin Albrow, *The Global Age: State and Society beyond Modernity*, 2nd ed. (Stanford: Stanford University Press, 1997).

17  Roland Robertson, "Glocalization: Time-Space and Homogeneity – Heterogeneity," in Mike Featherstone, Scott Lash, and Roland Robertson, *Global Modernities* (London: SAGE, 1995), 25-44. – Cascades could replace the singular event as the basic unit of historical analysis. Rosenau has developed some interesting ideas in this direction (applied to post-international politics) including thoughts about the scope, intensity, and duration of cascades; James N. Rosenau, *Turbulence in World Politics: A Theory of Change and Continuity* (Princeton: Princeton University Press, 1990), 298-305.

18  Alfred Wegener (1880-1930), a German meteorologist, developed the theory of continental drift. Wegener contended from 1912 on that the earth's continents were not fixed, and that a large landmass or supercontinent (*Pangaea*) had begun to split apart some 200 million years ago. Wegener's basic idea was debated back and forth during his lifetime; it was eventually confirmed by the development of the widely accepted theory of plate tectonics in the 1960s; Alfred Wegener, *The Origin of Continents and Oceans* (New York: Dover Publications, 1966). See A(nthony) Hallam, *A Revolution in the Earth Sciences: From Continental Drift to Plate Tectonics* (Oxford: Clarendon Press, 1973); Ursula B. Marvin, *Continental Drift: The Evolution of a Concept* (Washington: Smithsonian Institution Press, 1973).

19  Wolf Schäfer, "The New Global History: Toward a Narrative for Pangaea Two," *Erwägen Wissen Ethik* 14 (2003), 75-88; ibid., "Making Progress with Global History," *Erwägen Wissen Ethik* 14 (2003), 128-135; ibid., "Global Civilization and Local Cultures: A Crude Look at the Whole," *International Sociology* 16 (2001), 301-319.

20  Luhmann's approach is similar ("Wir gehen von einer ebenso trivialen wie aufregenden These aus: dass *alles, was geschieht, gleichzeitig geschieht*") but unhistorical ("Gleichzeitigkeit ist eine aller Zeitlichkeit vorgegebene Elementartatsache"); see Niklas Luhmann,

"Gleichzeitigkeit und Synchronisation," in Niklas Luhmann, *Soziologische Aufklärung*, vol. 5: *Konstruktivistische Perspektiven* (Opladen: Westdeutscher Verlag, 1990), 95-130, 98. The construction of contemporaneity as a fundamental fact outside history makes little sense for historians; we have to think of contemporaneity as a historical development and not as a given.

21  R. Buckminster Fuller, *Utopia or Oblivion: The Prospects for Humanity* (New York: Bantam Books, 1969), 208.

22  See Aeschylus' *Agamemnon*, 281ff. "Chorus: And at what time hath the city been sacked? Clytaemnestra: I say in the night that hath now brought forth this day. Chorus: And what messenger could come with such speed? Clytaemnestra: Vulcan [Hephaestus], sending forth a brilliant gleam from Ida; and beacon dispatched beacon of courier-fire hitherward (...)." Quoted after Gerard J. Holzmann and Björn Pehrson, *The Early History of Data Networks* (Los Alamitos, CA: IEEE Computer Society Press, 1995), 16-17 [available online at vvv.it.kth.se/docs/early_net/toc.html].

23  In 1837 Morse responded to a U.S. Senate call for proposals for a nationwide telegraph system. The senators were thinking of an optical system like the ones developed in France by Claude Chappe or in Sweden by Abraham Edelcrantz. Morse proposed an electromagnetic telegraph, and eventually won the government's support. The most important thing about Morse's telegraph, however, was not the use of electricity but what Carey has called the "effective separation of communication from transportation"; James W. Carey, *Communication as Culture: Essays on Media and Society* (Boston: Unwin Hyman, 1989), 203.

24  The message concerned the ending of the Sepoy Mutiny (1857-1858), a rebellion against British rule by Indian troops (sepoys) of the East India Company. The first successful transatlantic telegraph cable failed after a few weeks (the very first attempt in August 1857 had failed altogether). 732 messages were sent in 1858, each took over one hour; "it took twenty-six hours to get the first message across"; Steven Lubar, *InfoCulture: The Smithsonian Book of Information Age Inventions* (Boston and New York: Houghton Mifflin Company, 1993), 85.

25  See Edward Hagerman, *The American Civil War and the Origins of Modern Warfare: Ideas, Organization, and Field Command* (Bloomington: Indiana University Press, 1988), 87: "The Military Telegraph with its Morse equipment had largely taken over telegraphic field communications during the Gettysburg campaign. It connected Meade's headquarters to the headquarters of all corps and divisions. The army of the Potomac set organizational precedent when, 'for perhaps the first time in military history the commanding general of a large army was kept in communication during active operations with his corps and division commanders.'"

26  CNN boasted in 1991 that its reporter (Peter Arnett) was sending "for the first time in history" live pictures of an ongoing war to the entire world from behind enemy lines. But the American information policy took that into account; neither CNN nor the other networks could get through American censorship to cover American troop movements; Lubar, *InfoCulture*, 260.

27  Reinhart Koselleck, *Wie neu ist die Neuzeit?* (Munich: Oldenbourg 1991), 41.

28  Barbara Ward, *Spaceship Earth* (New York: Columbia University Press, 1966); Nigel Calder, *Spaceship Earth* (London: Viking, 1991).

29  Cf. Thomas L. McPhail, *Electronic Colonialism: The Future of International Broadcasting and Communication* (Newbury Park, CA: SAGE, 1987); Gerald Sussman and John A. Lent, eds., *Transnational Communications: Wiring the Third World* (Newbury Park, CA: SAGE, 1991); Edward A. Comor, ed., *The Global Political Economy of Communication: Hegemony, Telecommunication and the Information Economy* (New York: St. Martin's Press, 1994).

30  The newly reached parts of the planet did not immediately displace the traditional concerns of people. In 1584, the miller Domenico Scandella (Menocchio) still talked about the *Travels* of John Mandeville (a mid-14th century book). Ginzburg remarked: "It's well known that throughout the 16th century the circulation of descriptions of the Holy Land continued to outnumber those of the New World." Carlo Ginzburg, *The Cheese and the Worms: The Cosmos of a Sixteenth-Century Miller* (Baltimore and London: Johns Hopkins University Press, 1980), 42.

31  For the historical development of the theory and practice of Western dominance, see Michael Adas, *Machines as the Measure of Men: Science, Technology, and Ideologies of Western Dominance* (Ithaca and London: Cornell University Press, 1989).

32  For an excellent exposition of this change, see Margaret T. Hodgen, *Early Anthropology in the Sixteenth and Seventeenth Centuries* (Philadelphia: University of Pennsylvania Press, 1964), 389-390; also Johannes Fabian, *Time and the Other: How Anthropology Makes Its Object* (New York: Columbia University Press, 1983).

33  I translate from "Was heißt und zu welchem Ende studiert man Universalgeschichte?" in Friedrich Schiller, *Werke in drei Bänden*. Vol. 2 (Munich: Hanser, 1966), 9-22.

34  Quoted from the Universal Declaration of Human Rights (article 1, first sentence), which was completed by the U.N. Commission on Human Rights in June 1948 and adopted by unanimous vote by the General Assembly at its Paris session on Dec. 10, 1948 (with the members of the Soviet bloc, Saudi Arabia, and the Union of South Africa abstaining).

35  A village near the highest mountain (Großglockner) in Austria.

36  I translate from the German edition: Adolf Loos, *Sämtliche Schriften in zwei Bänden*. Ed. by Franz Glück (Wien and Munich: Verlag Herold, 1962), 280-281. A selection of Loos' essays has finally come out in English in 1998 but the translation is poor.

37  Ibid., 287 and 277.

38  The text is from 1913: "Er [Karl Kraus] steht an der schwelle einer neuen zeit und weist der menschheit, die sich von gott und der natur weit, weit entfernt hat, den weg. Den kopf in den sternen, die füsse auf der erde, schreitet er, das herz in qual über der menschheit jammer. Und ruft. Er fürchtet den weltuntergang. Aber, da er nicht schweigt, weiss ich, dass er die hoffnung nicht aufgegeben hat. Und er wird weiter rufen und seine stimme wird durch die kommenden jahrhunderte dringen, bis sie gehört wird. Und die menschheit wird einmal Karl Kraus ihr leben zu danken haben." Ibid., 328.

39  Ibid., 280, 286, 283 and 287.

40  This term was used by Ernst Bloch in "Bemerkungen zur 'Erbschaft dieser Zeit,'" in *Philosophische Aufsätze zur objektiven Phantasie*. Werkausgabe, vol. 10 (Frankfurt am Main: Suhrkamp, 1985), 31-53, 45.

41  The first edition of *Erbschaft dieser Zeit* states 1935 as the year of publication. However, the book was already distributed in November or December 1934 as we know from a letter that Walter Benjamin wrote to Gershom Scholem on 26.12.1934: "Da ist zum Beispiel seit

Wochen Blochs 'Erbschaft dieser Zeit' erschienen (...)." Walter Benjamin and Gershom Scholem, *Briefwechsel 1933-1940* (Frankfurt am Main: Suhrkamp, 1980), 182.

42 Ernst Bloch, *Heritage of Our Times* (Berkeley and Los Angeles: University of California Press, 1991), 97.

43 Ibid.

44 Ibid., 62.

45 Ibid., 113, 108 and 109.

46 Ibid., 185, 112 and 113; the latter quoted passage is printed in italics for emphasis.

47 Ibid., 110, 112 and 2.

48 Ibid., 108 and 102.

49 In a lecture on "Differenzierungen im Begriff Fortschritt," originally given in the German Democratic Republic (GDR) in 1955; Ernst Bloch, "Differenzierungen im Begriff Fortschritt," in *Tübinger Einleitung in die Philosophie*. Werkausgabe, vol. 13 (Frankfurt am Main: Suhrkamp, 1985), 118-147. – Bloch went into exile in 1933, first in Europe (1933-1938) and then in America (1938-1949). He remigrated to East Germany where he taught philosophy in Leipzig for a number of years before he was forced to retire from academic life (after the revolution in Hungary 1956). Bloch did not return to the GDR from a trip to West Germany after the erection of the Berlin Wall in 1961; he stayed in West Germany and became a Professor at Tübingen University. Bloch influenced the West German student movement in 1968 not least through his friendship with Rudi Dutschke (1940-1979), a charismatic student leader, and also an émigré from the GDR.

50 "(...) die gesellschaftlichen Stufen der Völker auf der Erde [sind] alles andere als 'gleichzeitig'. (...) die Topisierung verlangt, mindestens als universalhistorische, ein *Multiversum* – auch in der Zeit." Ibid., 128-129.

51 Bloch continued: "Diesen Kontinenten eben ist die weiße Vergangenheit nur knapp ihre eigene, und Geschichte überhaupt wird den mannigfach zukunftslos gewesenen Völkern dasjenige, was morgen beginnt." Ibid., 145.

52 "Der westliche Fortschrittsbegriff hat immerhin in seinen Revolutionen keine europäische (freilich auch keine asiatische oder afrikanische) Spitze impliziert, sondern eine (...) bessere Erde." Ibid., 146.

53 Ibid., 147.

54 Lothar Baier, "Das dumme Gefühl, an den Rockschößen des Zeitgeistes zu hängen: Gleichzeitigkeit – die heimliche Utopie der Westlichen Zivilisation," *Frankfurter Rundschau* (22.6.1991), 12.

55 Cheikh Hamidou Kane, *Ambiguous Adventure* (Portsmouth, NH: Heinemann, 1972), 79-80.

56 Cf. Helga Nowotny, "From the Future to the Extended Present," in Guy Kirsch, Peter Nijkamp and Klaus Zimmermann, eds., *The Formulation of Time Preferences in a Multidisciplinary Perspective: Their Consequences for Individual Behaviour and Collective Decision-Making* (Avebury 1988), 17-31, 26.

# Taking on the World

## Bell, Edison and the Diffusion of the Telephone in the 1870s

*W. Bernard Carlson*

Globalisation is one of the great buzzwords of the age, often used by journalists and commentators to emphasise how improvements in communications and transportation are increasing the speed by which capital, goods, and ideas move across national boundaries.[1] Focusing on how powerful a force globalisation seems to be – in weakening national economies, shifting the balance of power from one part of the world to another – we often make simplistic assumptions about it. First, it is tempting to assume that globalisation is a process that is only taking place in the present and that it did not necessarily shape the past. And second, it is easy to assume that the technologies involved in globalisation move easily from one place to another. Around the world, the inexorable forces of the marketplace lead managers to seek out new technologies in a determined quest for productivity and profits. In the struggle to survive, it is assumed that all economic players easily and readily take up whatever technology they need to survive.

In this essay, I want to investigate both of these assumptions. Like other papers in this volume, I will argue that globalisation is a process with a past, with a history. Individual entrepreneurs and nation states have been pursuing global strategies since at least the 1600s, and the particular dynamics of globalisation we see today were strongly shaped by the rise of specific technologies and business strategies in the late 19th century. But even more significant, we need to be aware that technologies do not necessarily move easily across political and cultural boundaries. Yes, there may be strong economic forces that prompt business people to investigate technological alternatives, but the exact ways in which a new technology is taken up is strongly shaped by cultural values and perceptions. Any discussion of technology and globalisation, in my view, must reckon with the reality of different cultures.

To wrestle with these issues, this paper looks at how and why American inventors chose to export their inventions and seek foreign patents. While historians of technology and business have often assumed that American business did not pursue global markets until the 20th century, I will argue here that, in the last decades of the 19th century, some American inventors and entrepreneurs eagerly promoted new products not only at home but throughout the world. As early as 1873, Thomas Edison and Elisha Gray travelled to England to secure patents for their improvements on the telegraph. Even a novice inventor such as Elihu Thomson sought to patent his first new devices in Europe; while working as a high school teacher in Philadelphia in 1878, Thomson spent significant time and money securing patents for his centrifugal creamer and telegraph relay in England and France.[2] By the 1880s, securing foreign patents seems to have become part of the standard business strategy of American inventors, and both Edison and Thomson filed patents to protect their inventions in Canada, Europe, South America, and Australia. But why did American inventors look to global markets as early as the 1870s? What do the early experiences of American inventors overseas tell us about the diffusion of technology around the globe?

To answer these questions, I will focus on the telephone as a case study. This is an interesting case, not only because the telephone has played a major role in globalisation, but because it is one of the first technologies in which America achieved global dominance. Invented in 1876 by Alexander Graham Bell, the telephone spread quickly around the world so that by 1911 there were roughly ten million telephones in use. Americans were particularly eager in taking up the telephone, and by that year, they used 70% of all telephones even though they possessed only 5% of the world's population. By comparison, all of Europe had only one-third as many telephones as the United States. But even more importantly, by the early 20th century, the United States had become the leader in developing and exporting telephone technology. As one commentator remarked:

> the United States may be generally recognized as the source of skill and authority on telephony.... Just as the wise buyer of to-day asks France for champagne, Germany for toys, England for cotton, and the Orient for rugs, so he will learn to look upon the United States as the natural home and headquarters of the telephone.[3]

To fully understand how America achieved global dominance in the telephone industry, one would need to investigate the histories of multinationals such as American Telephone, and Telegraph, Western Electric, and International Telephone and Telegraph.[4] While such an investigation would be interesting, I instead want to focus on the first efforts of Americans to take the telephone abroad. Consequently, this paper will discuss how both Bell and Edison sought patents and established operating companies in Britain in the late 1870s.[5] Remarkably, their efforts at exporting telephone technology came quickly, within 2-3 years of the invention of the first telephone. I will explore how Bell and Edison expected to make money from their domestic and foreign patents, what problems they encountered in Britain, how they believed that the telephone would change society, the intervention of the

British government in telephone affairs, and the slow diffusion of the telephone in Britain in the 19th century. In particular, Bell's pronouncements about telephone exchanges and Edison's comments about stirring up business practices reveal that both inventors were aware that they were exporting not only hardware but also values. Yet as we shall see, Bell and Edison soon discovered that these overseas ventures were extremely risky in all sorts of ways, often requiring them to become more deeply involved in local business problems. In recounting their stories, I wish to provide a historical perspective on globalisation, suggesting that the ways in which technology influences the process of globalisation are not unique to our time but indeed reach as far back as the 1870s.

## Patents and Profits

To understand why some American inventors pursued global markets in the 1870s, we should first consider the business strategies employed by inventors. We need to comprehend how inventors hoped that patents would allow them to make money both at home and abroad.

At first glance, it might seem like there should be a simple economic answer to the question why American inventors took out foreign patents. Having gone to all the trouble of perfecting an invention, why not patent it around the world? After all, the largest costs related to an invention come with experimentation and development, not with patenting; comparatively speaking, patents are relatively cheap, and global patenting presumably increases the opportunities by which an inventor could recover his initial investment. Hence, from an economic standpoint, it would make great sense for American inventors to secure as many foreign patents as they could.

This simple economic answer, however, fails to take into account the complexity and diversity of foreign patent systems. Having secured a U.S. patent, it was by no means an easy matter for a 19th-century American to secure patents in other countries. Then as now, different nations had different patent procedures. In Britain, for example, the patent was awarded not to the first person who conceived an invention (which was the case in the United States) but rather to the first person who filed an application. By contrast, Germany had an extremely rigorous examination procedure, and only granted patents to the original inventors of truly novel devices. In several European countries, particularly France, the recipient of a patent was expected to begin manufacturing the invention in the country granting the patent within a specified time; if an inventor failed to do so, the patent was invalidated. And in other countries (such as Austria-Hungary), there were fees and taxes that had to be paid every year, and the patent was lost if the fees were not paid on time. In general, securing foreign patents was a complicated and expensive business, and hence not necessarily a cost-effective means for increasing the opportunities for earning a return on an invention.

Instead, to understand why American inventors took out foreign patents, we need to investigate the ways in which they used patents to make money at home. 19th-century inventors had three basic strategies for making money from patents:

First, they could use the patents to create their own new business. Because the patent prevented others from manufacturing the product or using the process, the inventor earned a profit from his monopoly position. An example of this strategy is how George Eastman used his patented system of roll film to build up Eastman Kodak in the 1880s;[6]

Second, inventors could grant licenses to an established manufacturer. Under the license, the manufacturer might be required to pay inventors royalties for each item manufactured. For instance, Nikola Tesla received a royalty for each alternating current motor produced by Westinghouse; and

Third, they could sell their patents outright to another entrepreneur or business enterprise. The inventor would realise an immediate cash profit and would avoid the risks of having to manufacture and market his invention. Elmer Sperry, for example, developed an electrolytic process for white lead in 1904 which he sold outright to the Hooker Electrochemical Company.[7]

For the most part, historians of technology have assumed that inventors followed the first strategy, largely because that strategy led to the creation of long-enduring firms such as General Electric and Eastman Kodak. However, for the average 19th-century inventor, this strategy was highly risky, capital-intensive, and it required that the inventor master the intricacies of manufacturing and marketing. Consequently many 19th-century inventors preferred the second and third strategies. In particular, the strategy of licencing was seen as being highly profitable since one could grant a large number of licences to different firms or for use in different specified territories. With his incandescent lighting system, Edison and the Edison Electric Light Company made a handsome profit by granting licences to central station companies in dozens of cities. As a strategy, though, licensing had a down-side in that the inventor had to be ever vigilant against competitors infringing his patents, lest the licences lose their monopoly power. By not aggressively defending their patents in the mid-1880s, the Edison Electric Light Company inadvertently allowed several competitors to spring up, and one of those competitors, the Thomson-Houston Electric Company, eventually took over the Edison company to form General Electric in 1892.[8]

## Edison and Bell's Domestic Patent Strategy

During the 1870s, Munn & Company, the patent agency affiliated with *Scientific American,* strongly urged its inventor clients to pursue the licensing strategy.[9] However, curiously, two famous inventors, Thomas Edison and Alexander Graham Bell, eschewed licensing and initially pursued the strategy of selling their patents outright.

To some extent, Edison and Bell chose to sell their patents because of the ways in which the telegraph had evolved as a network technology in America. While in the 1840s Morse and other early telegraph inventors had licenced their inventions to different firms in different regions, it had resulted in a patchwork of companies and systems that were unable to communicate with each other. Recognising that the commercial potential of the telegraph lay in creating a nationwide system, Hiram Sibley aggressively bought up many of the regional companies to create the Western Union Telegraph Company. By 1867, Western Union controlled most of the telegraph business in the United States. Sibley's successor at Western Union, William Orton, was quick to recognise how technological improvements could be used to maintain the company's dominant position and he readily paid telegraph inventors such as Joseph Stearns significant sums of money for their patents.[10] At the same time, Jay Gould also recognised that new telegraph inventions could be used to create a system to rival Western Union, with the result that he too bought telegraph patents and effectively created a bidding war for the most promising inventions. Edison fully appreciated this highly competitive situation, and during the mid-1870s, he sold patents to both Orton and Gould. Edison's dealings with these two rivals were enormously complex, with each side claiming that Edison had sold them rights to the same invention, and thus earning for Edison the nickname the "Professor of Duplicity and Quadruplicity."[11] However, by establishing a reputation as a "hired gun" who could come up with inventions and patents, Edison generated sufficient income that he was able to build for himself a substantial laboratory at Menlo Park, New Jersey, in 1876.

Although younger and not as experienced as Edison, Bell too appreciated the potential for selling patents to Western Union. Bell may have taken up electrical inventing in 1872 after reading about Western Union's purchase of the two-message duplex patent of Joseph Stearns.[12] Bell hoped that he could come up with a similar blockbuster patent which could be sold to Western Union, and he pursued several lines of investigation, including a multiple-message telegraph, a facsimile telegraph, and of course, his speaking telegraph or telephone. Gardiner Hubbard, Bell's main backer and future father-in-law, also saw the opportunity for selling patents to Western Union. Even though Hubbard regarded Western Union as an evil monopoly which could destroy democracy in America, he offered Bell's multiple message and telephone patents to Orton in the fall of 1876 for $100,000. Orton de-clined to purchase the Bell patents that fall, and during the subsequent winter, Hubbard and Bell tried to sell them to several other businessmen. Clearly, at this point, Hubbard and Bell recognised that they did not possess the financial, market-ing, and engineering knowledge needed to exploit the telephone, and they thought it best to sell the invention to the highest bidder. At the same time, Bell was also anxious to marry Hubbard's daughter, Mabel, and so he was keen to sell his patents and have the income to start a family. However, Hubbard was unable to find a buyer for Bell's patents, and as a result, he and Bell set up the Bell Telephone Com-pany in July 1877 in order to develop the telephone in the United States.[13]

It was in this context that Edison and Bell approached pursuing foreign patents for their telephone inventions. Based on their experience with Western Union, both men had come to assume that the best business strategy would be to sell their patents outright. Both men had a need for ready cash: Edison to fund his labora-tory, Bell to support his new bride. What they were looking for were new backers who would pay cash for the privilege of exploiting their inventions in other coun-tries. When they turned their eyes overseas, then, they sought ready cash and not new markets to conquer.

Significantly, both Edison and Bell wanted potential backers to pay for the rights up front and to then secure patents for them in different countries. Both men were well aware of the expenses associated with securing foreign patents, and they did not wish to assume the burden of these costs. As early as the fall of 1876, Bell had begun to contemplate securing foreign patents, and he quickly realised that he could only do so by either borrowing money from his family or trying "to live on nothing in Boston."[14] For Edison, Western Union regularly covered the expenses associated with his American patents and he had no intention of covering the costs of securing foreign patents.

## Bell Goes Abroad

Even though Bell and Hubbard were unable to sell their patents in America and were forced to establish their own operating company, they did not abandon the idea of making money by selling the foreign rights to the telephone. In June 1877, they were approached by Colonel William H. Reynolds, a cotton goods broker from Providence, Rhode Island. Reynolds offered Bell $5,000 for five-eighths of any Brit-ish patent secured and $2,500 for one-half of the rights to the telephone in Russia, Spain, Portugal, and Italy. Bell accepted Reynolds' offer, and with these funds pro-mised, Bell married Mabel.[15]

As a honeymoon, Bell and his new bride travelled to Britain in the summer of 1877. Bell had intended to stay only a few months and leave it to Reynolds to establish an operating company in England. However, when Mabel became pregnant, Bell decided to remain, and he and his family did not return to America until November 1878.[16]

While waiting for his first child to be born, Bell became involved in the efforts to create an English telephone company. Reynolds' plan was to launch a joint-stock company capitalised at £500,000. During the fall of 1877, Bell and Reynolds had numerous inquiries from interested parties, and Reynolds arranged with a rubber company to manufacture telephones which could be offered for sale.

To launch a company at this level of capitalisation, Reynolds undertook an extensive publicity campaign. Reynolds hired Kate Field, an American émigré who supported herself by writing for newspapers. Field published a score of articles on the telephone in English papers as well as a pamphlet, *The History of Bell's Telephone*, in early 1878. To capture the public's imagination, Field boldly predicted that someday light as well as sound might be transmitted over a wire so "while two persons, hundreds of miles apart, are talking together, they will actually *see* each other!"[17]

In conjunction with Miss Field's efforts, Bell offered lectures before scientific societies which drew large crowds, sometimes up to 2,000 people. Like the American public, English audiences were captivated by the telephone as a scientific marvel, emblematic of the promises of technology. Sir William Thomson, who had been introduced to the telephone at the Philadelphia Centennial in 1876, praised Bell's invention, declaring it to be "one of the most interesting inventions that has ever been make in the history of science."[18] By the winter, Mabel found the shops full of "Domestic Telephones," consisting of two cans and a string. "Wherever you go," she wrote to her mother,

> on newspaper stands, at news stores, stationers, photographers, toy shops, fancy goods shops, you see the eternal little black box with a red face, and the word 'Telephone' in large black letters. Advertisements say that 700,000 have been sold in a few weeks.

At the end of 1877, the periodical *Punch* included the telephone in its list of New Year's resolutions: "To make myself thoroughly acquainted with the Eastern Question in all its bearings, the relations between Capital and Labour, the principle and construction of the telephone."[19]

Reynolds' biggest public relations coup was to have the opportunity to demonstrate the telephone to Queen Victoria. In January 1878, the Queen summoned Bell to Osborne House on the Isle of Wight, and Bell demonstrated the telephone by connecting the main house with a cottage and by transmitting conversation and music from Southampton and London. Miss Field also sang several songs into the telephone from an adjoining room. The Queen recorded in her diary:

> After dinner we went to the council room and saw the telephone. A Professor Bell explained the whole process which is the most extraordinary. It had been put in communication with Osborne Cottage, and we talked with Sir Thomas and Mary Biddulph; also heard some singing quite plainly. But it is rather faint, and one must hold the tube close to one's ear.[20]

Nevertheless, the Queen was impressed and asked if she could purchase a set of telephones from Bell. In response, he presented her with a pair of elaborately carved ivory instruments.

Miss Field followed up the demonstration for the Queen with a "Matinee Telephonique" for the press in order, as she put it, to "get one general chorus of gratuitous advertising." Two hundred people attended this demonstration and Miss Field reported that "the lunch was good and nobody wanted to leave."[21]

Reynolds now issued a prospectus for the Telephone Company, Limited and opened the stock subscription books to investors. Despite the careful publicity efforts, though, there were few takers for the stock. Potential investors were wary of the new company because Bell's British patent might not be valid. The problem lay with the intricacies of British patent law which stated that a patent was not valid if a description of the invention was published in Britain before the patent was applied for. Sir William Thomson had brought back Bell's telephone from the Philadelphia Centennial and had presented a paper about it at the 1876 meeting of the British Association for the Advancement of Science. Bell tried to appease the courts by dropping the claims which were revealed in Sir William's paper, but letters to *The Times* charged Bell with having stolen the idea of the telephone from Charles Wheatstone and Phillip Reis.[22] Fortunately, though, the illustration of the telephone receiver in Sir William's paper showed the metallic diaphragm bent away from the magnet (it had been damaged in transit). The British courts seized on this accident and bent the law in Bell's favour, declaring that the published paper had not disclosed a vital feature of Bell's telephone – the metal diaphragm – because the diaphragm could not work when it was bent away from the magnet.

As a result of these patent problems, Reynolds was not able to raise the anticipated capital of £500,000 and instead sold the British patent in March 1878 to a group of capitalists for £10,000 cash and another £10,000 in twelve months. From this sale, Bell received £500 for his expenses and services and the Bell trust received £3,000. The new group registered the new Telephone Company, Ltd. in June 1878 and capitalised it at £100,000. Bell was also named a director of the new company. [23]

As the company was being established, Bell addressed several technical problems. In particular, Reynolds was concerned that the numerous existing telegraph wires in London would, through induction, cause static on the sensitive telephone lines. To overcome this problem, Bell modified his circuit and developed a new cable. Rather than using a ground return with his telephone, he now used two wires to make the circuit and for the cable he insulated both wires and twisted them together.[24]

As important as these technical problem were, Bell was more concerned in getting his fellow directors to think boldly about how to market the telephone. In a printed letter, he argued that the telephone was unique among telegraph devices because it required no expert operators and could be used by anyone. Rather than simply selling pairs of telephones to be used on private telegraph lines, Bell urged that the company rent telephones to customers and establish central stations or exchanges. (The first such exchange had been established in the spring of 1877 by the E. T. Holmes Burglar Alarm Company of Boston, and Bell had followed the development of this exchange with great interest). By imitating gas and water companies, the telephone company could lay underground cables to connect "private dwellings, Counting Houses, shops, Manufactories, etc." with the central exchange. The exchanges, in turn, would be linked to each other, so that "a man in one part of the country may communicate by word of mouth with another in a distant place."

Recognising that individuals might be reluctant to install telephones in their homes or business establishments, Bell shrewdly suggested that the company install telephones in hotels (where they could be used to communicate from one room to another) and for free in selected shops. Bell suspected that, once a few shopkeepers discovered that customers would call in orders, then all shopkeepers would want to be connected to the central exchange. The company would make money, Bell suggested, by charging both a fixed annual rent for the service as well as a toll on each call made. "However small the rate of charge might be" for each call, Bell observed, "the revenue would probably be something enormous."[25]

Bell acknowledged that his ideas might seem "Eutopian" [sic] to the company's directors, but he nonetheless felt that they should take a long view of the business. The directors, however, did not see fit to pursue the central exchange plan and instead permitted McClure, the company's manager, to sell telephones out of a small shop in London. Determined to line his own pocket, McClure demanded that the company pay him royalties on his patented telephone with a call bell and button. Confident that the directors would not stop him, McClure published a new price list emphasising his telephone and not Bell's. Clearly, the short-term opportunities for selling telephones as a scientific toy were far more appealing to McClure than the hard work of building a telephone exchange.

McClure's actions enraged Bell. In July 1878, Bell submitted another letter to the company's directors which was printed and distributed. "[I]t has been one of my most cherished wishes to see this system in operation throughout the length and breadth of my native land," he wrote, and "You can, therefore, understand ... with what keen disappointment I view the possibility of its failure." Bell demanded that

McClure be fired and that the company focus its efforts on developing a system of telephone exchanges.[26] Although McClure was sacked, the Company continued to dither about exchanges, and in October 1878, Bell resigned as a director because of "the gross mismanagement of the Company's business and the personal discourtesy with which I have been treated by the Board of Directors and by the Acting Manager."[27]

It took the Telephone Company, Ltd. almost another year, until August 1879, to open its first exchange. Located in the City in London, this exchange had fewer than ten subscribers.[28] It charged its customers a flat rate of £20 per year for service.[29] But by then, Bell was not the only telephone business in Britain; Edison's men had arrived and were energetically promoting their system.

## "Making Slow Old England Hum":
## Edison's Telephone in England

Although Edison did not travel to England, he too became closely involved with the efforts to promote the telephone there. Edison's research on the telephone dated from 1875 when Western Union had asked him to study how different acoustic tones could be used to send multiple messages over a single telegraph wire. In this investigation of acoustic telegraphs, Edison designed a variety of devices which could transmit sounds over a wire but it did not occur to him to transmit speech. However, once Bell had demonstrated his telephone in 1876, Edison not only duplicated Bell's device but improved it. Anxious to block Bell and control this new area of acoustic telegraphy, Western Union contracted with Edison in March 1877 to develop a telephone superior to Bell's. Edison threw his energy into the telephone, and he sketched hundreds of telephones and perfected his carbon transmitter.[30] This transmitter was superior to Bell's magneto transmitter because it transmitted the voice more loudly and more clearly. Ever anxious to reassure his supporters at Western Union, Edison told them in May 1877 that his telephone was "more perfect than Bell's" and that they "need to have no alarm about Bell's monopoly as there are several things that he must discover before it [i.e., Bell's telephone] will be at all practical."[31]

While Western Union owned the American patents for Edison's telephone improvements, Edison was free to sell his inventions abroad. Like Bell, Edison hoped to sell the foreign rights for cash up front, particularly the patents for continental Europe. Consequently, he initially considered selling one-third of the rights for Russia, Spain, Italy, Austria, Germany, France, and Belgium to George Bliss, Cornelius Herz, and Stephen Field in September 1877 since Herz and Field were planning to travel to Europe shortly. In December, however, Edison changed his mind after meeting a Hungarian, Theodore Puskas. Although he sometimes claimed to be a count, Puskas had only married a rich countess. Puskas had come to America looking for opportunities to invest his wife's money and make his own fortune. In visiting Menlo Park, Puskas made quite an impression, arriving in a fancy carriage and flashing his cash roll of $1,000 bills. Edison took a liking to Puskas and showed him all of his current inventions, including the phonograph. Thrilled with everything he saw, Puskas offered to take out patents in Europe for all of Edison's inventions at his own expense in return for a one-twentieth interest.[32] With such a deal, one wonders whether Puskas was hustling Edison or Edison was hustling Puskas. Puskas proposed to Edison that telephone exchanges be set up in major cities, and he subsequently established a telephone exchange in Budapest. (One of the people Puskas employed in building this exchange was his nephew Nikola Tesla.)

While Puskas was given the continent, Edison pursued a different strategy for the telephone in Britain. At his own expense Edison filed a patent for his carbon transmitter in July 1877.[33] To help promote his telephone in England, he sent several instruments to William Preece, a telegraph engineer at the British Post Office, so that Preece could demonstrate them to his superiors. Edison apparently hoped that Preece might be his agent in England, but Preece may not have been able to take on this role and retain his position in the Post Office.[34] Consequently, Edison turned to another contact in London, Colonel George E. Gouraud, the resident director of the Mercantile Trust Company of New York.[35] Gouraud had attempted unsuccessfully to introduce Edison's system of automatic telegraphy in England in 1873, but he was more than ready to succeed with Edison's telephone four years later. Following a demonstration of Edison's carbon transmitter on a 115-mile telegraph line between London and Norwich, Gouraud put together a syndicate of capitalists who invested £100,000 in the Edison Telephone Company of Great Britain.

The sudden appearance of a rival was not lost on the Bell company who immediately claimed that the Edison Telephone Company was infringing on Bell's patent. Since Edison had a distinctive transmitter, the Bell interests seized on the fact that the Edison company was using a magneto receiver just like theirs. Undoubtedly aware that patent problems had scared investors away from the Bell company a year earlier, Gouraud panicked and begged Edison in January 1879 to provide him with an alternative receiver. Undaunted, Edison cabled back and promised a shipment of new receivers in ninety days.

In later recollections, Edison gave the impression that he invented an entirely new form of telephone receiver, his chalk drum receiver, in response to this crisis in England.[36] In reality, his sketches reveal that he had been using chalk drum receivers in some of his telephone experiments since April 1877. This receiver was based on his 1874 electromotograph which was a nonmagnetic relay. The electromotograph worked on the principle that a changing electrical current varied the friction on an electrode as it rubbed against a moist chalk surface. Edison adapted this principle to the telephone to create a receiver in which the listener used a small crank to turn a chalk drum in the receiver. Because he was simultaneously working on the electric light, Edison had his nephew, Charley Edison, continue to work on the chalk drum receiver during the winter of 1878-1879.[37]

Consequently, within a few weeks of receiving Gouraud's request, Edison was able to send his nephew abroad with six chalk drum receivers to demonstrate. Meanwhile, Edison put this receiver into production and shipped 600 devices to England within 90 days. With these new receivers, Edison recalled, went "a body of men on quick steamer; and an instructor went along, who during the voyage taught the men how to manipulate the new receivers, and how to make them if more should be required."[38]

Curiously, Edison's chalk drum receiver was not entirely unknown in England for Preece had described it in a paper he presented on the telephone at the summer 1877 meeting of the British Association for the Advancement of Science.[39] One cannot help but wonder why the Bell interests didn't use this prior publication to claim that Edison could not secure an English patent for the chalk drum receiver. Moreover, the chalk drum receivers were unpredictable, and Gouraud could never be sure if they would work reliably when he needed to demonstrate one to a prospective investor. To play up the scientific significance of this new receiver, Gouraud arranged for the distinguished physicist John Tyndall to lecture on it, but the lecture had to be postponed twice until an improved receiver was sent from Menlo Park.[40] However, in May 1879, Gouraud successfully demonstrated the chalk drum receiver before the Royal Society, and the audience included the Prince and Princess of Wales as well as several members of Parliament. On the strength of this demonstration, Gouraud increased the capital of the Edison Telephone Company from £100,000 to £200,000.[41]

The chalk drum receivers deflected the attack from the Bell interests and allowed the Edison Telephone Company to push ahead in building an exchange in London. Anxious to see this exchange established (and to learn from the experience of putting in this early installation), Edison dispatched his key lieutenants to England. In addition to his nephew Charley, these men included Charles Batchelor and James Adams who had conducted much of the telephone research as well as Edward Johnson, who had specialised in giving public demonstrations of the carbon transmitter.[42]

Along with the American workmen sent over earlier, these Edison men made quite an impression on the British workmen who were hired by the Edison Telephone Company. We know this because, one of the native workers was the playwright George Bernard Shaw. As he recalled years later in the preface to his novel, *The Irrational Knot*:

Whilst the Edison Telephone Company lasted, it crowded the basement of a high pile of offices in Queen Victoria Street with American artificers. These deluded and romantic men gave me a glimpse of the skilled proletariat of the United States; and their language was frightful even to an Irishman. They worked with a ferocious energy which was all out of proportion to the result achieved. Indomitably resolved to assert their republican manhood by taking no orders from a tall-hatted Englishman, whose stiff politeness covered his conviction that they were, relative to himself, inferior and common persons, they insisted on being slave-driven with genuine American oaths by a genuine and free American foreman. They utterly despised the artfully slow British workman who did as little for his wages as he possibly could; never hurried himself; and had a deep reverence for anyone whose pocket could be tapped by respectful behavior. Need I add that they were contemptuously wondered at by this same British workman as a parcel of outlandish boys, who sweated themselves for their employer's benefit instead of looking after their own interests. They adored Mr. Edison as the greatest man of all time in every possible department of science, art and philosophy, and execrated Mr. Graham Bell, the inventor of a rival telephone, as his Satanic adversary; but each of them had (or pretended to have) on the brink of completion an improvement on the telephone, usually a new transmitter. They were free-souled creatures, excellent company, sensitive, cheerful, and profane; liars, braggarts, and hustlers; with an air of making slow old England hum which never left them even when, as often happened, they were wrestling with difficulties of their own making; or struggling in no-thoroughfares from which they had to be retrieved like strayed sheep by Englishmen without imagination to go wrong.[43]

The engineering talent of Edison's lieutenants and the ferocious energy of the American workmen permitted the Edison Telephone Company to open its exchange in September 1879, one month after the Bell exchange was established. Located on Lombard Street in London, the Edison exchange attracted *The Times* as well as American companies such as the Pullman Car Association and Equitable Life Insurance as customers. Recognising the importance of exchanges for building up the telephone business, Edison Telephone offered its subscribers service at the rate of £12 per annum, thus undercutting the Bell company by £8.[44] Edison Telephone surged ahead of the Bell company, and by the spring of 1880 it had five exchanges and nearly 200 subscribers.[45]

Satisfied that the combination of the carbon transmitter and the chalk drum receiver had given his company a strategic advantage, Gouraud paid Edison $25,000 for his services.[46] Later in life, Edison described settling with Gouraud in much more colourful terms. Gouraud supposedly cabled Edison and asked if he would accept 30,000 for his services. Edison accepted this figure, but claimed that he was amazed that Gouraud paid him the 30,000 in pounds sterling when he had expected only $30,000.[47] While Edison would like us to believe that he was still the naive farm boy from Michigan, by 1879, he had become a shrewd business-man.

As profitable as the English telephone venture was for Edison, the episode took a heavy toll on his staff. James Adams, who had worked closely with Edison on the telephone experiments, drank himself to death while overseas. Nephew Charley fell ill and died while installing telephones in Paris.[48] Batchelor, Edison's right-hand man, also became sick while in London but he managed to return to Menlo Park to recover. Disturbed by all this, Edison wrote Johnson in the fall of 1879: "Hope you are not going to 'kick the bucket.' If you men are going to die off so, it would be better to have the large boxes [used to ship telephones] made a little longer, so that you can send the corpses back in them."[49]

## The State Intervenes, 1879-1880

The Bell and Edison telephone companies might well have competed head-to-head in Britain for several more years had not the Post Office stepped into the fray. Un-like the United States where the telegraph system was controlled by Western Union, a private corporation, Parliament had decided in 1869 that the telegraph system in Britain should be controlled by the Post Office. Through Preece, the Post Office had been monitoring both the Bell and Edison companies. In November 1879, the Postmaster-General concluded that the telephone was simply another form of the telegraph and that these companies were infringing on the Post Office's telegraph monopoly. When both companies refused to apply for licences, the Post Office took the Edison Company to court.[50] Even though the Edison interests were ably represented by Sir Charles Webster (who later became Chief Justice in Eng-land), they were nonetheless defeated, with the High Court of Justice ruling in fa-vour of the Crown. To drive home the point with the private companies, the Post-master-General secured permission from the government to set up Post Office tele-phone exchanges, and this gave the Postmaster the upper hand in negotiating with the private companies.

Faced with legal defeat, the Edison and Bell companies merged in 1880 to create the United Telephone Company. United then secured a licence from the Post Office to operate in metropolitan London, but under the terms of this licence, it was re-quired to pay a royalty of ten percent of its gross receipts to the Post Office. The Post Office then went on to license other telephone companies to serve additional cities in the United Kingdom. In 1890, these companies were brought together to form a single nationwide firm, the National Telephone Company, which still continued to pay a royalty to the Post Office.[51]

In the early years of the 20th century, engineers and lawyers on both sides of the Atlantic interpreted the triumph of the British Post Office over the private telephone companies as the major reason why the telephone industry grew so slowly in England. Anxious to stop the twin threats of the creation of municipally-owned local telephone companies and the possible nationalisation of long-distance telephony, lawyers for AT&T regularly cited the British case as evidence that government interference was detrimental to the development of the telephone. In particular, these commentators argued that, having sunk millions of pounds into its telegraph network, the Post Office did not wish to have a rival communications network spring up, and so it strangled the development of private telephone companies.[52]

One could, however, argue that the British government intervened because it did not agree with the competitive business practices of these American companies. Writing in 1880, Henry Fawcett, the Postmaster-General, explained that he favoured taking the Edison company to court because he believed that both telephone companies were more interested in eventually getting bought up by the State than in providing the public with efficient and economical service. It was not unreasonable for these companies to see the State as their ultimate customer, given that the Post Office already controlled telegraphy. The companies, Fawcett reported, were straining every nerve to look successful, going so far as to install telephones in homes and businesses of people who had never asked for the service and then offering a year of free service. As their workmen strung wires across the roofs of London and other cities, Fawcett feared that the companies were violating private rights and threatening public safety. Sooner or later, he concluded, this reckless competition would result in a public outcry and lead to demands that the Post Office take over the telephone. Better to quash these companies now, concluded the Postmaster-General, than to have to spend millions to buy a poorly built network from them later.[53]

## The Spread of the Telephone in Britain

As a result of these efforts, Bell, Edison, and their companies generated a great deal of interest for the telephone in England and they established a few embryonic exchanges. Writing in 1882, the telephone expert J. E. Kingsbury, conveyed something of the ongoing enthusiasm associated with the telephone:

> In England its use is now rapidly extending. A resident in the suburbs, having his house connected with the Telephone Exchange, has had his letters read to him from his office, dictated his replies to a shorthand writer at the City, communicated with his broker, solicitor, or banker, and all without leaving his bedroom;

sermons delivered in church have been heard by invalids when reclining on their sofas; operas performed in the crowded theatre have been listened to in the quiet library; dancing has been carried on to music which I have myself played more than ten miles away.[54]

But despite such positive pronouncements, the telephone spread slowly in Britain. Taking London as an example, in 1888 the United Telephone Company had only 4900 subscribers in this vast metropolis.[55] Likewise, by 1911, there were only 600,000 telephones in all of Britain; in contrast, by that year, the United States had seven million telephones.

Both the Post Office and the private companies blamed the other for this slow growth. To the Post Office, the slow growth was a result of United Telephone enforcing its control of the telephone patents and demanding exorbitant royalty payments from new companies trying to establish exchanges. In the eyes of United Telephone, the Post Office's demand of 10% of its gross receipts was exorbitant and a burden that prevented its growth.[56] But along with these problems, there were also social reasons for the slow spread of this new technology. First, the telephone had to compete with two existing and effective forms of communication: the Penny Post and messenger boys. During the late nineteenth century, Britain had a remarkable postal system, and within London, mail was delivered several times daily, making it possible for a letter to cross the city in two or three hours.[57] In discussing the differences between American and English use of the telephone to a Parliamentary committee in 1879, Preece admitted

> [T]here are conditions in America which necessitate the use of such instruments more than here. Here we have a superabundance of messengers, errand boys, and things of that kind. ... The absence of servants has compelled Americans to adopt communication systems for domestic purposes. Few have worked at the telephone more than I have. I have one in my office, but more for show. If I want to send a message – I use a sounder or employ a boy to take it.[58]

Hence one of the problems confronting the spread of the telephone was that it did not serve a unique niche in British commerce.

Second, the telephone was greeted by some as a disruption in the already hectic life of British businessmen. Rather than being seen as a way to increase productivity, (as the telephone was seen in America in the 1880s) it was viewed by some in Britain as a potential source of trouble. As *The Times* commented

> It is a common complaint that the conditions of modern life, and especially of mercantile life, have been rendered well-nigh intolerable by the telegraph; and

the addition of the telephone must inevitably 'more embroil the fray.' In old times a man of business could arrange his affairs for the day after the delivery of the morning post, and the perpetual arrival of telegrams has served to add new stings to existence.... The despatch of a telegram gives some little trouble, and therefore almost requires to be justified by some sort of occasion. With the new instrument hanging over his desk, the merchant or banker will be liable to perpetual interruptions from telephonists, who will begin with some such phrase as, 'Oh, by the bye.' But there are limits to human endurance, and those who are threatened by such an evil will probably discover some means of keeping it within reasonable bounds.[59]

This quote suggests that at least one commentator saw that the telephone meant different social practices. While it was perhaps acceptable for democratic Americans to be at the mercy of every telephone call, it was not appropriate for a proper British businessman who aspired to be a gentleman.[60]

Overall, the British seemed to have viewed the telephone with the dialectic response that we find associated with the introduction of so many other technologies. On the one hand, the telephone was admired as a marvel of science and ingenuity. On the other hand, it was quickly perceived as a device which would speed up daily life.

## Conclusion

To borrow a phrase from Mark Twain, the story of Bell, Edison, and the telephone in England is a story of innocents abroad. Both inventors approached foreign patents with the intention of making a quick killing; their interest was in securing cash for their inventions while not getting too deeply involved in the troubles of introducing a new technology in a foreign country. Both Bell and Edison, however, soon found themselves drawn into solving a myriad of problems. Each inventor had to tangle with the intricacies of British patent law, find a reliable representative who could raise capital, undertake a publicity campaign, choose a marketing strategy, and develop improvements suitable for the competitive situation. But all of these challenges were really cultural negotiations, in the sense that Bell and Edison were trying to find ways in which the telephone – an American artifact – could reside in British culture.

This story of Bell and Edison should serve as a cautionary tale about the global diffusion of technology. As we stand at the start of the 21st century, marvelling at the global spread of the Internet and the World Wide Web, it is easy for us to assume that soon everyone everywhere will be communicating with each other.[61] Such breathless predictions remind me of the enthusiasm with which people greeted the telephone in the 1870s; they too expected that the telephone would dramatically alter society. Central to these predictions is a belief that people throughout the world are the same, and indeed, have the same needs for information and communications. And yet, if the story of taking the telephone to England reveals anything, it shows us that there are always differences between cultures. Bell and Edison both went abroad assuming that the English would take up the telephone just as easily as Americans, and they were astonished by the challenges that they encountered. As we look at the diffusion of other technologies around the globe, we need to be careful not to be taken in by the breathless predictions and wind up being surprised like Bell and Edison. The global spread of new technologies may not be the imposition of one culture's values upon another as much as it is a process of cultural negotiation undertaken again and again as inventors and promoters introduce new technologies in different cultures.

# Notes

1 For a discussion of how transportation and information technology are shaping globalisation, see W. Bernard Carlson, "The World since 1970," in W. Bernard Carlson, ed., *Technology in World History* (New York: Oxford University Press, forthcoming), vol. 6, chap. 3.

2 W. Bernard Carlson, *Innovation as a Social Process: Elihu Thomson and the Rise of General Electric, 1870-1900* (New York: Cambridge University Press, 1991), 73-78.

3 Herbert N. Casson, *The History of the Telephone,* 4 ed. (Chicago: A. C. McClurg, 1911), 272.

4 See, for example, Stephen B. Adams and Orville R. Butler, *Manufacturing the Future: A History of Western Electric* (New York: Cambridge University Press, 1999).

5 One could tell an equally interesting story about how Bell's and Edison's telephones were introduced into other European countries. In particular, it would especially valuable to look at France and Germany since in both countries individual entrepreneurs and the State played different roles than in Britain. However, I have chosen to concentrate on the British case here because both Bell and Edison personally played a part in shaping how the technology was imported, and their papers give us detailed insight into the process by which telephone was transferred from America to another country. For a general overview of European telephone systems in the early 20th century, consult Casson, *The History of the Telephone*, 255-272. For a technical discussion of each national system, see A. R. Bennett, *The Telephone Systems of the Continent of Europe* (London: Longmans, Green, 1895; reprinted New York: Arno, 1974).

6 Reese V. Jenkins, *Images and Enterprise Technology and the American Photographic Industry, 1839 to 1925* (Baltimore: Johns Hopkins University Press, 1975).

7 Thomas P. Hughes, *Elmer Sperry: Inventor and Engineer* (Baltimore: Johns Hopkins University Press, 1971), 91-93.

8 Harold C. Passer, *The Electrical Manufacturers, 1875-1900: A Study in Competition, Entrepreneurship, Technical Change, and Economic Growth* (Cambridge, Mass.: Harvard University Press, 1953), 151-164.

9 *The Scientific American Reference Book* (New York: Munn & Co., 1877), 47-50.

10 Paul Israel, *From Machine Shop to Industrial Laboratory: Telegraphy and the Changing Context of American Invention, 1830-1920* (Baltimore: Johns Hopkins University Press, 1992).

11 Robert Conot, *A Streak of Luck* (New York: Seaview Books, 1979), 91.

12 Robert Bruce, *Bell: Alexander Graham Bell and the Conquest of Solitude* (Boston: Little, Brown, 1973), 93.

13 W. Bernard Carlson, "The Telephone as Political Instrument: Gardiner Hubbard and the Formation of the Middle Class in America, 1875-1880," in Michael T. Allen and Gabrielle Hecht, eds., *Technologies of Power Essays in Honor of Thomas Parke Hughes and Agatha Chipley Hughes* (Cambridge, Mass.: MIT Press, 2001), 25-56.

14 Quoted in Rosario Joseph Tosiello, *The Birth and Early Years of the Bell Telephone System, 1876-1880* (New York: Arno Press, 1979), 41-42.

15 On Reynolds, see Bruce, *Bell*, 231. Bell was anticipating additional income from the sale of patent rights in other countries, and he was anxious that this income support his new wife and future children. Consequently, Bell set up a trust for this income and asked Hubbard to manage it for him. See Bruce, *Bell*, 243.

16  Ibid., 237.

17  Kate Field, *The History of Bell's Telephone* (London, 1878). The copy I consulted was in the Brundy Library, Dibner Institute for the History of Science and Technology, Cambridge, Mass.

18  Casson, *The History of the Telephone*, 249.

19  Both quotes are from Bruce, *Bell*, 242.

20  Quoted in Catherine Mackenzie, *Alexander Graham Bell: The Man Who Contracted Space* (New York: Grosset & Dunlap, 1928), 193.

21  Ibid., 194.

22  For a discussion of Reis and Bell, see W. Bernard Carlson, "Electrical Inventions and Cultural Traumas: The Telephone in America and Germany, 1860-1880," in Klaus Plitzner, ed., *Elektrizität in der Geistesgeschichte* (Bassum: Verlag für Geschichte der Naturwissenschaften und der Technik, 1998), 143-154.

23  Bruce, *Bell*, 243-244, and Albert Anns, "The History of the National Telephone Company, Part I," *National Telephone Journal* 5 (Nov. 1911), 156-163, reprinted in Neil Johannessen, ed., *"Ring up Britain": The Early Years of the Telephone in the United Kingdom* (London: British Telecommunications, 1991), 156.

24  Bruce, *Bell*, 244.

25  For the full text of Bell's letter to the Directors of the Telephone Company, 25 March 1878, see Mackenzie, *Alexander Graham Bell*, 202-206.

26  Alexander Graham Bell to the Directors of the Telephone Company, Limited, (printed circular), 25 July 1878, in AGB-Telephone Co., Ltd.-England-Management-1878, Box 1103, AT&T Archives, Warren, New Jersey.

27  Bruce, *Bell*, 245.

28  Peter Young, *Person to Person: The International Impact of the Telephone* (Granta Editions, 1991), 16.

29  Anns, "The History," 156.

30  W. Bernard Carlson, "Invention and Evolution: The Case of Edison's Sketches of the Telephone," in John M. Ziman, ed., *Technological Innovation as an Evolutionary Process* (New York: Cambridge University Press, 2000), 137-158.

31  Quoted in W. Bernard Carlson and Michael E. Gorman, "Thinking and Doing at Menlo Park: Edison's development of the Telephone, 1876-1878," in William S. Pretzer, ed., *Working and Inventing: Thomas Edison and the Menlo Park Experience* (Dearborn: Henry Ford Museum and Greenfield Village, 1989), 91.

32  Draft Agreement with George Bliss, Cornelius Herz, and Stephen Field, 19 Sept. 1877 and Edward Johnson to Uriah Painter, 17 December 1877, both In R. A. Rosenberg et al., ed., *The Papers of Thomas A. Edison* (Baltimore: Johns Hopkins University Press), vol. 3, 555-558 and 676-679.

33  British Provisional Patent Specification: Telephone and Phonograph, 19 July 1877, *Edison Papers*, 3: 446-451.

34  I am grateful to Paul Israel for telling me that Edison hoped that Preece would be his agent. On Preece, see E. C. Baker, *Sir William Preece, F.R.S.: Victorian Engineer Extraordinary* (London: Hutchinson, 1976).

35  Forrest McDonald, *Insull* (Chicago: University of Chicago Press, 1962), 16.

36  George Parsons Lathrop, "Talks with Edison," *Harper's Monthly* 80, 425-435, on 433, and Frank L. Dyer and Thomas C. Martin, with William Henry Meadowcroft, *Edison: His Life and Inventions*, 2 vols., 2 ed. (New York: Harper & Brothers, 1929), vol. 1, 184.

37  Paul Israel, *Edison: A Life of Invention* (New York John Wiley, 1998), 184.

38  Lathrop, "Talks with Edison," 433.

39  W. H. Preece, "The Telephone," *Nature* 16 (6 September 1877), 403-404.

40  Matthew Josephson, *Edison: A Biography* (New York: McGraw-Hill, 1959), 151.

41  Israel, *Edison*, 184-185 and Anns, "The History," 156.

42  Anns, "The History," 151-152.

43  George Bernard Shaw, *The Irrational Knot* (New York: Brentano's, 1905), ix-xi.

44  Anns, "The History," 156.

45  Young, *Person to Person*, 16-17.

46  Conot, *A Streak of Luck*, 147. Israel reports that Gouraud paid Edison $5,000 as an advance on the chalk drum receiver and that Edison gave $1,000 to his wife and used the rest of the money to buy 500 books for his library; see Israel, *Edison*, 185.

47  Dyer and Martin, *Edison*, 185.

48  Conot, *A Streak of Luck*, 146 and 155-156.

49  Quoted in Josephson, *Edison*, 154.

50  Baker, *Sir William Preece*, 177-180.

51  Ibid., 187-194, and *The Post Office. An Historical Summary*, reprinted in Johannessen, "Ring up Britain," 88-91.

52  See, for example, Herbert Laws Webb, *The Development of the Telephone in Europe* (London: Electrical Press, 1911).

53  Baker, *Sir William Preece*, 183.

54  Quoted in Young, *Person to Person*, 19.

55  Preece attributed the slow growth in London in part to the fact that it was very difficult for telephone companies to secure permission (wayleave or right-of-way) from owners to string lines on their property. See William Henry Preece and Julius Maier, *The Telephone* (London: Whittaker, 1889), 482.

56  Ibid., 481.

57  Young, *Person to Person*, 22.

58  Quoted in Young, *Person to Person*, 11-12.

59  Quoted in ibid., 18-19.

60  As Leslie Hannah observed at the conference, telephones in 19th-century Britain were designed with three modes to handle incoming calls: the telephone would ring in response to an incoming call, it could have a busy signal if the line was already engaged, or it could be set to indicate to the caller that the owner of the telephone was not taking any calls.

61  See, for example, Thomas L. Friedman, *The Lexus and the Olive Tree*, rev. ed. (New York: Random House, 2000).

# Towards a Global Telephone Network

## Technological Advances in Long-Distance Telephony

*Helge Kragh*

## Introduction

The vast telegraph system which developed from the 1850s onwards was the first technology that made global communications a reality. Yet it was the humble telephone rather than the telegraph that became the true starting point of the international communications network that came to play such a dominant role in the culture, business, and politics of the second half of the 20th century. Originally a means of communication suited only for conversations over small or medium distances, from about 1920 telephony began to conquer the longer distances as well, and even compete with the telegraph. During this process telephony formed the backbone of a new multi-purpose communications network that came to span the entire globe. Indeed, the telephone marked a new and vigorous phase in the globalisation of technology. It was a key factor in the trend towards the global information society that has so drastically transformed the world during the latter part of the 20th century. The development has been extremely complex and cannot be easily described in its totality.[1] In this essay I focus on certain aspects of the development of long-distance telephone technology that illustrate lessons of a more general character to historians of modern technology.

Although it is beyond doubt that social, cultural, economic, and political factors played a very important role in the development, these are not central to my paper. It focuses on the technological progress that has been such a characteristic feature of a century-long development and undoubtedly will continue to be so in the 21st century. In general, cultural and socio-political contexts cannot be separated from the technological contexts. Communication technologies are, like other technologies, significantly shaped by cultural and social forces.[2] In many cases, so-called technical reasons are thoroughly integrated with reasons of a social and cultural nature. All the same, this does not imply that it is meaningless to speak of technical considerations or that scientific and technical factors have no explanatory power. A considerable part of the development of modern long-distance communications can only be understood if close attention is paid to these factors, that is, to the possibilities opened up by a series of scientific and technical innovations.

## Telephone Cultures

The earliest phase of telephony was characterised by the telephone companies' attempts to create a public need for the new technology. Graham Bell's invention was not the result of such a need and when the telephone entered the market it was not quite clear what kind of instrument it was and what it should be used for. The unsettled character of the "real" nature of an emerging technology is typical for many inventions that are not made as responses to definite needs or for definite purposes. The applications and social attitudes attached to the telephone first had to be established until the technology was defined and people knew what a telephone was.[3]

In the United States, Bell's vision of the telephone as an instrument of general communication was relatively quickly accepted, in part because of its resonance with cultural values characteristic of the American society. In Europe, the telephone was received much more reluctantly.[4] There were many reasons for this, one of them being that telephone conversation was widely seen as unfit for the European mind. The striking technology gap between the New and the Old World was not the result of the telephone being an American invention or otherwise rooted in differences in technical knowledge and practices. The main reason seems to have been different cultural attitudes and expectations that, in the case of Europe, resonated much better with the telegraph than with the telephone. "What strikes and frightens the backward European almost as much as anything in the United States is the efficiency and fearful universality of the telephone," wrote Arnold Bennett, a British telephone expert, in 1912. As to European telephone culture, he observed: "Many otherwise highly civilized Europeans are as timid in addressing a telephone as they would be in addressing a royal sovereign. The average European middle-class householder still speaks of his telephone, if he has one, in the same falsely casual tone as the corresponding American is liable to speak about his motor car."[5]

The telephone evolved to become a great agent of democratisation and leveling of social strata, but for a long time it was restricted to the upper and middle classes. It appealed to active people such as entrepeneurs, businessmen, and industrialists, who tended to appreciate the active and unpredictable mode of telephonic communication. It was a mode of communication that caused many military officers to dislike the introduction of the telephone.[6] Nor did it appeal to many literary men, who found the telephone distasteful because it intruded their privacy. The traditional European upper class, the aristocracy, also had difficulties accepting the telephone. They typically considered it a profane apparatus that penetrated the sanctuaries of their privileged lives. The nature of telephony – its pugnacity, immediacy, reciprocity, and irreverence – was widely felt to be incompatible with aristocratic values. It threatened the elaborate system of protocols and etiquette that gave people of noble birth a special position in society. Franz Joseph, the last emperor of the

Austro-Hungarian empire, hated telephones and other modern technologies (including typewriters, automobiles, and electric light) that heralded a new age hostile to his beloved aristocratic order. The emperor refused to install telephones in his castle in Vienna, but of course his obstinate opposition to modern technology changed nothing.[7]

About the turn of the century the telephone had passed its childhood. It was increasingly accepted, indeed eagerly welcomed, by many people who no longer considered it a toy but a useful means of communication over medium distances. In America, more than in Europe, it was widely perceived as a necessity and its value rarely questioned. In an acute analysis of the social impact of modern technology, the sociologist Thorstein Veblen challenged the consensus view by reverting the standard metaphor that "necessity is the mother of invention" into "invention is the mother of necessity." As Veblen saw it, modern technology was dangerously close to becoming autonomous: "Any such innovation that fits workably into the technological scheme, and that in any appreciable degree accelerates the pace of that scheme at any point," he wrote, "will presently make its way into general and imperative use, regardless of whether its ulterior effect is an increase or a diminution of material comfort or industrial efficiency." According to Veblen, the telephone was precisely such an innovation. It forced an unnatural rythm on peoples' life and caused an "increase of nervous disorders and shortening of the effective working life of those engaged in this [telephonic] traffic."[8] However, Veblen's critical attitude was far from representative of the American response to the telephone.

If the telephone should ever hope to compete with the telegraph it had to be effective over distances of more than a few hundred kilometers. It was the long-distance capabilities that made possible the formation of telephony as a large network technology or integrated system. Without a long-distance transmission system it would have remained what the early telephone historian Herbert N. Casson called a neighborhood affair.[9] The importance of increasing telephonic range was recognised by the Bell System and the more progressive of the European telephone companies. They realised that control over the long lines was essential not only to satisfy the customers but also in the competition with local companies. In 1901 an AT&T officer described the long-distance lines as "the nerves of our whole system" and emphasised "that it is extremely important that we should control the whole toll line system of intercommunication throughout the country."[10] AT&T decided to embark on a program to extend long-distance telephony, not because there was a widespread demand for communicating over long distances (which there was not) but primarily because it would improve the company's competitive situation.

It soon turned out that it was technically difficult to transmit speech of acceptable quality over very long distances. The difficulties threatened to slow the pace of the telephone industry and make it a less serious competitor to the telegraph system. In the terminology of Thomas Hughes, the problem constituted a "reverse sa-lient," that is, a bottleneck in an expanding system that hampers the growth of the entire system. The long-distance problem was not the only reverse salient in early telephony, but it was one of the most serious. As is often the case with reverse salients, efforts to solve the long-distance problem resulted in important techno-logical advances, many of which were unrelated to the original aim.

## Phases of Progress in Long-Distance Telephony

The concept of long-distance telephony is not well defined. Not only has the mean-ing of "long distance" changed considerably over time, it also involves speech com-munication over wires and cables as well as various forms of radio and microwave communications. I shall mostly concentrate on wire technologies, that is, transmis-sion either through open wire circuits or through wires arranged into underground or submarine cables. (There is no clearcut distinction between wire and cable tech-nologies; cables may be arranged on open systems, that is, between poles, but in what follows cable telephony will mainly refer to land underground or submarine cables.) The main part of the technological development of long-distance tele-phony can be classified under five different categories or traditions. Although these did not follow each other consecutively – in fact, they often coexisted and over-lapped – by and large they map the chronological order of progress.

*Phase I.* When the need for speech transmission over long distances arose in the 1880s, the solution of the telephone engineers was modeled on the theory and practice that governed the transmission of telegraph signals. For more than two de-cades a powerful "telegraph paradigm" framed the development of telephony over long distances. Mistakenly adopting William Thomson's celebrated telegraph the-ory to the new art, it was concluded that in order to reduce the attenuation that the product of the line's capacitance ($C$) and resistance ($R$) per unit length should be minimised. Moreover, insofar as the self-inductance ($L$) was considered at all, it was considered a harmful effect that could be largely avoided by using wires of copper instead of iron. "The effect of self-induction materially affects the clearness of arti-culation of telephones, and seriously reduces their efficiency," the authoritative *Manual of Telephony* told its readers.[11] In accordance with the telegraph paradigm, cables were constructed of thick copper cores insulated with guttapercha, that is, es-sentially the same kinds of cables as used in telegraphy. With such cables and open wire systems the speaking distance was considerably increased. The first interna-tional submarine connection, the 498-km Paris-London line, was opened for traffic in 1891.[12] The following year the New York-Philadelphia line over 1,442 km marked a new distance record. However, transmission quality was poor and because of the high fares – $9 for a 5-minutes call – it carried only low traffic. The traditional and somewhat unimaginative solution to the long-distance problem did not allow economically feasible lines much longer than 1,000 km. At the turn of the century it was all too evident that the traditional approach to extending the range of telephony had reached its limit. As the trade journal *Electrical World* expressed it, there was a great need for "a solution of perhaps the most important electrical problems which now confront us – submarine rapid telegraphy and telephony, and long distance land telephony and rapid telegraphy with conductors of moderate cost."[13] Whether these were needs for the customers or the communication companies, the journal did not say.

*Phase II.* The first major innovation in long-distance telephony was based on the theory of telephone current transmission proposed independently in 1887 by Oliver Heaviside in England and Aimé Vaschy in France.[14] According to this theory, the attenuation varied (under certain conditions) approximately as the square root of $R^2C/L$, implying that a line "loaded" with self-inductance would carry speech signals over longer distances than a traditional line. Only in 1900-1902 was this theoretical insight turned into a an engineering theory and from there into practical methods of how to add self-inductance to wires and cables. George Campbell, a Bell Telephone (or AT&T) researcher, and, independently, the physicist Michael Pupin developed schemes for discrete loading by means of induction coils.[15] Carl Krarup, a Danish engineer, invented an alternative by winding the copper conductors continuously with thin wires of soft iron.[16] The continuous method was widely used for submarine cables, whereas the coil loading method – often known as "pupinisation" – dominated land lines. In 1912, less than ten years after the loading method had been introduced, a total of 143,000 km of American telephone lines was equipped with Pupin coils. At the same time, inductive loading was widely used in European submarine telephone lines, either discretely (Pupin coils) or continuously (the Krarup method).[17]

The loading system was continuously improved through a series of innovations. In 1916 AT&T researchers developed the iron powder core, which was smaller, magnetically more stable, less wasteful in electrical energy, and better suited for repeater circuits. By 1921, Western Electric's manufacture plant at Hawthorne, Illinois, produced more than 25,000 pounds of iron powder per week.[18] Even more important was the AT&T invention in 1925 of induction coils made of a new iron-nickel alloy called permalloy. The new alloy was excellently suited for Pupin coils because they were smaller, cheaper, and had a higher magnetic permeability (hence smaller energy loss) than traditional coils. During the years 1928-1931 more than four million permalloy core coils were manufactured for the Bell System alone.[19]

*Phase III.* The real revolution in long distance telephony, as in telecommunication in general, was caused by the introduction of the triode vacuum tube as a means to amplify or "repeat" the weak speech currents. Harold Arnold and his staff at AT&T developed Lee De Forest's triode into a practical vacuum tube repeater, and in Germany Siemens & Halske and AEG joined forces to develop Robert von Lieben's gas-filled tube into a commercial device.[20] In January 1915, AT&T's tube repeater proved its worth by securing telephone conversation over the new transcontinental line from New York to San Francisco. The opening of the line (in the presence of the aging Graham Bell) was a landmark in long-distance telephony and a triumph for the new electronic repeater. The physicist Robert Millikan, who participated in the opening ceremony, later rationalised: "From that night on, the electron – up to that time largely the plaything of the scientist – had clearly entered the field as a potent agent in the supplying of man's commercial and industrial needs. ... It was a great day for both science and industry when they became wedded through the development of the electronic amplifier tube."[21]

Tube-repeater lines played an important role during World War I and after 1918 they formed the basis of the first long-distance telephone networks in Europe and the United States.[22] The partly integrated European cable networks were also of great importance in the politics, culture, and economy of Europe in the late 1920s, when it became possible, for the first time, to speak from one end of the continent to the other (Figure 1).[23] For example, in 1927 direct telephone connections over cables were opened between Stockholm and London over a 2,456-km line that included several submarine cables. Tube repeater engineering was chiefly responsible for the remarkable progress that occurred in European telephony around 1930 when England, Germany, France, Sweden and most other countries were interconnected with 22-25 other European countries. Only Albania was outside the new European cable network. Impressive as the European network was, technically it was inferior to the American telephone system which was both longer and operated more reliably. Figure 1 gives an impression of the development for which tube technology was primarily responsible, whether in the form of a repeater for cable telephony or as part of radio links.

It should be pointed out that vacuum tubes, as well as loading coils, were used for many other purposes than extending the range of telephony. Whereas the loading coil was invented as a long-distance device, and subsequently used for other purposes, the vacuum tube was not originally conceived as an amplifier for currents in long lines. In both cases, the technology was also used to lower costs for shorter distances and to build faster networks of local communications. Mass-production of standardised components resulted in improvements in manufacturing processes that contributed to the integration of communications systems by decreasing the costs of components.[24] By lowering the costs and improving the quality of cable communications, they allowed telephone companies to overcome transmission bottlenecks and connect cities and less populated regions. Different companies used the versatile technologies in different ways, depending on the companies'

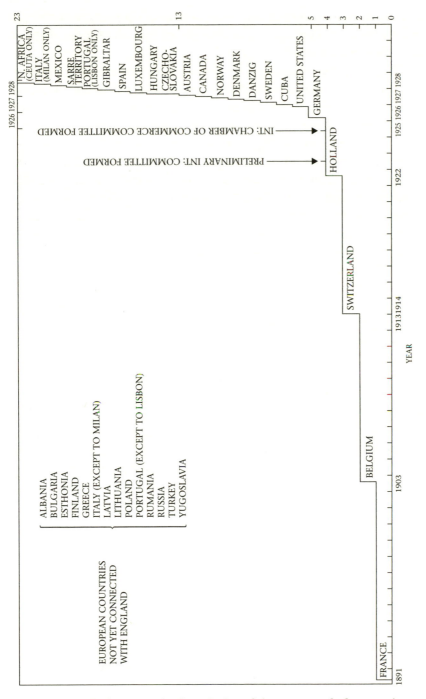

*Figure 1: Global telecommunications, I. Growth in overseas telephone service with Great Britain 1891-1928.*[25]

strategies, local problems, traditions, and competitive situations. As far as the vacuum tube is concerned, its use as a repeater in long lines was of relatively little importance in the overall picture.

In no area of telephony was the power of the vacuum tube repeater more impressively demonstrated than in long-distance submarine telephony. Ever since 1876 engineers had dreamed of telephoning across the Atlantic, and in 1928 AT&T made the first serious proposal of designing a transatlantic non-repeater cable based on a new type of continuous loading.[26] However, nothing came of the plan and with the development during World War II of submerged tube repeaters it was realised that this was the method to be used in a future transatlantic cable. The first cable crossing the Atlantic, named TAT-1, was completed in 1956 as a joint project of AT&T, the British Post Office, and the Canadian Overseas Telecommunication Corporation. The heart of the 4,244-km cable was the 51 submerged tube repeater units. Extensions from London to other European cities made the 7,917-km circuit between Copenhagen and Montreal the world's longest telephone cable line.[27] Subsequent ocean telephone cables were even longer. In 1961 the 60-circuit CANTAT-1 cable offered connections between Canada and England and a distance record was achieved two years later with the laying of a transpacific cable between Canada and Australia over a distance of nearly 11,000 km. Whereas the first generation of trans-oceanic cables used vacuum tubes in the repeater units, from the mid-1960s tubes were increasingly replaced by transistors. One of the first cables of this type was an 800-circuit cable laid in 1970 by AT&T between the United States and Spain.

*Phase IV*. TAT-1 made crucial use of another very important innovation in telephone technology, namely the frequency-division-multiplex (FDM) coaxial system. This invention goes back to the method of carrier wave telephony where the information (speech or in any other analog form) is carried in the sidebands' frequency intervals. Based on theoretical work by John Carson and others, in 1918 AT&T inaugurated the first commercial carrier system and ten years later AT&T's carrier system had expanded to a length corresponding to 368,000 km of single-wire lines. The first patent for a coaxial cable carrier system was filed in 1929, again by AT&T researchers (H. A. Affel and Lloyd Espenscheid).[28] Only two years later the system was put into practical use with the laying of a new Havana-Key West cable with six frequency bands. Later multichannel coaxial cable systems relied heavily on the invention of the negative feedback amplifier by Harold Black, another of AT&T's ever-inventive scientists. His idea of 1927 (a patent was only granted in 1937) has been compared with Lee De Forest's invention of the vacuum triode. "Without the stable, distortionless amplification achieved through Black's invention," the President of Bell Telephone Laboratories wrote, "modern multi-channeled trans-continental and trans-oceanic communication systems would have been impossible."[29]

The TAT-1 coaxial cable included 36 voice channels and in later transatlantic cables the number of circuits increased drastically. For example, the transistorised TAT-6 cable from 1976 had a capacity of 4,000 channels. The largest cable project of the traditional coaxial type is the 15,000-km ANZCAN cable between Canada and Australia which started service in 1984. Investments amounted to $500 million and each of the 1,124 transistorised repeaters cost nearly $100,000. ANZCAN was not only the largest system of its kind, it was also the last. By 1984 an entirely new cable technology was under development.

*Phase V.* The last chapter so far in the history of long-distance cable telephony consists of the successful development of cables made by optical fibers.[30] Fiber optics for telecommunication purposes relied on the solution of two critical problems, the invention of a coherent and strongly focused light source and the development of low-loss optical fibers. The source problem was largely solved with the invention of the laser in 1960 and its further development into the LED (light-emitting diode) some ten years later. In a classic paper of 1966 Charles Kao and George Hockham of Standard Telecommunication Laboratories in London showed theoretically that the attenuation of glass fibers needed to be reduced from about 1,000 dB (decibel) per kilometer to at least 20 dB/km. By 1970 a team of researchers at Corning Glass Works had prepared experimental fibers with an attenuation constant as low as 16 dB/km. Further development work reduced in 1975 the loss to 4 dB/km.

It took another decade until fiber-optical communications had truly transformed from an invention to a practical innovation and the first commercial fiber cables came in operation. Among the most important uses of the new technology were submarine cables, the first one being the 1986 link between England and Belgium. Two years later the first transatlantic optical fiber cable, named TAT-8, was opened for service between England and North America. The innovative project, a collaboration between AT&T, British Telecom, and France Telecom, had a capacity corresponding to 40,000 telephone conversations or almost double the existing cable capacity across the Atlantic. TAT-8 was followed by a fiber-optic link between the United States and Japan that went into service in 1991.

Fiber optics has continued its rapid development through the 1990s, during which decade the capacity of commercial optical fiber communications systems has more than doubled every two years. Since 1990, transatlantic capacity has increased dramatically. Ten years after TAT-1 went in operation, the total capacity was about 100 Gigabits per second, corresponding to 1.5 million telephone channels. One of the most important innovations was the invention in 1987 of a way to amplify signals in an optical fiber by inserting directly in the line a fiber doped with ions of the rare-earth element erbium. Together with the development of fiber lasers, the erbium-doped amplifiers initiated a new phase in optical fiber communications.[31]

## Rival and Complementary Technologies

Long-distance telephone cable technology was part of a larger complex of communications technologies that included other systems with the same function, that is, communication over long distances. In the same way that the development of railways in the 20th century cannot be properly understood if alternative transportation technologies such as motorcars and airplanes are ignored, so telephony developed in competitive interaction with alternative communications technologies of which telegraphy and radio links were the most important. The three kinds of technologies – cable telephony, cable telegraphy, and radio links – developed alongside and affected each other, partly as rivals and partly as supplements. Cable telephony, the main subject of the present paper, cannot be isolated from the other telecommunications technologies, and I therefore need to consider also cable telegraphy and wireless.

Harmeet Sawhney has called attention to certain evolutionary patterns that seem to be common for the even larger class of infrastructure technologies, including not only electrical communications but also canals, highways, bridges, and railroads.[32] According to Sawhney a technology typically starts as a collection of "infrastructure islands," that is, isolated projects of a restricted and largely demonstrational value. If the technology is found to be locally viable it starts "feeding" on an existing, functionally similar technology that will inspire and inform the newcomer. At this stage, the two technologies will still be in a complementary rather than competing relationship. It is only with the creation of long-distance capabilities and the ensuing development of an integrated system that the new technology finds itself in competition with the old and – until then – predominant one. The new and progressive technology eventually subordinates or annihilates the older rival until it will itself be challenged by a newcoming technology.

Although much of this quasi-Darwinian picture fits reasonably well with the development of telephony, Sawhney's scheme tends to exaggerate the degree to which a certain technology dominates a field at the expense of other technologies. In the development of communications technology it has been a characteristic feature not only that alternative methods of long-distance communications have co-existed for extended periods but also that they have, in some cases, merged into an integrated system where they interact collaborativelly rather than antagonistically.

Still in the 1920s traditional cable telegraphy, based on the vast system of submarine cables, was the dominant communication technology over very long distances.[33] In 1914 the submarine telegraph system totaled a length of almost 500,000 km distributed on some 2,000 cables of which the seventeen transatlantic cables were the most important. It was a truly global network dominated by British political and industrial interests. Politically and commercially important as the system was, seen from a technological point of view it was relatively conservative and based on cables that were largely of the same construction as those laid in the 1870s. In order to increase the traffic speed, cables became thicker and more expensive, as illustrated by the "Jumbo," a late transatlantic cable laid by the Commercial Cable Company in 1923. The cable contained 269 kg of copper per km, which resulted in a record transmission speed of almost 500 letters per minute. It marked the zenith of an unimaginative continuation in cable technology and belonged to the same kind of "dinosaur technology" as exemplified by telephone cables around 1900.[34] In both cases progress in performance was secured simply by making the cables thicker. Around 1920 it was no longer possible, or rather economically viable, to increase telegraphic speed in this way.

The immediate solution to the technological crisis in cable telegraphy was to make use of the method of inductive loading that had proved so successful in telephony. Because of the differences between speech signals and telegraph signals, the method could not be simply adopted from telephony but had to be reconsidered from a scientific and technological perspective. The theory of loaded telegraph cables was ready in 1920, to a large extent based on the work of Henry Malcolm in England.[35] Loaded cables became a reality a couple of years later with the invention of permalloy, whose magnetic properties proved to be excellently suited for telegraph purposes. The innovative work at Western Electric involved both mathematical theories, laboratory experiments and elaborate series of testing. As a result of the extensive research the first continuously loaded telegraph cable was constructed and laid in the fall of 1924 between New York and the Azores. The 3,730-km permalloy-loaded cable performed exceedingly well. The operating speed was 1,920 words per minute, a phenomenal record that not only raised transatlantic telegraph speed with almost 400% but also necessitated the construction of special high-speed recorders.[36]

The striking success of Western Electric's permalloy-loaded cable revitalised transoceanic telegraphy by adapting a technology from telephony. Several new loaded cables were laid during the following years, the longest of which was the 6,422-km Pacific cable from Bamfield in Canada to Suva in the Fiji Islands, from where there were further connections to Australia and New Zealand. The 1926 cable duplicated a cable of the traditional type laid in 1902, but whereas the old cable only allowed a speed of 135 letters per minute, more than 1,000 letters could be sent over the new cable each minute.

The development of loaded high-speed ocean cables was the first significant change in telegraph cable technology for half a century and promised a new life for the old and venerable industry. By 1929 nine cables of the new type were in operation, together stretching a distance of about 32,000 km and comprising about 7% of the world's total ocean cable mileage. The efficiency of the invention is illustrated by the fact that the two loaded transatlantic cables of 1924 and 1926 carried a traffic capacity almost as large as the combined capacity of the seventeen nonloaded cables that bridged North America and Europe before 1924. However, with the new cables the need for long-distance telegraphy was saturated. Since 1929 no more loaded cables were laid and both the number and mileage of telegraph cables began to decline. The reason was not a decline in traffic over very long distances, but that an increasing part of the messages was sent by means of the competing wireless technology, either as telegrams or, increasingly, telephone messages. Much later, in the 1960s, the development in tube-repeater submarine telephony and satellite transmissions made ocean telegraph cables obsolete.

The wireless alternative was technologically rooted in the same modest component that had revolutionised long-distance cable telephony, that is, the vacuum tube. The Bell System recognised early on the potential importance of wireless and its relevance for telephone business, if only a practical amplifier could be developed. In a memorandum of 1909, John Carty wrote that "Whoever can supply and control the necessary telephone repeater will exert a dominating influence in the art of wireless telephony when it is developed. ... A successful telephone repeater, therefore, would not only react most favorably upon our service where wires are used, but might put us in a position of control with respect to the art of wireless telephony should it turn out to be a factor of importance."[37] And, indeed, it did turn out to be a factor of importance. Experimental radio telephony across the Atlantic was first achieved by AT&T in 1915 and in 1923 the company collaborated with RCA (Radio Corporation of America) in establishing a one-way experimental telephone link between England and the United States.[38]

Transoceanic and transcontinental wireless had greatly progressed, but it was still an expensive and somewhat clumsy technology that depended on ever more gigantic longwave stations. The situation changed after 1924 when shortwave radio transmission directed by parabolic reflectors or antenna arrays were introduced (Figure 2). The new shortwave technology that emerged about 1926 saved radio from the dinosaur syndrome that threatened to block progress, in much the same way as loading and tube-repeatering had helped long-distance wire telephony by offering alternatives to the traditional method of increased wire size. Shortwave radio links appeared shortly after the loaded telegraph cable and effectively blocked further development of the latter technology.

In January 1927 the first commercial transatlantic radiotelephone service, a longwave link, started operation between London and New York. Later the same year it was supplied with a shortwave connection and within a year it was possible to speak between Stockholm and Chicago, or between Paris and Boston. These first lines were not the result of a manifest demand to speak across the Atlantic, but were largely built ahead of demand. An important factor in the construction of the lines

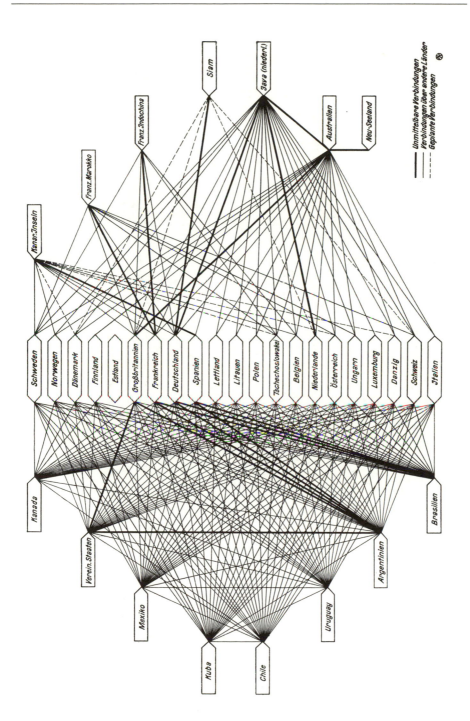

*Figure 2: Global telecommunications, II. European international wireless links about 1930.[39]*

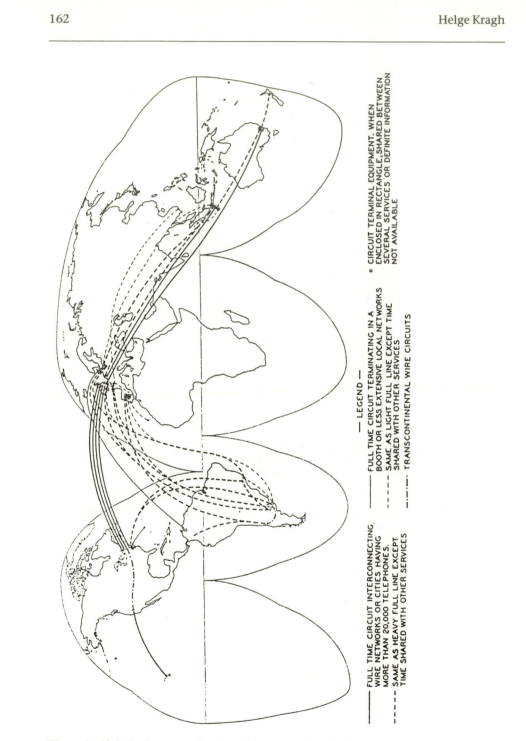

*Figure 3: Global telecommunications, III. International telephone circuits of the world as of January 1932. Only circuits over 1,000 km are shown.*[40]

| Route | length | opening | ownership |
|---|---|---|---|
| London-New York | 5,550 | June 1927 | GPO/AT&T |
| London-New York | 5,550 | June 1928 | GPO/AT&T |
| London-New York | 5,550 | June 1929 | GPO/AT&T |
| London-New York | 5,550 | Dec 1929 | GPO/AT&T |
| London-Buenos Aires | 11,140 | Dec 1930 | GPO/ITT |
| London-Sydney | 17,000 | Apr 1930 | GPO/WA |
| Paris-Buenos Aires | 11,060 | June 1930 | TSF/ITT |
| Paris-Saigon | 10,120 | Apr 1930 | TSF |
| Berlin-Buenos Aires | 11,920 | Sep 1930 | RPM/ITT |
| Madrid-Buenos Aires | 10,060 | Oct 1930 | ITT |

Selected intercontinental radiotelephone links 1927-1930, their lengths given in km. Abbreviations: AT&T: American Telephone and Telegraph Company; GPO: British Post Office; ITT: International Telegraph and Telephone Company; RPM: Reichpost Ministry; TSF: Companie Télephone Sans Fil; WA: Wireless Australasia.

was, to quote from Carty's 1909 address, to put AT&T "in a position of control" of the new technology and its possibilities. Reflecting the situation, initially the rates for transatlantic wireless telephony were very high ($75 on a three-minutes basis between London to New York) and the traffic correspondingly low, less than four calls per day. Yet, potential customers soon found the lines to be useful; or to put it differently, a demand was created in conformity with the expectations of AT&T and other involved companies. Rates declined rapidly and by the end of 1929 the average daily number of transatlantic radio calls had increased to 45. Not an impressive number by later standards, but it was only a beginning. By 1930 there was speech communication over the combined radio and cable telephone network between 14 countries in North America (U.S., Canada, Mexico, Cuba) and Europe (Spain, France, Great Britain, Switzerland, Luxemburg, Belgium, the Netherlands, Germany, Austria, and Czechoslovakia). The rapid development of shortwave radio telephony was a direct threat to the system of cable telegraphy, whereas it was not in the same way antagonistic to ordinary telephony over wire or cable.

In fact, it was soon realised that cable telephony and radio links were complementary rather than rival technologies. During the 1920s a growing number of telephone connections consisted of radio and cable in combination. The first large-scale example of such a hybrid communications system was AT&T's link between Havana and Santa Catalina off the Californian coast established in 1921. The link consisted of a new inductively loaded Havana-Key West cable connected to the New York-San Francisco line which continued in a radio connection to Santa Catalina. By thus combining radio and cable telephony a record distance of telephone transmission was achieved over more than 8,000 km. Truly international telephony, defined as circuits joining different continents over a distance of more than 1,000 km, was still limited to radio links (see Table and Figure 3). In the early 1930s such links totaled a length of about 280,000 km of which the four circuits between London and New York were the most important. Many of the intercontinental connections combined radio with cable transmission, a method that was impressively demonstrated with the first round-the-world telephone conversation on 25 April, 1934. In this AT&T demonstration the total distance covered was 37,300 km of which 31,200 were wireless.

In 1965, the technological competition between cable and radio telecommunications took a new turn with the launching of the first active communication satellite, Early Bird (or Intelsat-1).[41] With its 240 telephone circuits Early Bird was merely a beginning and by itself unable to challenge the new transatlantic telephone cables. But it was quickly followed by a series of geostationary satellites with much higher traffic capacity and much lower rates. By 1977 the eight Intelsat-4 satellites offered 40,000 telephone circuits to six continents and provided an almost global communication system. The major share of intercontinental telephony was transmitted wirelessly through satellites rather than through cables. As mentioned, as a result of the introduction of fiber-optical transmission lines, from the mid-1980s the global balance between wired and wireless telephony began to change in favor of cables. And yet it is far from clear that the future belongs to fiber-optical systems, for recently satellite systems have experienced a remarkable renaissance based on new types of antennas and breakthroughs in satellite technology. Many experts now believe that future long-distance communications will rely on a mixture of optical fiber cables and a system of both geostationary and low-orbit satellites where the major part of the telephone traffic will go through the satellite services.[42]

The new international cable-wireless network of the late 1920s was part of a large restructuring in the communications business structure.[43] In early 1928 an Imperial Wireless and Cable Conference was held in London with participation of British private communications industries and the governments of Great Britain, Australia, and Canada. It resulted in a big merger between private and government interests and also between wireless and cable business. The new unified communication company of 1929 was organised in a holding company and an operating company, the Cable and Wireless, Ltd. The new British communication giant, based on cable telegraphy and radio, included at its foundation 253 cable and radio stations throughout the world and its cable system made up 262,000 km, or more than half of the world's total mileage. The merger was in part effected with the purpose of protecting the telegraph cable network, but it could not prevent the reduction in cable traffic that forced a gradual shrinking in the telegraph cable mileage during the 1930s.

To a large extent the British merger was a defensive action against a threatening American dominance led by the new and aggressive International Telegraph and Telephone Company (ITT) founded in 1920. As part of an involved struggle in American communications politics and economics, in 1925 ITT took over most of AT&T's international business, including International Western Electric (which was renamed International Standard Electric) and its manufacturing plants in London and Antwerp. Two years later, ITT established cooperation with or bought decisive shares in the All American Cables Co., the Commercial Cable Co., and the Mackay cable group. The new American-based giant communications trust was further strengthened by agreements with Western Union and independent European companies including the Marconi group in England and Telefunken in Germany. By 1930 telecommunications had not only become big business; it had also become a highly monopolised and multinational business in which national communications interests to a large extent were determined by an opaque network of companies and capitals operating across the borders. At that time, globalisation and monopolisation might seem to be almost synonymous.

## Progress in a Science-Based Technology

Nowadays the notion of technological progress cannot be taken for granted. It has sometimes been questioned and it is indeed often difficult to establish clear criteria for what constitutes such progress. Yet it seems intuitively clear that certain areas of technology have evolved through an almost uninterrupted series of more and more successful devices and methods and in this way exhibited a steady progress. Electrical telecommunications in general, and long-distance cable telephony in particular, is such an area of technology. Contrary to some other fields of technology, progress in telephony and similar communications technologies can be assessed relatively easily and objectively by means of reliable quantitative indicators. For example, the dissemination or popularity of telephony can be measured either by the telephone density – the number of telephones, say per hundred inhabitants – or the number of daily calls per inhabitant. Such indicators measure the quantitative growth in telephony but not necessarily what we would want to associate with technological progress. The increased use of a certain technological artifact may be the result of technical improvement, as is indeed often the case; but it may also be the result of lower prices, better marketing, fashion, or numerous other factors not related to technological progress. There are many ways in which to illustrate the progress in telephone transmission performance. To mention only one, in addition to those already mentioned, since the end of World War II the relative annual cost per telephone circuit has decreased by a factor of about ten.

It would be hard to deny technical progress in long-distance telephony. Whether such progress is also progressive in the wider sense, say from an ethical or political point of view, is of course a different question. It belongs to the realm of philosophy and I shall limit my discussion to the technological sphere. An attractive definition of technological progress is to equate it with increase in efficiency, as suggested many years ago by Henryk Skolimowski.[44] But in *what* does efficiency consist, more exactly? A more efficient solution to a technological problem may be one which is more durable, more accurate, or have a higher capacity than an alternative solution. In general it is problematical to compare the efficiencies of two technologies, for other reasons because the criterion of efficiency will typically consist of several components that may well be in conflict. (If the range of a cable is longer than that of another, equally expensive cable, but the latter carries more circuits, which is the more efficient?) Moreover, what counts as efficiency is ultimately dictated by a socially set problem. If it was not deemed socially desirable to speak over very long distances, long-distance and multi-channel telephony would not be "efficient."

It may be useful to distinguish between *performance progress* and *integration progress*. The technical performance of a long-distance cable can be reasonably measured by the maximum length of cable or wire through which speech of good quality can be transmitted. It is beyond doubt that the range of cable telephony has increased continually and dramatically through more than a century. On the other hand, transmission over very long distances is not the only component of performance progress. The other component that evidently enters is the traffic capacity as measured by, for example, the number of circuits per cable. Growth in this respect has been no less continual and dramatic than with respect to distance. It should be noted that progress cannot simply be estimated by some combination of the two measures, such as their product, but that economical and other factors have to be included as well. To these other factors belong reliability, durability, and speech quality, of which the latter depends directly on cultural norms.

In discussing progress in technological performance we are interested in practical and commercial technologies, not experimental state-of-the-art technologies that for various reasons do not enter the market. So far as commercial cables are concerned they had to compete on the market with alternatives and for this reason, among others, their performance included economical and other factors. We may imagine an advanced cable type anno 1920 with a maximum range of 10,000 km and including 5,000 circuits; such a cable could in principle have been constructed, but it would be prohibitively expensive, allow only transmission of bad quality, and perhaps be very unreliable. It would therefore not be used commercially and its remarkable technological performance would be illusory.

Almost all technological traditions include what may be called *demonstration technologies*, namely, technological devices that function extremely well or perform remarkably efficiently, but are not constructed under the constraints of market conditions. They are typically constructed in order to demonstrate to potential buyers and investors the power of a certain innovation and to show what this innovation can in principle achieve. They may turn up at exhibitions or trial competitions, where the socio-economic ambience is widely different from that of real-life situations. (Racing cars is a well known example – they may demonstrate the wonderful performance of a new motor design, but are useless in, and not intended for, ordinary traffic.) The history of long-distance telephony offers several examples of such demonstration technologies. Thus, as early as 1882 Cornelius Herz reportedly transmitted speech signals over a distance of no less than 1,100 km of aerial wire by means of specially designed and very complicated (and very expensive) telephone apparatus. Similarly, the Belgian engineer François van Rysselberghe's impressive results on American lines in the late 1880s – he transmitted speech from Chicago to New York through a specially designed circuit system – must be considered to belong to this class of demonstration technologies. The performance of van Rysselberghe's system was not of demonstrational value only, but it depended on techniques that were too complicated and too expensive to be used commercially on a large scale.[45]

Many large-scale and expensive technological projects are just the opposite of avant-garde demonstration technologies. In such projects, reliability and security, and not technological sophistication, are given maximum priority. They are technologically conservative and rely on tested rather than on new and higher-performance inventions. For example, TAT-1 used ordinary tube technology in its repeaters although in 1956 the new and more efficient transistor was available. As two AT&T engineers argued, "Proved reliability is an essential requirement in a pioneering and costly venture of the difficulty of a transatlantic cable."[46] Again, the later ANZCAN cable used the thoroughly tested metallic coaxial technology rather than the technically superior fiber-optic solution. In the late 1970s, when planning for ANZCAN started, the development of fiber optic cables was in a more or less experimental stage and it was considered too risky to base the huge project on a technology that had not yet proved its worth in practice.[47]

In continuation of earlier remarks concerning rival and complementary technologies I would like to suggest that technological progress includes also a quantity that relates to how easily a technology can be integrated into a larger technological system. Such *integration progress* is not easily quantifiable but it is no less important for that. The progress in the modern communications system consists not only in improved performance of individual technologies but also in a diversification with the invention of new devices (television, fax, telex, computers, internet, etc.) that have become integrated in the larger system. Ever since the first integrated cable-radio links in the 1920s, telecommunications have increasingly developed in a systemic way which in itself must be counted as part of the progress. Both performance and integration progress are largely of a technological nature, for the only ways to extend the range significantly, to increase the traffic capacity, and to integrate different communications and information technologies (and to do so under market conditions) have been by means of new innovations and technical improvements. Efficiency, in Skolimowski's sense, seems to be well encapsulated by the two aspects of performance combined with the integrative measure.

This does not mean that social and cultural factors can be ruled out in considerations of technological progress. Concepts such as "efficiency" and "integration" are rarely reducible to a purely technical level, such as illustrated by several examples from the history of telephone communications. Thus, in the early phase of submarine telephone lines engineers discussed how to measure the efficiency of loaded cables, without being able to reach a consensus based on technical reasons alone. Although expressing their views in a neutral technical language, the engineers' arguments depended to a considerable extent on their training, cultural standards, national environment, and commitment to known technologies.[48] Another example is provided by the controversy over the transmission unit that occurred in the 1920s and eventually resulted in the global acceptance of the decibel system. That this controversy evolved as it did had more to do with national traditions and cultural standards than with technical arguments.[49]

Apart from progress, the development of long-distance telephony is characterised by its strong foundation in scientific methods and practices. It is indeed a prime example of a science-driven technology, although far from the simple and long discarded "linear model" of technology as merely applied science. Most of the major innovations of 20th-century communications technology have not been developed in purely empirical ways but have been rooted in scientific theories. These are, however, not the theories of pure science but rather engineering theories of various types and generality. Consider the kind of theoretical reasoning that entered in the first breakthrough in long-distance telephony, the construction of the loaded cable. The 1887 theories of Heaviside and Vaschy were guided by and designed to illuminate a general technological problem, the transmission of speech currents over long distances. Rather than applying basic electromagnetic theory in its most general sense, Heaviside derived from Maxwell's theory what has been called "limited-reference theories," that is, theories based on such approximations that refer to and are guided by practical situations.[50] "We shall never know the most general theory of anything in Nature," Heaviside wrote in 1887, "but we may at least take the general theory so far as it is known, and work with that, finding out in special cases whether a more limited theory will not be sufficient, and keeping within bounds accordingly."[51] On another occasion Heaviside stressed the importance of a basic theory with which the technologically oriented limited-reference theory is linked: "The advantage of a precise theory is its definiteness. ... we may elaborate it as far as we please, and be always in contact with a possible state of things. But in making applications it is another matter. It requires the exercise of judgment and knowledge of things as they are, to be able to decide whether this or that influence is negligible or paramount."[52]

Whereas a basic scientific theory deals with "a possible state of things," the object of an engineering theory is to investigate "things as they are." Even though less general than a theory of fundamental physics, such reference theories are not limited to definite technological devices or applications. They are abstract and general, only to a more limited extent than the truly fundamental theories. Because of its origin in the approximations on which it is based a limited reference theory – or engineering theory – provides a practical approach to the solution of engineering problems, but it is an approach that is not directly transformable into technological practice. The engineering theory is typically related to an artifact of some kind and for this reason the relevant scientific theory has to be reformulated in ways that are not initially evident but depend on the development of the artifact.

The theory of Heaviside and Vaschy was an engineering theory insofar as it included the nomopragmatic prescription "in order to increase speaking distance, increase the self-inductance."[53] But it did not tell how to design cables or wires with increased self-inductance and it was therefore unable to act as what Edwin Layton has called "instruments for implementing goals through the design process."[54] Such an instrument was only provided with the Campbell-Pupin theory which was specifically designed in order to solve a real technological problem, although not so specifically that it was limited to a particular kind of line or apparatus. The Campbell-Pupin theory was, like the Heaviside-Vaschy theory, a limited-reference theory in the sense that it included approximations originating in practical considerations, only these approximations were more specific and goal-oriented.

I have focused on the early development of the loaded cable (phase II above) because the case is relatively simple and has been studied in detail by historians of science and technology. Far from being a unique example of engineering science, it is fairly representative for the kind of scientific theories that have played a crucial role also in other innovations in the history of telecommunication. During the decades following the invention of the loaded cable, advanced engineering mathematics became a branch of direct technological usefulness in the design process and a major goal of the large research-oriented companies such as AT&T, Siemens & Halske, and Standard Electric.[55] These and other institutions used science consciously and systematically to develop generalised engineering theories that could be useful in the design of concrete technologies. For example, the study of noise in tube amplifiers, as made by Walter Schottky in 1918 and Harry Nyquist in 1928, was mathematically complex and not directly useful for solving design problems.

Yet it turned out to be important as a general framework from which possible technological solutions could be better understood. On an even more abstract level may be mentioned the work of Claude Shannon, the Bell Laboratories mathematician whose 1948 general theory of information was mathematically as well as conceptually abstruse but which, nonetheless, led to results of profound value to the coming era of digital communications technologies.[56] It is today generally accepted that science and technology should be viewed as separate spheres of knowledge rather than standing in a derivative or hierarchical relationship. However, in some areas, such as telecommunications, the separation is far from strict and a substantial part of the technology's knowledge content is intimately linked to scientific knowledge. As pointed out in a recent review, for almost a century the development of marketable communications technology has been closely connected with the application of the latest discoveries in physics and materials science.[57]

## Conclusion

I have sketched the development of long-distance telephony during the century 1890-1990 and argued that this area of technology has been characterised by steady progress. There are many ways in which progress in technological performance can be achieved; one of them would be extending the scale of existing technological solutions. This may lead to what I have called the dinosaur syndrome, that is, the growth of a technology until it approaches a limited size. The alternative is of course development by means of technological innovation, this being based on scientific insight, or not. It is this kind of innovative progress that has been characteristic during most of the history of telecommunications. I have suggested to distinguish between two kinds or measure of technological progress, performance progress and integration progress, where the first relates to how well a technology performs and the latter to its ability to enter into coordination with other technologies in a larger system. Moreover, I have called attention to the difference between, on the one hand, practical or commercial technologies and, on the other, demonstration technologies that are not governed by the market forces. Finally, I have stressed the close links between telecommunications technologies and scientific knowledge and briefly indicated the sort of engineering theories that have played an important and fruitful role in 20th-century telecommunications.

## Notes

1  For overviews, see Anthony R. Michaelis, *From Semaphore to Satellite* (Geneva: International Telecommunication Union, 1965) and Laszlo Solymar, *Getting the Message: A History of Communications* (Oxford: Oxford University Press, 1999).

2  The social shaping of communication technologies has been examined by many authors. For an overview, see David E. Nye, "Shaping communication networks: Telegraph, telephone, computer," *Social Research 64* (1997), 1067-1091. For the claim that technological knowledge is social through and through, see Donald MacKenzie, *Inventing Accuracy: A Historical Sociology of Nuclear Missile Guidance* (Cambridge, Mass.: MIT Press, 1990).

3  For the reception of the telephone and early telephone culture, see Ithiel de Sola Pool, ed., *The Social Impact of the Telephone* (Cambridge, Mass.: MIT Press, 1981); Renate Genth and Joseph Hoppe, *Telephon! Der Draht an dem wir hängen* (Berlin: Transit, 1986); Claude S. Fischer, *America Calling: A Social History of the Telephone to 1940* (Berkeley: University of California Press, 1992); and Helge Kragh, "Transatlantic technology transfer: The reception and early use of the telephone in the U.S. and Europe," in Dan C. Christensen, ed., *European Historiography of Technology* (Odense: Odense University Press, 1993), 68-90.

4  For the transfer of telephone technology and comparisons between Europe and America, see Kragh, "Transatlantic technology tranfer"; Werner Rammert, "Telefon und Kommunikationskultur: Akzeptanz und Diffusion einer Technik im Vier-Länder-Vergleich," *Kölner Zeitschrift für Soziologie und Sozialpsychologie 42* (1990), 20-40; James Foreman-Peck, "International technology transfer in telephony, 1876-1914," in David J. Jeremy, ed., *International Technology Transfer: Europe, Japan and the USA, 1700-1914* (Aldershot, England: Edward Elgar, 1991), 122-152; and W. Bernard Carlson, "Electrical inventions and cultural traumas: The telephone in Germany and America, 1860-1880," in Klaus Plitzner, ed., *Elektrizität in der Geistesgeschichte* (Bassum: Verlag für Geschichte der Naturwissenschaften und der Technik, 1998), 143-154.

5  *Harper's Monthly 125* (July 1912), 192. Here quoted from Sola Pool, *The Social Impact of the Telephone* (note 3), 152.

6  Helge Kragh, "Telephone technology and its interaction with science and the military, ca. 1900-1930," in Manuel J. Sànchez-Ron and Paul Forman, eds., *National Military Establishments and the Advancement of Science and Technology: Studies in 20th Century History* (Boston: Kluwer, 1995), 37-68. As McLuhan pointed out, "It is not feasible to exercise delegated authority by telephone. The pyrimidal structure (...) cannot withstand the speed of the phone to bypass all hierarchical arrangements." Marshall McLuhan, *Understanding Media* (New York: New American Library, 1964), 234.

7  Stephen Kern, *The Culture of Time and Space 1880-1918* (London: Weidenfeld & Nicolson, 1983), 91-92 and 315-316.

8  Thorstein Veblen, *The Instinct of Workmanship and the State of the Industrial Arts* (New York: Macmillan, 1914), 314-316.

9  Herbert N. Casson, *The History of the Telephone* (Chicago: McClurg, 1913), 172.

10  Quoted in John V. Langdale, "The growth of long-distance telephony in the Bell System: 1875-1907," *Journal of Historical Geography 4* (1978), 145-159, on 148.

11  William H. Preece and A. J. Stubbs, *A Manual of Telephony* (London: Whittaker & Co., 1893), 13.

12  David G. Tucker, "The first cross-Channel telephone cable: The London-Paris telephone links of 1891," *Transactions of the Newcomen Society 47* (1974-1976), 117-132. After six years of service, traffic was about 250 messages per day.

13  *The Electrical World 23* (1894), 666.

14  On Heaviside, see Ido Yavetz, *From Obscurity to Enigma: The Work of Oliver Heaviside, 1872-1889* (Basel: Birkhäuser, 1995), and Paul J. Nahin, *Oliver Heaviside: Sage in Solitude* (New York: IEEE Press, 1988). On Vaschy, see M. Atten, "Physiciens et télégraphistes français face à la théorie de Maxwell (1860-1890)," *Recherches sur l'Histoire des Télécommunications 2* (1988), 6-40. The mathematical details of the theory are outlined in Helge Kragh, "Ludvig Lorenz and the early theory of long-distance telephony," *Centaurus 35* (1993), 305-324.

15  Neil H. Wasserman, *From Invention to Innovation: Long-distance Telephone Transmission at the Turn of the Century* (Baltimore: Johns Hopkins University Press, 1985); James E. Brittain, "The introduction of the loading coil: George A. Campbell and Michael I. Pupin," *Technology and Culture 11* (1970), 36-57, reprinted in Terry S. Reynolds, ed., *The Engineer in America* (Chicago: University of Chicago Press, 1991), 261-282.

16  Helge Kragh, "The Krarup cable: Invention and Early Development," *Technology and Culture 35* (1994), 129-157.

17  *Loading Coils for Telephone Circuits*, Western Electric Bulletin 4006 (London, 1913); J. G. Hills, "The loading of submarine cables: A comparison between coil-loaded and continuously-loaded cables," *Electrical Review 71* (1912), 892-894, 931-933, 973-975.

18  T. Shaw and W. Fondiller, "Development and application of loading for telephone circuits," *Bell System Technical Journal 5* (1926), 221-281.

19  T. Shaw, "The evolution of inductive loading for Bell System telephone facilities," *Bell System Technical Journal 30* (1951), 149-211, 447-489, 721-778, 1221-1243.

20  The history of electronic tubes is described in Gerald Tyne, *Saga of the Vacuum Tube* (Indianapolis: H. W. Sams & Co., 1977). For the work at AT&T, see Lillian Hoddeson, "The emergence of basic research in the Bell Telephone System, 1875-1915," *Technology and Culture 22* (1981), 512-544; and for the development in Germany, K. Skowronnek, "Zur Entwicklung der Elektronenverstärker-Röhre (Lieben-Röhre)," *Archiv für Geschichte der Mathematik, der Naturwissenschaften und der Technik 13* (1931), 225-276.

21  Robert A. Millikan, *The Autobiography of Robert A. Millikan* (London: MacDonald, 1951), p. 136.

22  Kragh, "Telephone technology." See also Bancroft Gherardi and Frank B. Jewett, "Worldwide telephony – its problems and future," *Bell System Technical Journal 11* (1932), 485-519.

23  Frank J. Brown, *The Cable and Wireless Communications of the World* (London: Pitman & Sons, 1930); P. Craemer, ed., *Zwei Jahrzehnte Deutsche Fernkabel-Gesellschaft 1921-1941* (Berlin: EF Verlag, 1941). See also Harm G. Schröter, "The German long distance telephone network as a large technical system, 1919-1939, and its spin-offs for the integration of Europe," in François Caron, Paul Erker and Wolfram Fischer, eds., *Innovations in the European Economy Between the Wars* (Berlin: Walter de Gruyter, 1995), 83-105.

24  In the case of Germany, this is documented in Hartmut Petzold, "Zur Bedeutung der Bausteintechnik für die Entstehung des elektrischen Telekommunikationssystems," *Technikgeschichte 56* (1988), 193-205.

25 Frank Gill, "International telephony," *Electrical Communication 7* (1929), 190-199, on 190.

26 Helge Kragh, "History and prehistory of the first transatlantic telephone cable," *Polhem 13* (1995), 246-271.

27 Robert M. Black, *History of Electric Wires and Cables* (London: Peter Peregrinus, 1983), 204-209.

28 D. G. Tucker, "The early history of amplitude modulation, sidebands and frequency-division-multiplex," *The Radio and Electronic Engineer 41*:1 (1971), 43-47; A. F. Rose, "Twenty years of carrier telephony," *Bell Telephone Quarterly 17* (1938), 245-263.

29 Quoted in John Bray, *The Communications Miracle: The Telecommunication Pioneers from Morse to the Information Superhighways* (New York: Plenum Press, 1995), 140.

30 Jeff Hecht, *City of Light: The Story of Fiber Optics* (New York: Oxford University Press, 1999); Bray, *The Communications Miracle*, 269-298; Sami Faltas, "The invention of fibre-optic communications," *History and Technology 5* (1988), 31-49; Morton I. Schwartz, "Optical fiber transmission – from conception to prominence in 20 years," *IEEE Communications Magazine 22* (1984), 38-48.

31 Alastair M. Glass, "Fiber optics," *Physics Today 46*:10 (1993), 34-38.

32 Harmeet Sawhney, "The public telephone network: Stages in infrastructure development," *Telecommunications Policy 16* (1992), 548-552.

33 Vary T. Coates and Bernhard Finn, *A Retrospective Technology Assessment: Submarine Telegraphy* (San Francisco: San Francisco Press, 1979); Daniel R. Headrick, *The Invisible Weapon: Telecommunications and International Politics 1851-1945* (New York: Oxford University Press, 1991).

34 In general a dinosaur technology may be defined as a technology in which improvement has reached its practical limit simply by extending the system to bigger and more powerful versions.

35 H. Malcolm, *The Theory of Submarine Telegraph and Telephone Cable* (London: The Electrician Printing and Publ. Co., 1917).

36 Oliver E. Buckley, "High-speed ocean cable telegraphy," *Bell System Technical Journal 7* (1928), 225-267.

37 Quoted from Federal Communication Commission, *Proposed Report. Telephone Investigation* (Washington D.C.: U.S. Government Printing Office, 1938), 212. Note that the keyword "control" appears also in the AT&T quotation from 1901 (note 10).

38 Brown, *The Cable and Wireless Communications of the World*; Hugh G. J. Aitken, *The Continuous Wave: Technology and American Radio, 1900-1932* (Princeton: Princeton University Press, 1985).

39 P. Craemer and E. Franke, *Länderkarten des Europäischen Fernsprechnetzes* (Berlin: Verlag Europäischer Fernsprechdienst, 1931), 46.

40 Gherardi and Jewett, "World-wide telephony," 490.

41 Early Bird was preceded by "passive" satellites, starting with ECHO-1 in 1960. See John R. Pierce, *The Beginnings of Satellite Communication* (San Francisco: San Francisco Press, 1968).

42 Joseph N. Pelton, "Telecommunications for the 21st century," *Scientific American 278*: 4 (1998), 68-73.

43 Anthony Sampson, *The Sovereign State: The Secret History of ITT* (London: Hodder and Stoughton, 1973); Peter Young, *Power of Speech: A History of Standard Telephones and Cables 1883-1983* (London: Allen & Unwin, 1983); Daniel R. Headrick, "Shortwave radio and its

impact on international telecommunications between the wars," *History and Technology 11* (1994), 21-32; Headrick, *Invisible Weapon*, 201-213.

44  Henryk Skolimowski, "The structure of thinking in technology," *Technology and Culture 7* (1966), 371-383, followed by Ian C. Jarvie, "The social character of technological problems," ibid., 384-390.

45  On Herz's system, see Comte du Moncel, "The telephonic system of Dr. C. Herz," *The Electrician 6* (1881), 192-193. An account of Van Rysselberghe's system is given in D. G. Tucker, "François van Rysselberghe: Pioneer of long-distance telephony," *Technology and Culture 19* (1978), 650-674.

46  Quoted in Black, *History of Electric Wires and Cables*, 121.

47  Lewis Coe, *The Telephone and its Several Inventors: A History* (Jefferson, North Carolina: McFarland & Co., 1995), 153.

48  Kragh, "The Krarup cable," 147-150.

49  Helge Kragh, "The decibel: Historical roots of a technical unit," *Polhem 16* (1999), 157-166.

50  Ido Yavetz, "Oliver Heaviside and the significance of the British electrical debate," *Annals of Science 50* (1993), 135-173; Ido Yavetz, "From Obscurity to Enigma" (note 14), 233-235. Limited-reference theories are largely the same as the "artifact theories" discussed in Eda Kranakis, "Technology, industry, and scientific development," in Tore Frängsmyr, ed., *Solomon's House Revisited: The Organization and Institutionalization of Science* (Canton, Mass.: Science History Publications, 1990), 133-159.

51  Oliver Heaviside, *Electrical Papers* (New York: Chelsea Publishing Co., 1970), vol. I, 120.

52  Ibid., 403.

53  For nomopragmatic statements, see Mario Bunge, "Toward a philosophy of technology," in Carl Mitcham and Robert Mackay, eds., *Philosophy and Technology* (New York: The Free Press, 1972), 62-76.

54  Edwin Layton, "Science as a form of action: The role of the engineering sciences," *Technology and Culture 29* (1988), 82-97.

55  According to Campbell, "Electricity is now preeminently a field for mathematics, and all advances in it are primarily through mathematics." G. A. Campbell, "Mathematics in industrial research," *Bell System Technical Journal 3* (1924), 550-557, on 551.

56  Claude E. Shannon and Warren Weaver, *The Mathematical Theory of Communication* (Urbana, Illinois: University of Illinois Press, 1949); John R. Pierce, "The early days of information theory," *IEEE Transactions on Information Theory 19*:1 (1973), 3-8.

57  W. F. Brinkman and D. V. Lang, "Physics and the communications industry," *Reviews of Modern Physics 71* (1999), S480-S488.

# A Passing Technology

## The Automated Teller Machine

*Richard Coopey*

The first Automated Teller Machines (ATM) appeared on the streets in the mid-1960s. Since then there has been an inexorable international spread of these machines. Certainly among the developed economies ATMs are now commonplace, their use an expectation rather than a novelty. They provide access to a range of services, only the most prominent of which is to obtain cash, reshaping the parameters of time and space in banking transactions. They provide banking services at all times, becoming progressively standardised and networked nationally and internationally. This chapter will trace the origins of the ATM, through a complex network of individual, institutional, social and cultural contexts until it reaches its globalised form. It will also explore some of the inherent paradoxes revealed in the history of the ATM, notably that the technologies involved are formed together in many ways that often reflect the inertias in society rather than ideas of progress; that the ATM represents a clearly ephemeral and transient technology yet displays increasing persistence and tenacity, usurping the technology of a cash*less* society; and that the technology which facilitates travel and redefinition of urban and global space, is itself a product of the increasing difficulties of travel. It will also question the part played by the ATM in globalisation – seemingly an inextricable part of globalisation in terms of, for example, communication and cultural homogenisation, and yet uneven in its use from nation to nation, or within nations on the basis of class, or status.

Tracing the origins of the ATM, like all technologies, involves an examination of a range of tributary developments. The ATM is best viewed as the consolidation of a series of technologies and systems, developing independently, and some in turn picking up impetus from the development of the ATM itself. Later we will address some of the broader contextual factors pushing and pulling the development of the ATM. Firstly though some of the more concrete technological trajectories need to be outlined.

## Card Technology

The first "technology" to examine might be cash itself, developing through a series of actual and representative values, or indeed, the evolution of banking and credit systems, the cheque and so on. However, for expediency the story of the ATM is perhaps best picked up in the 20th century with the advent of card based credit and money transfer.

Though the ATM is largely a debit system, the card which it is based upon owes at least part of its origins to the development of credit cards, not least in terms of establishing a culture of use. Credit cards have a long and complex history, their origins lying largely outside the banking system. In the U.S. and Britain a large increase in the provision of credit grew in the early decades of the 20th century.[1] In the U.S. credit "cards" were in circulation before World War One, and were used as a means to identify charge account holders by hotels, oil companies, and department stores. The early mechanisation of the credit card transaction process can be traced in the development of "charga-plates" in 1928, and subsequently used by department stores. In an early mechanisation of the credit process these metal plates were embossed with the customers details, enabling an imprint to be taken at the time of the transaction. These early cards were circulated to ensure brand loyalty, particularly useful to oil companies, for example, where the mobility of motorists encouraged brand switching. Initially the creation of a culture of use involved the mass unsolicited distribution of cards (resulting in a high level of fraudulent use – a topic to which we shall return).[2] Further early developments pioneered by the retail sector included the advent of revolving credit in the 1930s by Wanamaker's of Philadelphia. The development of network arrangements encompassing a syndicate of department stores began in the 1940s, based around the charga plate system.[3]

"Universal" credit cards, not tied to any specific retailer, began to develop in the 1940s in the U.S., and here we see the beginnings of bank involvement. The Flatbush National Bank of Brooklyn, New York implemented the Charg-It scheme based on a local network of community credit. By 1955 there were over 100 banks in the U.S. with credit card plans. The first large scale applications continued to come from outside the banking sector, however, with the growth of travel and entertainment (T&E) cards such as Diners Club, American Express and Carte Blanche. Diners Club, for example, was formed in 1949 and was initially connected with restaurants, but soon expanded into a wide range of services including hotels, petrol stations and airlines across the U.S. Use of the card expanded globally by the mid-1950s, particularly into Europe, despite strong resistance from indigenous hotel associations.[4]

Bank based universal credit cards in the U.S. grew from the late 1950s led by the Bank of America and Chase Manhattan, though not without teething problems involving losses for pioneering banks. The Bank of America was initially the more successful, building upon its large Californian branch network. In 1966 the bank licensed BankAmericard throughout the U.S., leading to the establishment of the rival Interbank Card Association (ICA) set up by other banks to compete at a national level.[5] In 1969 the ICA purchased the rights to Western States Bank Card Association's Master Charge card. The following year the Bank of America spun off Bank Americard to form National BankAmericard Inc. (NBI). These two organisations, ICA and NBI, independent of the banks, went on to dominate the credit card industry as Mastercharge/Mastercard and Visa, the latter identity chosen by NBI to reach global markets. The control exerted by the big two in credit cards was later to be a key factor in banks' attempts to retain control of ATM systems.

Credit cards expanded their use fairly dramatically, meeting head-on resistance from storecards, for example, and overcoming it. Established in the U.S., these two companies also began a global push. From 1966 onwards BankAmericard established operations in 52 countries. The major link to Europe was through Barclaycard – the pioneer in British credit cards launched by Barclays Bank in June 1966 – which had been originally set up using the software developed by BankAmericard. In response to Barclaycard the remaining British clearing banks had established the Joint Credit Card Company (JCCC). JCCC's Access card went on to align itself with ICA, as did Eurocard.[6]

The growth of the credit card industry attuned a very large proportion of the population to the idea of plastic card based transactions. Through a series of aggressive marketing campaigns targeted at successive groups in society, the credit card companies had built up a very large base of customers. By 1978 some 52 million Americans owned "at least two bank cards" and $44 billion was being spent annually using card-based credit.[7] When Barclaycard was launched the immediate target was one million cardholders and 30,000 retail outlets.[8]

## Cash Machines

Though the U.S. pioneered the widespread use of credit cards, the first cash machines were introduced in Britain. John Sheperd-Barron, had worked for De La Rue's Instrument division in the development of automated petrol dispensing equipment which was operated by tokens. Sheperd-Barron persuaded Barclays Bank that the same technology could be adapted to dispense cash. The Barclaycash machine was unveiled at Enfield, near London in June 1967, one of six machines in a pilot project. Barclay customers were issued with vouchers for the machine which carried information in punched-card form. Even though Barclays had had cash counting technologies in place inside their banks for around ten years this was, however, not incorporated into the cash machines.[9] Instead they dispensed standard packs of £10. The vouchers, which were valid for six months, were signed then inserted into a drawer in the "robot cashier," and the customer typed in a six digit identity number to verify the transaction. This transaction was later processed like a cheque during normal banking hours. The machines were not on-line, though they were operational 24 hour per day.[10] Somewhat typically, this new technology, hailed as "the first step in a major banking breakthrough" was not trusted at first. As actor Reg Varney became the first customer to use the machine it was operated manually, to avoid an embarrassing public failure.[11] Other British banks followed Barclays lead, the Westminster bank installing their first machine, made by Chubb and Sons Lock and Safe Co., in July 1967. This machine retained the card it was operated with, which was subsequently returned through the post for re-use.[12] By 1970 the bank (now operating as the National Westminster) had installed over 200 machines in the UK. The Midland Bank installed its first dispensers in 1968, incorporating a plastic card with information stored in a magnetic stripe. (Customers paid a fee of 10 shillings for this card). This system still dispensed fixed amounts of cash and was not on-line.[13]

The development of on-line machines began in the 1970s in Britain as Lloyds Bank introduced the first on-line "Cashpoint" dispenser late in 1972. The machine was developed in conjunction with IBM and incorporated the ability to withdraw variable amounts of cash. This was followed in January 1975 by National Westminster's Servicetill, manufactured by NCR. Like Lloyds Cashpoint the first Servicetills were installed inside bank halls and were restricted to operation during banking hours only. The first external machine, installed at Croyden in September 1975, was Europe's first fully functioning 24-hour ATM.[14] It enabled customers to withdraw up to £100 per day in variable amounts, check balances, print statements, transfer money between accounts, request new cheque books, change PIN numbers and pay bills.[15] The NCR 770 Servicetill brought ATMs into line with credit cards being operated with a plastic card with a magnetic stripe. The new generation of machines also operated with video screen technologies. From 1975 onwards, both Barclays and National Westminster installed the NCR 770, Barclays installing 257 machines by the end of the year, each averaging 72 withdrawals per week.[16] By 1990 there were over 17,000 ATMs in Britain, Barclaybank alone dispensing £130 million per week, 220 million transactions per year. Growth continues with over 22,000 currently in use in the UK.[17] On-line cash machines gave several advantages, not least of which was security. Transactions could be checked against balances each time the card was used. More than this a list of stolen cards could be readily checked against the card being used. Whether it also meant a reduction in processing time and costs for the bank, is a point to which we shall return below.

Other countries were slower to adopt the ATM than Britain. The first U.S. manufacturer to enter the field was Docutel, following the example of European firms like De La Rue and Chubb. Docutel machines were incorporating a magnetic stripe by 1969. By the early 1970s several rival U.S. ATM manufacturing companies had entered the market including Diebold, Mosler and Burroughs. The first Docutel ATM was installed in 1969.[18] Once off the mark, however, the U.S., and Japan moved rapidly ahead of Britain in the use of cash machines and ATMs. Of the 20 million debit cards in circulation worldwide in 1977, 70% were in the U.S., 22% in Japan, and 6.25% in Britain. No other country had more than 158,000. By 1981 Japan's share of ATMs had risen to 32% compared to 38% in the U.S., the use of debit cards in Japan outnumbering that of credit cards.[19] By 1990 there were nearly 600,000 installed worldwide.[20] A boost to the use of ATMs, and a reconvergence occurred, with the merger of credit and debit cards – as credit cards were adapted to use in ATM machines in the later 1970s.

## Deeper Technologies
## – Real Time Computing and Magnetic Stripes

In examining the history of ATMs so far we have focused rather narrowly on the card and the machine in terms of their spread and function. However both these technologies rest on a foundation of broader technological developments – in plastic materials development, dispensing machine technologies, telecommunications and computing, for example. The latter example is perhaps the most graphic and strongly contingent. The ATM in its general form – an on-line interactive connection to an electronic database – was dependent on the development of several computing technologies including real-time computing and the magnetic stripe storage medium.

The magnetic stripe, when it was introduced by American Airlines and American Express for ticket vending at O'Hare airport in the mid-1960s, came at the end of a cycle of development and progressive refinement of drum, tape and disk storage. The stripe was available for use in the first ATMs but was not immediately utilised. This was partly due to a lack of confidence in the reliability of "invisible" information stored in magnetic or electronic form on behalf of customers and the banks themselves. Work by JoAnne Yates on the adoption of magnetic tape storage over punched cards, has shown the comparative radicalism involved in moving away from hard copy – albeit in the digitalised form of punched cards.[21] Distrust of ATM and Electronic Funds Transfer (EFT) in general is evidenced by the continuing issuance of paper receipts, cluttering up the transaction process. Distrust is also revealed in the widespread and persistent belief in "phantom transactions" – the unacknowledged withdrawal of funds from customer accounts, with no apparent cause. Disputes of this kind (which must of course have a logical explanation in machine failure or fraud) are comparatively rare occurrences, yet they receive widespread publicity, and have become part of popular folklore.[22] The most recent panic involves the unauthorised withdrawal of cash, following the use of ATMs by foreign tourists in the Russian Republic.

In terms of computing, the banks' role in taking up this technology is a very important, if neglected area. Whether or not the banks were rationalising their operations as a means of competing through non-financial factors is a debate we shall return to below. It is clear that this sector has often been wrongly neglected in accounts of technological modernisation and business. In Britain, for example, where the argument over national technological capabilities and economic decline has been the most vigorous, there is strong evidence that the banking sector has been at the forefront of innovation. Wardley has recently shown that banks in the earlier 20th century in Britain led the field in rationalising managerial structures and labour markets and in installing automated systems.[23] This is certainly the case in the adoption of computing from the 1950s onwards. The Bank of Scotland claimed to be the first in Britain after having installed a converted series of IBM tabulators in 1959 in their Greenside branch in Edinburgh.

Real-time computing developed outside the banking system, originating in the military sector and later taken up by air ticketing systems, for example.[24] The banking sector was prescient, however, in being on the forefront of general commercial applications, making use of hardware developments, and, importantly, developing software – a considerably greater difficulty at the time. In 1959 the Bank of Scotland claimed a first in data transmission between banks using the Post Office Telex system.[25] By 1966 the Midland Bank made the decision to put all its branches on-line and "to develop a system that would be one of the most advanced in the world."[26] The banking system in Britain rapidly developed a series of local and wide area networks (LANs and WANs). In 1970 Lloyds Bank became the first in the UK to become totally networked, using a total of 2,350 terminals at branches and sub-branches.[27] The early use of teleprocessing between banks, coupled with the increasing use of EFT meant that as national and international data highways became established they were in a position to use them to maximum effect.

## Competition, Cooperation and Control – Interconnections, Networks and Systems

In order to understand the spread of ATMs, nationally and throughout the globe, we need to look beyond the development of tributary technologies, important as these are, and consider also corporate, social and cultural determinants or conditioning factors. If we begin with corporate factors we need to understand the strategies of product innovation within both ATM manufacturers and banks. Manufacturers emerged from a range of sectors each with their own competitive dynamic. These sectors included cash register manufacturing in the case of NCR, dispensing machines in the case of Docutel; instrument making in the case of De La Rue; computer Manufacture in the case of Burroughs, IBM and Fujitsu; and security systems in the case of Chubb. In terms of the banks we also need to understand more general strategies in terms of competition and cooperation in the banking marketplace.

From the earliest, the success of ATMs, as with credit cards, was seen to be dependent on the widest possible geographic spread. Though early experimental systems were limited to local areas, banks realised that there were significant advantages to be gained from forming linked networks. In many ways it is unsurprising that banking networks chose cooperative routes since there was a strong precedent for national and international cooperation in transferring funds. The culture of cooperation is embedded within national banking industries through the process of clearing funds. With card based systems, however, we can follow the development of distinct phases of competition and cooperation.

Networking is essential in establishing a broad geographic base for debit or credit card use. Competing nationwide networks were rapidly established, each formed from strategic alliances within the industry. Standardisation was also important. In the U.S. the thrift institutions established a joint on-line Communications and Specifications Committee in the early 1970s, for example. By 1982 there were six national ATM networks operating, Plus, RIA, Exchange/ADP, Express Cash, Cirrus and Continent. Later in the 1980s the credit card networks integrated into this system as Mastercard bought Cirrus and Visa bought Plus.[28] In the UK by the mid-1980s there were four main shared networks, one based around the Midland Natwest and the TSB Group, a second shared by Barclays, Lloyds and the Royal Bank of Scotland, the third being the MATRIX system operated by one group of building societies, and finally the LINK system which included building societies and other financial institutions. International networks were also established including the credit card networks plus a Eurocheque international system and a joint Link/Plus system covering the U.S., UK and Japan.[29] Many of these groups have formed joint operating agreements into the 1990s, forming meta-networks.

We need to be careful in periodising the trend of cooperation in different settings. For example, from the early 20th century there had been an overt culture of cooperation in British banking in the form of a cartel involving the major clearing banks. This lasted until the early 1970s when competitive forces began to emerge. This change coincided more or less with the introduction of ATM banking – seen as a key factor in promoting competitive advantage. ATMs were adopted as cooperation was declining. This may explain the long time lag before banks in Britain interconnected their ATM systems. For example, it was not until 1987 that Barclays, Lloyds, the Bank of Scotland and the Royal Bank of Scotland formed a combined network.[30] Similarly in the 1970s banks in the U.S. competed for customers on the basis of service when government legislation precluded interest rate competition for deposits.[31]

## Towards the Virtual Bank

If the growth of ATM networks can be partly explained through the development of inter-firm competition or cooperation, can it also be linked strongly to internal corporate strategies, for example in terms of cost reduction or managerial control? The move by banks to automate, to create the fully networked "robot branch" is often portrayed as a strategy directly aimed at increased productivity, based on reducing costs. Certainly costing was touted as a factor in the initial switch to EFT/POS and ATM systems. In 1982 cheque processing costs in the U.S. were 55 cents per transaction, nearly two-thirds of which was labour cost. In 1984 in the U.S. there were 3.6 billion cheques written in supermarkets alone, generating labour costs in excess of a billion dollars.[32] This argument holds perhaps for POS transactions, but is rather weaker for ATMs. ATMs represent considerable capital investment and need sufficient throughput to justify a purely cost criteria. The break-even level of ATM was calculated at around 8,000 transactions per month in the U.S. in the 1980s. In the first years of use ATMs were only operating at 15% efficiency. By 1982, use levels had picked up but were still averaging only 7,200 transactions per month. By 1987 this had fallen to around 5,000.[33] Bank responses were either to bear the cost or to impose a surcharge, though the latter has fluctuated in response to competitive pressure between banks. In 1999 in Britain, Barclays, having recently joined the dominant Link network attempted to impose a blanket charge on ATM transactions, a move resisted primarily by the building society sector.

Cost justification alone cannot then be sufficient to explain the banks' enthusiasm for automation. When computerising in the first instance, banks in Britain considered direct costs a minor factor in purchasing systems. Indeed it seems that the majority of computer users in the early years of computing in the U.S. or Britain had little, if any, accurate idea of the cost benefits of computing.[34] There were, however, strong incentives to automate, driven by labour control policies within banks.[35] Banks in Britain for example faced some difficulties in staff recruitment in the late 1960s and computerisation "went a very long way to solving the acute staff problems" that were facing banks in the London area at that time.[36] Computerisation and automation in general was not simply seen as a sophisticated accounting tool replacing human labour, but rather as a "management tool" supplying information for monitoring and decision-making.[37] ATMs formed part of a chain in the process of managerial rationalisation and control *within* the banking sector.[38]

The same trend can be applied to ATMs. The first ATMs in Sweden were seen as "a sophisticated alternative to manual tellers."[39] The initial idea to proceed with the Barclays ATM was driven by the problems resulting from the London clearing banks deciding to close on Saturday due to staff difficulties. A clear indication that ATMs were originally introduced as part of a process of staff rationalisation, rather than extended service provision, is evident in the siting and limited accessibility of early machines. When first installed the majority of ATMs were inside banks, operating during normal banking hours only, and aimed purely at alleviating queues.[40] That 24 hour remote banking did not occur as a possibility to banks at first can be judged from Lloyd's initial assertion that customers would not be able to operate the machines in the street while holding briefcases and umbrellas.[41]

A strong justification for the cashless banking system could be made in terms of security, as part of this trend towards managerial control. Certainly EFT reduced the scope for fraud within the bank, as did the automation of cash handling and counting.[42] However, ATMs represent stubborn resistance to this trend, keeping cash in the system and generating a new range of problems relating to security.[43] ATMs themselves were immediately vulnerable to attack on the street, if not from thieves then vandalism. One early trend involved shaking beer bottles which were then opened against the card slot.[44] Initially attempts were made to design ATMs in a bland, unobtrusive way. Later, more sophisticated security screens were incorporated.[45]

Beyond vandalism there were also a range of thefts and frauds to consider. Electronic banking introduces the opportunity for electronic theft, but the ATM also presented a vestigial opportunity for cash or "near cash" thefts. Theft of cash cards has escalated the problem of cash theft in societies since it can involve a multiplier effect over cash stolen – i.e. by theft of the means to obtain cash. Thefts have ranged from crude robberies – muggings at the site of withdrawal, or in some cases stealing the ATM itself with the aid of earthmoving equipment or a fork lift truck. Personal robberies have led to revisions over the appropriate siting of ATMs. Some states in America have enacted legislation ensuring proper lighting and public information about personal security in using ATMs. The Washington Mutual Bank, for example, was being sued in the late 1990s in a case which claimed that the siting of one of its ATMs failed to take account of public safety.[46]

Credit and debit and ATM cards have embodied a range of security devices within the card itself. These range from personal identification in the form of signatures or photographs to general anti-counterfeiting measures, echoing banknote technology most graphically in the form of imprinted holograms – too elaborate to be easily reproduced by the average forger. Ironically the cash card has no use for this traditional cash security device. Instead the measure most applicable to ATM cards is the PIN number verification system which came in with the very first ATMs and was designed to mitigate the effects of theft by providing virtual identification. Initially, however, the security number was mailed together with the card, resulting in a high level of mail theft. In addition there were growing fears of theft from within the banking system, or its subcontractors, resulting in PINs eventually being printed inside a sealed envelope, invisible to bank employees.[47] The banks need to rely on the customer to maintain the security of the PIN, and this involves interesting legal questions of property rights and obligations, since "the issue of an ATM card and PIN places a powerful instrument in the hands of the cardholder."[48] More sophisticated thefts have developed over time, ranging from the setting up of fake security video cameras which record PIN numbers as entered, to staging auctions where customers are asked to key their PINs into a portable terminal, later to be used in conjunction with fake, encoded cash cards.[49] Arguably more serious is the threat of fraud through hacking into the bank's system, though this is more a general worry with EFT systems than with ATMs specifically, since they operate with a physical cash limitation.

## Creating a Card Culture. Demand or Supply?

In order for a technological system to succeed – to become widely adopted – it must secure a critical mass of users. A culture of use and acceptance needs to be established. ATM card use, where it has flourished, has been built upon a user base created in society by the marketing push of firstly the credit card companies, and later the banks through debit cards distribution. Initially, mass unsolicited mailings in the U.S. in the late 1960s for example, though costly and prone to encourage fraud, did succeed in promoting a widespread plastic card culture.[50] Plastic cards subsequently went on to be commonly used for a range of applications, for example in keys, identification cards and public phone cards. The latter becoming so ubiquitous as to generate a hobby rivalling stamp collecting.

The ATM fed off these processes, but also generated its own culture of use, subsequently spun off into other areas. Attempts in the 1970s to automate ticket sales at Laguardia and O'Hare airports in the 1970s failed due to unfamiliarity. The same programmes restarted successfully in the 1980s once a culture of card use had been established. When the Avis car hire company began to use terminals for automatic rental in 1984 they were seen to be "piggybacking on and reaping the benefits of the financial industry's customer education efforts relative to ATMs."[51] The generation of ATM culture in Britain reached its extreme in 1992 when Barclays bank installed a dummy ATM in a museum for children in Halifax for "school children to experiment on."[52] Some sense of the level of penetration of the ATM into popular culture can be gained from the comments of Eric Jukes, interviewed in 1992, who at the age of 45 had never used an ATM; "I suppose I should use one once. I don't want on my epitaph, 'he never used a cash machine in his life.'"[53]

The spread of the popularity of ATMs can also be attributed to market demand of course. The most obvious points are the attractiveness of 24 hour availability in a culture of shifting work patterns and local travel difficulties generated by the concurrent increase in urban traffic congestion. Though somewhat paradoxical early

ATM studies found that queuing time was increased overall by ATM customers since they made ten times more frequent trips to the ATM than they made to the teller in a normal system.[54] Convenience and time may not be the sole factors in the demand for ATMs, however. There is evidence that bank customers liked the impersonal relationship of machine banking. Just as early fixed-price ticketing was favoured by shop customers wanting to avoid the potential embarrassment of asking the price, in case it could not be afforded, so bank account holders could consult ATMs over balance enquiries, with impunity. This trend towards secrecy was relished by the very earliest of cash machine customers. As Luther Simjian – who holds a claim as one of the ATMs inventors – noted of the first trials: "It seems the only people using the machines were a small number of prostitutes and gamblers who didn't want to deal with the tellers face to face."[55]

## The Failure of a Cashless Society

With the advent of electronic financial transactions, storage and processing from the 1950s onwards – firstly within banks, then between banks, and then between banks and their customers – the idea of a "cashless society" began to emerge. The banks themselves have promoted this as far as possible – as can be seen in recent history where the banks have been at the forefront of many technological innovations. The advantages of a cashless system are numerous – not least security, reduced labour costs and managerial control within banks. However the limits of such a system have become apparent, and somewhat ironically the same technologies which provided the opportunities to eliminate cash have been the very ones to ensure its continued provision.

From the point view of security, banks have long been anxious to limit large cash transfers. As part of this process the banks in Britain received a great boost in the number of ordinary current accounts they possessed during the 1960s and 1970s, as employers throughout the country, in order to eliminate large cash transactions on pay day, were encouraged to pay wages by cheque or direct transfer to bank or building society accounts. The banks were central to this process which compelled mainly non-staff employees to open new accounts, creating what might be termed the "accountisation" of society. This was an essential precursor to the spread of the ATM, closing the supply of cash in the form of wages. However, the continued demand for cash, for reasons outlined below, simply created pressures which underscored the switch from bank tellers to ATMs.

The development of the ATM cannot be separated from a general process of rationalisation in banking based around electronic fund transfer (EFT). This process grew from intra- and inter-bank information processing, as we have seen, and spread to include ATMs and point of sale (POS) systems whereby retail transactions were linked direct to bank accounts. Early POS systems were pioneered in the U.S. In 1971, for example, the City Bank and Trust Company of Ohio ran the "Post" experiment, placing on-line terminals in a range of retail outlets, linked to the BankAmericard system and using magnetically encoded cards.[56] The introduction of the bar-code in 1973 dovetailed with the POS system in the automation and synchronisation of stock control and sales in retailing. Just as POS terminals spread throughout a range of retail outlets, so ATMs spread their locations to include railway stations, department stores and retail parks, airports, office buildings and, in the U.S. at least, casinos. Perhaps one of the most incongruous sitings to date being the Barclays ATM in the House of Lords in Britain.[57]

The sitings of ATMs say something about the bank's conceptions of urban space and also reveal how strategy reflected and reinforced class-based discrimination in some societies. Many early machines were sited in distinctly middle class areas – the first non-bank locations in the UK for example were in Selfridges and John Lewis stores.[58] Sitings became more rapidly diffused, though the siting of an early Chase Manhattan cash machine in Grand Central Station shocked the *Banker* which noted the "tough, even vicious, reputation" of the location.[59] As noted above, banks can be held liable for the siting of ATMs in what might be termed insecure areas.

The moves towards a cashless EFT/POS system has been inexorable in most advanced economies, even if the pace of change has been determined by different cultural and institutional settings. The spread of cashless transactions has developed unevenly between countries and regions in such a way that there is clearly a core and periphery effect. Within advanced societies there remain divisions (partially reflecting the class differences recognised and promoted by card issuers). These divisions are reflected in the scale of enterprises, indeed in the scale of transactions, which form an economic boundary where a cashless transaction, or the installation of EFT/POS equipment, makes little economic sense. Small shops (or pubs), dealing with low price sales are the obvious example. To be sure the trend in many advanced societies is shifting away from the small shops to large scale chain stores and retail parks. There is however a growing reaction to this process, evidenced in recent cases involving Walmart in the U.S., and the limitations on retail park building in Britain in the 1990s.

Despite the spread of card culture, and the continued efforts of banks to eliminate cash transactions, many other areas remain impervious to this process. These include personal or black market transactions – the former constituting a very large sector indeed, encompassing general second-hand sales, garage sales and the 1980s growth phenomenon of car boot sales in the UK. Black market transactions might include cash-based work to avoid tax payment, widespread in most economies, through to the illicit drugs sector, entirely cash based, even on the largest scale, witnessed by the continual need to launder money through elaborate, often international processes.

Card culture, or ATM culture also developed unevenly throughout the global economy. As we have seen above, national systems developed at an uneven pace, dependent partly on corporate strategy in the banking and related sectors of individual countries. This could partly explain the, albeit brief, British lead in some aspects of ATM development. Uneven spread is also clearly linked to international demand side variables, narrowly or broadly conceived in different societies. The ascendency of Japan, for example to the top of the league table in ATM use per capita, is at least partly to be explained in terms of the widespread adoption, trust and indeed thirst for technological systems in society generally. The more limited spread in France, or the attempt to leapfrog into "higher" technology smart cards, may again be explicable in terms of a broader tradition, particularly in the post war period, promoting advanced, complex national technological systems, reflecting a unique variant of techno-nationalism.[60]

In global terms, while there remain variances in the level of use in advanced countries, the spread of ATM use outside these countries remains polarised to a large extent. Just as the geographic spread of ATMs within advanced economies varies on a geographic basis, particularly along a progressively widening urban-rural division,[61] so the global spread of ATM systems exhibits wide variances. The global spread of the ATM has been pronounced where international travel is likely to take place. Indeed international travel has been facilitated by, and in turn has promoted the spread of the ATM. Bank and hotel lobby sitings are to be found throughout the, predominantly urban, regions which comprise tourist or business destinations for travellers from advanced economies, for example. Beyond this phenomenon, however, the take up of ATMs is limited by a number of factors. In the ex-Soviet Union and transitional economies ATM use remains comparatively low. This may be partly due to the lack of a banking infrastructure, since these countries have long had a non-institutional cash saving culture. A more general cause may be that these societies are significant *dollar* cash societies. Long held suspicions and distrust over the long-term stable value of domestic currencies such as the rouble, hrivna or lei have meant that savings have most frequently been held in U.S. dollars. Clearly, though, these are stubborn cash societies; they are based on the "wrong" cash in terms of that which could be dispensed legally from a local ATM.

## Cash Versus the Virtual World

Given that there remain real limits to a cashless society, what the technology of the ATM has done is to provide the means to enable the emergence of "immediate cash" societies. As societies have moved towards urban transport saturation and difficulties in reaching banks during normal working hours have emerged, ATMs have had to be provided to enable cash to be obtained with temporal and spatial flexibility. The ability and willingness to travel through the urban environment, to obtain goods and services, is shaped by social and cultural conventions, which change only slowly in response to available technological systems.

Another indication of cultural inertias which have frustrated the trend towards the cashless society is perhaps the slower than predicted growth of internet shopping. The cash transactions which are not amenable to EFT outlined above – small transactions, illegal transactions etc. – apply equally to internet buying. Recent trends towards grocery shopping internet systems delivered by van are highly urban specific and have been slow to expand in the U.S. The British began investing heavily in these systems in the late 1990s, operating initially at a loss in the hope that a culture of use will eventually be generated.

If successful, internet grocery shopping will replace an interesting "intermediate" alternative to the ATM, which has arisen in the 1990s. In order to reduce cash stocks in supermarkets, customers using debit cards have been offered the facility of cash-back at the check-out – effectively turning the check-out operative into a cash machine – or rather a bank teller. This resiting of the banking labour function may well be ephemeral itself, however. There are moves, pioneered in Holland and adopted in the UK, to replace checkout with customer self-checkout systems, using hand held bar-code readers. This system, which is based on a security sampling and a trust relationship, will eliminate the cash-back option – restoring the need for ATMs.

In general, internet shopping, and its telematic and mail-order predecessors, though offering all the convenience of travel-less transactions, have not realised their rational potential. There may have been exceptions, for example in the early years of mail-order in the U.S., where extreme travel constraints fostered the growth of catalogue giants like Sears, Roebuck and Montgomery Ward, or in post war Britain where catalogue companies built a customer base on credit provision by exploiting kinship, social and neighbourhood networks.[62] Internet shopping remains well below its technological potential, at least partly as a result of confidence and familiarity issues, but also because people still like to shop.[63] To a large extent shopping, remains a social and leisure activity in the advanced economies.

The internet has recently extended very much the possibilities and effectiveness of home banking. Phone banking, begun in 1973 at the Seattle First National Bank with its "Dial a Computer" system, and spread gradually throughout the 1980s.[64] As with the internet generally, and the explosion in the sale of domestic PCs into the 1990s, internet connection and software availability has meant that home banking is now a real growth area. In terms of non-cash transactions, an increasing number of account holders no longer need to travel to the bank, thus realising an early ambition of Wally Olins, a prominent bank marketing consultant, that banks should recognise that they are "financial supermarkets" with a range of products, of which cash transactions are a marginal feature. Olins advised Barclays to drop the word "bank" from their corporate identity.[65] If the banks do disappear from the High Street, or remain in unrecognisable form, and much of the business of banking fades into the virtual world of the internet, the "robot" teller will remain, going from strength to strength, using the technologies of a cashless society to effortlessly dispense foreign currency and the necessary means to buy a round of drinks.

In 1908, E. M. Forster envisaged a world where travel had been eliminated as the global networking of technology had made it superfluous.[66] This is slow in becoming a reality. Here the central paradox emerges. ATM technology, which has facilitated international transactions, being an essential part of the trend in increased international travel, has itself been part of the process of resistance to the elimination of local travel. The continued, if uneven, growth in the implementation of ATM systems is symptomatic of many such paradoxes. The technology itself can be seen to stem from a wide range of tributary technological streams, and from organisational and competitive strategies within differing national banking sectors. Equally important, and ultimately determining that the technologies of a cashless society are frustrated or resisted, are a wide range of inertial cultural characteristics in both advanced, transitional and developing economies.

## Notes

1　Martha L. Olney, *Buy Now, Pay Later: Advertising, Credit and Consumer Durables in the 1920s* (Chapel Hill: University of North Carolina Press, 1991), 86-134; Susan Strasser *Satisfaction Guaranteed: The Making of the American Mass Market* (New York: Pantheon, 1989), 239-242.

2　Lewis Mandell, *The Credit Card Industry: A History* (Boston: Twayne Publ., 1990), 17-19.

3　Ibid., 23-25.

4　Ibid., 26.

5　Ibid., 30-31.

6　Eurocard had been formed in 1965 by the merger of the Rikskort card of Sweden and the British Hotel and Restaurant Association card.

7　Mandell, *The Credit Card Industry*, 48.

8　"Barclaycard," Barclays Group Archives.

9　*Barclays Bulletin* No. 8 (Autumn 1967).

10　Peter Nye, "Instant Cash at Enfield," *Spreadeagle* 4 (1967), 326-328; "Barclay's Open World's First Mini-bank" *Barclays Bulletin* No. 8 (Autumn 1967).

11　Nick Nuttall, "At Last the True Story of the Hole in the Wall Gang," *The Times* (27 June 1992).

12　"Cash Machines" Cairs Acc. No. 0007132, Natwest Group Archive (NGA).

13　A claimant to the "invention" of the cash machine is Luther Simjian, who persuaded Citicorp to run a trial in the mid-1960s.

14　Though Barclays make an identical claim for their NCR 770 installed at Oxford around the same time. "Barclaybank: A History" Acc. 447/1, Barclays Bank Group Archive (BBGA); *Barclays Bulletin*, Spring 1975.

15　"Money Round the Clock Shuffle," *The Banker* (October 1975), 1220.

16　"Barclaybank: A History."

17　Ibid.; "News From Barclays" (17 June 1997).

18　Mandell, *The Credit Card*, 21-22.

19　Mandell, *The Credit Card*, 127-129.

20　"News From Barclays" (17 June 1997).

21　JoAnne Yates, "Using Giddens' Structuration Theory to Inform Business History," *Business and Economic History* 26 (1997), 168-177.

22　"Losing at Cards: An Investigation into Consumer's Problems with Bank Cash Machines," National Consumer Council, 1985; "Automated Teller Machines," Submission of the APCS, 20 and 25.

23　Peter Wardley, "Commercial Banking and its Part in the Emergence and Consolidation of the Corporate Economy in Britain Before 1940," paper presented at the International Economic History Congress, Madrid, August 1998.

24　Martin Campbell Kelly and William Aspray, *Computer: A History of the Information Machine* (New York: Basic Books, 1996), 157-180; Paul N. Edwards *The Closed World: Computers and the Politics of Discourse in Cold War America* (Cambridge Mass.: MIT Press, 1996); Arthur L. Norberg and Judy E. O'Neill, *Transforming Computer Technology: Information Processing for the Pentagon 1962-1986* (Baltimore: Johns Hopkins University Press, 1996), 68-118.

25　"Banking Computers Come of Age," *Intercom* (July 1980).

26  UK Computer Industry, House of Commons Select Committee on Science and Industry, Session 1969-1970, Vol. II, 211.

27  *Computer Weekly* (29 October 1970), 6.

28  Mandell, *The Credit Card Industry*, 123 and 128.

29  "Automated Teller Machines," Submission of the APCS, 9-10.

30  "History of Cash Dispensers 1967-1997," Barclays Group Archive.

31  Mandell, *The Credit Card Industry*, 122.

32  David Van L. Taylor Jr., "Debit Cards" in Federal Reserve Bank of Atlanta, *Payments in the Financial Services Industry of the 1980s*, Quorum 1984, 12-13.

33  Mandell, *The Credit Card Industry*, 125 and 127.

34  Richard Coopey, "Management and the Introduction of Computing in British Industry, 1945-1970," *Contemporary British History* 13:3 (1999), 59-71.

35  "New Age Banking," *The Economist*" (2 March 1957).

36  *UK Computer Industry*, 210.

37  Ibid., 212.

38  G. Masson, "Spotlight on Organisation and Methods Department," *Intercom* No. 30 (March 1974).

39  *The Banker* (September 1975), 1138.

40  "The Robotic Branch," *The Banker* (December 1984), 72; "Lloyd's New Cash Dispenser," *The Banker* (February 1973), 225.

41  "Cashpoint – The World Outside," *The Banker* (November 1974), 1460.

42  "Into the Eighties with New Technology," *Intercom* No. 61 (March 1982).

43  A stronger case could be made for the precursor of the ATM – the automated petrol dispenser – which aimed to remove cash from the prime robbery site of the gas station in the U.S.; see Linda Fenner Zimmer, "ATMs," *Payments in Financial Services*, 7-8.

44  *The Banker*, March 1974, 298. See also Nye, "Instant cash at Enfield," 326.

45  "Autotellers Launched," *Intercom* No. 56 (March 1980).

46  *The Seattle Times* (2 February 1998).

47  *Intercom* March 1980. One of the biggest problems in the early days of ATMs was preventing field engineers stealing cash from machines; see Mandell, *The Credit Card Industry*, 126.

48  "Automated Teller Machines," Submission of the APCS, 29.

49  "At Last the True Story of the Hole in the Wall Gang," *The Times* (27 June 1992).

50  Mandell, *The Credit Card Industry*, 34-37. Unsolicited mailing was eventually banned in the U.S. by the EFT Act of 1978, though no such restriction has been enforced in the UK to date. "Automated Teller Machines," Submission of the APCS, 31.

51  Fenner Zimmer, "ATMs," 7-8.

52  "News From Barclays" (17 June 1997).

53  "At Last the True Story," passim.

54  Inter-Bank Research Organisation, Reid Report; see Frank Land, "The first business computer: a case study in user-driven innovation," *Annals of the History of Computing* 22:3 (2000), 16-26.

55  *The Times* (24 November 1998).

56  "Credit Cards and Cash Dispensers," *The Banker* (September 1972), 1217.

57  "Cash Machine in House," *Barclays News* (April/May 1996).

58  *The Banker* (November 1974), 1460.

59  "Cash on the Rail," *The Banker* (May 1974), 534.

60  Another example of this may be the early promotion of the national Minitel system and subsequent comparative resistance to the more "standard" internet.

61  The progressive withdrawal of local bank branches in Britain for example, driven partly by the complimentary growth of ATMs, has contributed, as with the rise of car dependence, to the isolation of many rural communities, or their reconfiguration as dormitory commuter communities.

62  Richard Coopey, Sean O'Connell and Dilwyn Porter, "Mail-Order Retailing in the United Kingdom 1880-1960: How Mail-Order Competed With Other Forms of Retailing," *The International Review of Retail, Distribution and Consumer Research* (July 1999).

63  Paul Foley and David Sutton, "Forecasts and Trends for Electronic Commerce 1996-2000," Leicester Business School, Occasional Paper No. 49, 1998; "Selling-by-Internet Remains Boxed In," *The Guardian* (10 August 1998).

64  *Intercom* No. 64, July 1983; *Intercom* No. 68, February/March 1986; *The Banker* (December 1984), 72.

65  Wally Olins, *Corporate Identity: Making Business Strategy Visible Through Design* (London: Thames and Hudson, 1989), 56-66.

66  Edward M. Forster, *The Machine Stops*, from *The Eternal Moment and Other Stories* (London: Sidgewick and Jackson, 1928).

# The Globalisation of Transport?

## Computerised Reservation Systems at American Airlines and French Railways

*Nathalie N. Mitev*

This case study examines the troubled introduction of a computerised reservation system (CRS) at French Railways (*Société Nationale des Chemins de Fer Français* or SNCF). *Socrate*, based on the American Airlines *Sabre* system, had a disastrous beginning. It was badly received by the French public, led to strikes and government inquiries, and had to be substantially modified. This study challenges beliefs and assumptions about the obvious success of technologies such as *Sabre* and uses the notion of "symmetry," from the sociology of technology, to demonstrate how failures express the same dynamics as successes, and technological choices are not always obvious.

Differences between air and rail transport, between American and European transport deregulation and between the needs of national identity, regional development and public access to transport, are all reflected in the question of "yield management." Yield management is a crucial component of CRS and was first adopted during the deregulation of the American air transport industry in the early 1980s. It requires complex optimisation software designed to manage passenger revenues and control demand by manipulating the availability of full and discounted fares. Price differentiation is buried within the computer so that pricing, ticketing, and the choice of routes and trains are hidden from staff and customers alike.

The notion of "translation" helps us analyse how the *Socrate* project borrowed from airline pricing, with the aim of gaining competitive advantage by changing passengers' travelling behaviour and thereby identifying profitable market segments. The *Socrate* case exposes fundamental changes in transport. They are associated with the role of computer technology in deregulated and global markets, its effect on the concept of national identity and sovereignty in transport policymaking, and the relationship between global reservation travel systems and the future of European transport industries.

## I.

Analysing the use of computer technology in organisations requires the appreciation of issues at micro and macro levels and of how they relate to each other. However the usual notion of information technology failure is unhelpful here. It belongs to a managerial discourse in which information technology (IT) is seen as unproblematic. Managers and computer practitioners tend to envisage IT as being neutral and this belief needs to be questioned. Managerial discourses have a truncated understanding of organisations; they are characterised by a belief in "rational" management; a denial of continuing power relations and conflict; a desire to eliminate organisational politics, through the use of IT; a tendency to see organisations as individual closed entities and a limited focus on the business environment which neglects broader perspectives.

This narrow understanding of organisations effects the narration of IT failures and successes. The explanations commonly found in management literature are as simplistic for successes as they are for failures. In the case of failures, they try to find something or someone to blame, as if using information technology was a neutral, rational exercise, which in the "normal" course of events is unproblematic. More useful would be the incorporation of the accounts of various groups at different times; this would lead to a richer and more complex picture of the use of information systems in organisations. This analysis therefore moves away from managerial explanations and includes wider "environmental" perspectives.

## II.

Analyses of information systems failures often reflect a dichotomy between the technical and the social.[1] Sociologists of science and technology have argued that the boundary between the social and the technical is a matter for negotiation and represents no underlying distinction, in other words "the fabric has no seams."[2] Technical and social choices are constantly negotiated and constructed, and their construction follows the same logic in success as it does in failure. Conversely, disentangling the interplay of actors and choices can be done by focusing on "failure"; it can show that choices are not as obvious as they appear to be in a successful project. Failure studies also allow for more elaborate explanations of human action and better explain the complex links between technical choices and social environment.

> Like the sociology of science, the sociology of technology has chosen as its methodological principle to use the same explanatory resources when reporting on successful and unsuccessful innovations. However, to challenge the impression of obviousness which can be given by technical choices that lead to devices which 'perform well,' there is no better strategy than concentrating on failure cases to show that it is impossible to distinguish between good and bad decisions. Moreover, in failures and controversial cases, actors facilitate the researcher's

work since they express the more complex relationships between technical choice and social environment.[3]

Historians and sociologists of technology, borrowing from the sociology of scientific knowledge, argue that failures are of as much interest as the success stories. The sociology of scientific knowledge sees controversy as an important subject for research since controversy is about the truth or falsity of a belief in solving social problems. Different groups will define the problem differently and also its success or failure.[4]

The history and sociology of technology also suggests that the development of artifacts should be interpreted within an analysis of "systems" or "networks." The *constructivist* approach to the study of technology turns from technical, social, economic or political distinctions in technological development to the use of "seamless webs," or "actor-network" metaphors. For example, Callon refuses to categorise the elements in a system or network "when these elements are permanently interacting, being associated, and being tested by the actors who innovate."[5] *Actor-network theory*, a more extreme constructivist approach, uses the higher abstraction of "actors," who subsume science, technology, economics and politics. "Human" and "non-human" actors are the heterogeneous entities that constitute a network. In contrast to Callon, Bijker, Hughes and Pinch preserve the social environment and argue that the social groups play a critical role in defining and solving the problems that arise during the development of an artefact. Problems are defined within the context of meaning assigned by a social group. And because social groups define the problems of technological development, there is flexibility in the way things are designed and their design is not always the best.[6]

## III.

This case study reveals fundamental changes taking place in air and rail transport. The troubled implementation of an airline CRS at SNCF is symptomatic of the difficulties of globalisation and the use of information and computer technologies. SNCF adopted knowledge, information technology and management concepts developed by the U.S. carrier *American Airlines* in the 1970s and 1980s. SNCF was fascinated with air transport, seemingly because of the technological prestige in the late 20th century, compared to rail transport. CRS are information technologies with the potential to undermine the concept of national sovereignty. Combined with transport *deregulation*, they are beginning to erode the state's responsibilities towards public transport and the normal transformation of economic progress into citizens' welfare. Thus there are tensions between transport systems perceived as national infrastructure and global computer technology.

According to the notion of "translation" *actors* must have their attributes defined for them, or "translated," so that they can play their assigned roles in scenarios conceived within a socio-technical actor-network.[7] In order for an actor to secure the support of others, it must make itself indispensable to them by "translating" their interests; the network becomes constructed according to the "translation's" own logic.

Fieldwork on this case study at SNCF began early 1994, six months after the introduction of *Socrate*. Research access was relatively easy, the timing was judicious and most interviewees were willing to talk at length. Liberal access was given to documentation covering the initiation and development of the *Socrate* project, starting from 1989. Several of the original members of the *Socrate* executive team were interviewed, as were SNCF senior managers, yield management experts, marketing, human relations and training managers, sales staff, union representatives, CRS experts and travel agents.[8] Secondary sources included SNCF documents and government reports, technical documentation and trade unions' and consultants' reports.

## IV.

SNCF introduced *Socrate* (*Système Offrant à la Clientèle des Réservations d'Affaires et de Tourisme en Europe*), a computerised reservation system in April 1993, having bought *Sabre* from *American Airlines* in 1989 in order to build it. One of its aims was to transform SNCF's commercial activities through the instigation of a new philosophy of selling, based on importing techniques used in the airline industry. One of the marketing slogans used by SNCF at the time was, "*Avec la SNCF tout est possible,*" which seems ironic since even the worst proved "to be possible."[9] *Socrate* is one of the first software system that provoked nation-wide strikes when it was introduced and which attracted massive media criticism. For such an ambitious project, and perhaps because of it, the number and type of problems encountered were spectacular: problems in its design, development and implementation, in consultation, in ergonomics, in training, in communication and the fact that it was linked to a highly controversial commercial strategy.

When SNCF began the *Socrate* project in 1989, its aim was to reposition the enterprise in a new European competitive environment characterised by substantial traffic expansion.[10] *Socrate* would offer a better quality of service and support the diversification of services.[11] The initiators of the project also emphasised the importance of maximising revenue, since SNCF had been a semi-public – as opposed to a strict public-sector – nationalised utility since 1982. One of their most important objectives was to instigate a new philosophy of marketing based on yield management techniques.[12] SNCF bought *Sabre* (*Semiautomatic Business Environment Re-*

search), the *American Airlines* CRS and an information system which claimed to have provided competitive advantage for a major airline.[13] Several years were spent adapting this software to the conditions of the railway industry and a French national institution.[14]

When first implemented, however, both SNCF staff and its customers rejected *Socrate* and its underlying ticketing, pricing and selling philosophy. This was widely reported and examined by SNCF, the French trade unions, passenger associations, and the French government which commissioned a public inquiry into its failure. Technical malfunctions, poor management and user resistance led to a chaotic introduction.[15] The project management team gave only secondary consideration to the databases and input sets. Staff training was inadequate and did not prepare sales people for real-life problems such as tariff inconsistencies and printing errors. The "user interface" was designed using the logic of airlines rather than railways and the new ticket proved unacceptable to customers. Moreover public relations failed to prepare the people for such a dramatic change.[16] The inadequate database information on timetable and routes of trains, inaccurate tariff information, and the unavailability of ticket exchange capabilities caused major problems for the SNCF sales force and customers alike. Impossible reservations on trains, inappropriate tariffs and wrong train connections led to large queues of irate customers at major railway stations and to a public outcry in France. Online reservations available through the Minitel public network failed, tickets were booked for non-existent trains whilst other trains ran empty, the railway unions went on strike, and passenger associations sued SNCF.[17]

These events, widely reported in the media, contributed to the upheaval of the French railways scene, which had been relatively unchanged, particularly regarding the services on offer. The new ticketing and pricing policies introduced through *Socrate* changed railway users' and workers' practices, which were both grounded in the cultural dimensions of French society. In contrast to previous technical innovations (such as the successful introduction of high-speed trains in the early 1980s, which took place in a stable and well-established SNCF), *Socrate* indicated a new phase of forced global innovation in an enterprise facing strategic imperatives. The environmental setting was one of European integration, which opened transport to deregulatory moves and to the growth of competition across modes (i.e. rail, air and road).

## V.

As a response to a growing demand for reservation management, the previous CRS, known as *RESA*, was introduced in the early 1980s at SNCF ticket offices and was also made available to private homes through the Minitel public network. It needed to be improved and extended, however, since it was reaching saturation point at about 50 million reservations a year. It was considered that there would be a need for 130 million reservations a year by 1995.[18] SNCF therefore decided in 1988 to change its CRS completely and adopt *Socrate*. Important decisions about pricing strategies were also taken, which contributed to the difficulties experienced in 1993.[19]

One of the fundamental changes in database design was the disappearance of the railway station as the basic "unit," to be replaced by the "relation" between two railway stations, i.e. the origin-destination concept of the airlines. Design difficulties arose since *Sabre* was written for a maximum of 80 "relations" with very few intermediate stops. SNCF discovered that it had to be rewritten to cope with the 22,000 important "relations" in the French rail network and its 2,400 stations. If the "relation" has not been pre-recorded (because there was not enough demand in small stations) the transaction had to be done manually by sales staff and took twice as long. This important fact was overlooked and only a small number of the most profitable "relations" were pre-recorded for the launch in March 1993. This was one of the main reasons for the queues in railway stations, and SNCF had to rapidly deploy staff to record more relations and facilitate the work of the sales staff.[20] Another, more significant problem with *Sabre* was that it was designed for air fare structures which are much simpler than for rail travel. American computer scientists had to be brought in to help adapt the system and by 1993 *Socrate* had already cost 1.3 billion francs. Design and programming were carried out in Paris and Lille, with three super computer mainframes. They control the network of sales workstations and automatic ticket machines in stations, to which is connected the SNCF server accessible via communications networks. *Socrate*, like *Sabre* and other airline CRS, e.g. *Amadeus* (Air France) or *Galileo* (British Airways), run for travel agents, is also a global distribution system or GDS. The major U.S. airlines have used GDS to dominate distribution channels and eliminate weaker competitors. *Socrate* supports connections with other European and global CRS for travel and tourism distribution channels.

*Socrate* was envisaged as a tool which could also manage, control and modify demand in order to maximise profits and allocate resources. By using a database management system together with a commercial yield management, SNCF hoped to reproduce the strategic success and competitive advantage that *Sabre* was credited with having given *American Airlines* in the 1980s. Yield management techniques were applied to ensure optimal filling of trains, combined with maximum profit for each seat filled, through optimising the average price/rate of occupation ratio per seat. Beyond booking and ticketing, the optimisation software aims to redirect demand – not by altering prices, but by changing the number of seats on offer at normal and reduced prices (the pricing *mix*) according to demand.[21] This system limits access to certain prices, particularly reduced prices, on a train per train basis, and is intended to make customers book their seats as early as possible. If customers buy their tickets near to the time of departure, they are unlikely to be entitled to reductions, e.g. old-age pensioners, children, families, etc. This highlights an important difference between European train and air travel: there is a social dimension to rail travel, which is not present in air transport. *Socrate* also includes software (called *Thalès*) which accumulates statistical profiles of types of seats sold and fares paid per individual train, in order to be able to make future modifications to the pricing *mix* for each individual train. The pricing mix is therefore constantly modified on the basis of past statistical data, marketing surveys, socio-economic characteristics of origin-destination "relations," air and road competition on that "relation," and the value that customers find in the service.[22] Moreover, associated software (called *Aristote*) was connected to SNCF accounting systems and introduced detailed reporting information on the costs and profits of trains and specific route operations.

## VI.

Labour unions condemned SNCF's new strategic objectives as early as December 1991 with arguments about social costs and environmental consequences, including under-utilisation of rail infrastructure, road traffic saturation, pollution, increased accidents, and effects on regional development.[23] Instead of competition across different transport sectors, they argued that there was room for co-operation between them in the interest of the travelling public; *Socrate* could be used to support this objective and integrate different transport modes. While anxious not to be seen as "Luddite" or blaming the technology, the unions saw *Socrate* as a means by which SNCF and the government could realise their political objectives and as a way of tackling the SNCF's budget deficit prior to privatisation.[24] Some contended that fare increases for captive travellers on profitable lines, such as Paris-Lyon and Paris-Lille, might improve profits,[25] but if carried too far and on too many lines, demand would fall and passengers would travel by car instead. This was one of the reasons why sales fell after *Socrate* was introduced.[26] This decrease was also due to the technical problems outlined above, which turned passengers away, as well as the ensuing problem of lack of public confidence in SNCF.

The strategic choice was also in opposition to existing organisational skills and culture within SNCF. The technological choice of *Socrate* and the new strategic direction adopted by SNCF, were not accepted by some of the computer staff, managers and workforce. It was seen as being driven by financial motives rather than the principles of public service. The interests of the various SNCF divisions diverge, particularly those of regional, intercity and high-speed services.[27] Conflicts arose because *Socrate* concentrated on high-speed connections. Regional trains suffered because regional timetable information was not readily available through *Socrate*; and reservations for regional trains remained as time-consuming as they were before *Socrate*. The organisational climate, already poor due to budget deficits and staff cuts, became increasingly tense and conflict-ridden; rivalries between divisions worsened and staff became demoralised. Sales staff were particularly prone to this. Before the launch of *Socrate*, training sessions were only five days in duration; three days were spent explaining the new commercial policies and the rationale for the new pricing structures.[28] It was judged inadequate by staff and unions on the grounds that it did not provide enough information on the user-computer interface. Unlike its predecessor, which was almost self-explanatory and transparent, the new system required a thorough understanding of what happens "behind the screen." A computer-based simulation was used but it was criticised for being unrealistic and was soon abandoned.[29] Moreover, sales staff qualifications and promotions were structured around a thorough knowledge and understanding of fare structures; their professional ethos was to create good relationships with the passengers and find the best possible routes and fares for them. For sales staff their knowledge of fares became irrelevant, the computer having taken over that role. Dialogue with clients became difficult because staff had to keep looking at a complicated and cluttered screen; their role degenerated to one of merely reporting to customers what was displayed on the screen. Customer choice became more complex and the staff-client dialogue more difficult, because it was framed by a complex and difficult dialogue between staff and the computer. SNCF's management claimed that since staff did not look at the screen whilst talking to customers, work breaks were unnecessary. This added to stress levels experienced by staff, who had to deal with long queues of angry and confused customers. This was also in contrast to the new commercial attitudes staff were expected to adopt, for instance through the use of words such as "customers" and "clients" instead of "passengers" or "users."[30] At the same time as introducing the new computerised system, SNCF implemented a monitoring system, which keeps track of the number of transactions, the time taken for each transaction, and the type and price of tickets sold, for each sales employee. Sales staff were therefore subjected to a change of computer system and its user interface together with a whole catalogue of other minor revolutions: i.e. changes in training, qualifications, promotions and job prospects (cheaper and less qualified staff was now employed part-time in small stations and staff numbers were reduced), professional ethos, working conditions, handling of performance monitoring and reporting.[31] It was not surprising, therefore, that they took the side of the passengers, joined in protests and took industrial action by issuing open tickets. In the end, ticket controllers and train agents refused to inspect tickets, which was naturally highly popular with passengers.

# VII.

We now turn to the complex political, cultural and socio-economic context of the European transport industry, which cannot be dissociated from the problems experienced by SNCF with *Socrate*. The transfer of a U.S. airline CRS to a European railway was bound to be anything but straightforward since there are divergences in two dimensions: between the U.S. and Europe, and between air and rail transport.[32]

With American air deregulation in the 1980s, it was expected that airlines would become more efficient by reducing costs and thus be able to lower prices. The results were not so straightforward however. While short routes with low profits were abandoned other routes were restructured in star-shaped networks with "hubs and spokes," leading to economies of scope; meanwhile fare structures became more complex, necessitating gigantic reservation information systems.[33] The European aviation market differs in several major respects from the U.S. domestic market and liberalisation in Europe may not produce the same results as in the U.S. Indeed the "transferability" of American air transport deregulation to Europe has been questioned by experts. Button and Swann have laid out some of the obstacles to the transfer of the air deregulation model across the Atlantic.[34]

Their arguments can be extended here to the transferability of deregulation from air to rail, as well as from the United States to Europe and are presented in tabular form in Table 1.

*Table 1: Comparison of U.S. and European air and rail transport.*

|  | U.S. | Europe |
|---|---|---|
| Transport Market | Long distances. <br> Unique liberalisation regime | Short to medium distances <br> Densely populated <br> National liberalisation regimes |
| Air | Intramodal competition <br> Concentration of operators <br> Hubs and spoke networks | Intramodal pan-European competition <br> Many national operators <br> Intermodal national competition between air, rail and road |
| Rail | Rail passenger transport now insignificant, what remains is mostly freight/ <br> No intermodal air/rail competition. | High-speed and normal trains <br> Many stops, dense networks <br> Costly infrastructures <br> National intra and intermodal competition <br> Little pan-European competition |

Some of the important points are:

- The nature of the markets is different, for example rail infrastructure is far more costly than air transport infrastructure.
- There are geographic and historical differences, for example, distances are much shorter in Europe, which means that air, road and rail are much closer substitutes in Europe than in the U.S.[35]
- The rail emphasis in Europe is on high-speed trans-European networks; high-speed trains, such as the TGV (*Trains à Grande Vitesse*), and planes compete directly on certain routes, in particular 500 to 700 kilometer segments.
- The rate of liberalisation varies from country to country; for instance, former president of Deutsche Bahn (DB), Heinz Dürr, decided not to separate track from operations, unlike SNCF and British Rail. On the other hand, he planned to open DB to competition from other operators. His successor, Johannes Ludewig, by contrast, has stated that the real competitors to rail are road and air, and has initiated co-operation between SNCF and DB on the Paris-Metz-Frankfurt route.[36]
- Europe is much more densely populated, routes are shorter, and there are many more stops on a train line than on an air route, which makes railways more complex operationally. Different countries have different network configurations.[37]

Transport deregulation in Europe differs from the U.S. in that it has to consider intermodal competition as well as intramodal competition. One aim of European liberalisation is to harmonise standards (technical, economic, social, financial and fiscal) so that rail and air transport companies can operate freely in any European member state. Since the late 1980s the European Union (EU) has introduced measures to abolish market restrictions in the air and rail sectors. The first measures taken by the EU have been the clarification of the relationship between nation state and transport companies, an emphasis on high-speed networks, and the abolition of public service obligations and subsidies.[38]

The 1991 EU Directive 91-440 on the liberalisation of rail transport (adopted in France in 1995) aims to revitalise rail transport through market forces; but it also believes in supporting trains since they pollute less, and envisages that increased intra-European exchanges through high-speed train networks will reduce road traffic congestion. Applying the free market model to rail transport might bring economies of scope in the design, production and operation of infrastructures, but adverse consequences such as the disappearance of short routes are contested in smaller and more densely populated countries. This is particularly apparent in the decisions surrounding the French TGV routes. The TGVs are regarded as a great technological success in France, but financing its special infrastructure is extremely costly, and opinions are split as to its benefits. In the face of opposition in many countries, it remains unclear whether the EU will achieve its aim of opening all European freight and passenger rail transport to competition.

## VIII.

SNCF and the French government have been hostile to the liberalisation of European rail transport on the grounds that the national rail network would be weakened and that deregulation ignores the cultural and public service differences between countries. And SNCF has expressed strong opposition to the opening of domestic routes to competing operators.[39] Various French governments have appeared to protect France from a liberal EU agenda, but nevertheless SNCF has had to respond to competition and increase its profitability. It has become more accountable and has had to reorganise its activities into purchaser/supplier relationships. The French government eventually decided to divide infrastructures and trains operations into two companies in 1996. Continuing deficits at SNCF and organisational difficulties have led to several government investigations; the Martinand report, for example, identified decreasing revenues, low productivity and poor returns on investments.[40] The *Rapport de la Cour des Comptes* criticised SNCF for its inflated traffic estimates on the TGV Nord and claimed that this over-estimating was deliberately made to justify the investment in the line. Interestingly, the TGV building programme itself (1981-1994) was not blamed, but its financing. Several governments are seen as having neglected to arrange proper financal structures for the investment. On the other hand, there are claims that SNCF pushed TGV technology to the detriment of its traditional intercity network. Moreover, it is alleged that the TGV's manufacturer, GEC-Alsthom possibly overcharged a captive SNCF buyer; and ignored requests by SNCF to look into alternative and cheaper technologies such as "tilting" high-speed trains which run on existing tracks.[41]

Decisions, roles and responsibilities about rail infrastructure are crucial and there has been an ongoing and very heated debate in France between the company, the government, the trade unions and the public. SNCF unions rejected the proposed 1995-2000 "*Contrat de Plan*," arguing that it should include a clear government commitment to clear the debt and take responsibility for infrastructure costs, rather than impose job cuts and continuing budget deficits. The government proposed a SNCF reform in early 1996, withdrew it in late 1996, and then relaunched it in January 1997 after arduous negotiation and bargaining. The newly created public infrastructure company, the *Réseau Ferré de France* (RFF) took on the SNCF debt of 125 billion francs and inherited assets worth 135 billion francs. A deal was struck to freeze SNCF's track fees at 6 billion francs a year until 1999 and RFF received 26 billion francs from the French state in 1997. In exchange for resolving the debt crisis, the government negotiated cost reductions at SNCF including reorganisation and productivity improvements. Some problems remained on how much SNCF would pay to use RFF's track, but overall the French railway network remained intact, the national monopoly preserved and the public service still in place. During these events, the role of SNCF was reconsidered in a climate of general questioning of public sector performance.[42] An important aspect of this was the controversy over the choice of the TGV high-speed technology. The growth of the TGV network, contrary to expectations, was seen as creating a "discontinuous" space and reinforcing rural "desertification."[43] The TGV is more profitable the fewer stops it makes and investment concentrates on profitable segments, which are becoming saturated to the detriment of peripheral zones. As a result, intermodal competition increases on profitable segments, for example Paris-Lyon, between the TGV and the airlines.

These issues strongly coloured the public reaction to the introduction of *Socrate*. The price differentiation policies created by the new system were interpreted as forcing passengers onto the more expensive TGV to recoup the infrastructure costs and compete with air transport. This was to the detriment of the national intercity lines, to which the French public and SNCF employees – the "cheminot" culture – were very attached and keen to protect.[44] Having already built the most profitable lines, SNCF would face further debts if it invested in new TGV lines without French state or European aid. Consequently, there has been a series of decisions and counter-decisions concerning the construction of the *TGV Est* route and the project was dropped (1996) and then re-launched (1998) after complex negotiations involving local, regional, national and European government figures.

More significantly, there is evidence of a rethinking of a global transport strategy, with a "Plan Rail" which is moving away from the strong emphasis on TGV technology or "*Tout TGV*," as well as from "*Tout Autoroute*."[45] This is some achievement since the French are still extremely proud of the TGV – a classical example of "techno-nationalism." A more balanced view is evident in the consideration of "tilting" TGVs, which can use existing tracks, and in decisions to increase budgets for regional networks. The association of rail transport with regional development and national identity are strongly expressed through these "transformations," but in new ways: the irrational and technocratic reverence towards the TGV is questioned and its destructuring effects condemned. It is worth noting that the trade unions had already argued some of these points, for example that SNCF should not use the TGV to compete with the airlines for wealthy business customers on a few profitable segments, but should instead make trains accessible to all and offer a true public transport service, which competes with road transport. Similarly, SNCF demanded a "level playing-field" between rail and road transport.[46]

These changing priorities in French rail transport have been realised to accommodate EU liberalisation objectives such as accounting for infrastructure and operations separately, getting rid of public debt, and recognition by the state of its responsibility in financing infrastructure. In fact national rail monopolies in Europe have appeared to *co-operate* rather than *compete*, and the Paris-London *Eurostar* and the Paris-Brussels-Amsterdam *Thalys,* to mention just two examples, would appear to contradict Brussels' intended liberalism. However, the SNCF deficit was less than 1 billion francs in 1997 and passenger traffic was increasing.[47] One major reason was a pricing revolution which accumulated revenue through lowering prices. This strategy had been abandoned when the primary aim was the highest yield per unit. *Socrate* and the TGV initially resulted in a fall of 15 per cent of passenger traffic between 1994 and 1996. Thereafter revenues increased because traffic increased, pricing was simplified from four to two differentiated pricing levels (thereby making parts of *Socrate* software redundant) and discounts were introduced. These changes mark a return to the conception of the railways as mass public transport, although whether this is a challenge to the rail liberalisation that the EU is seeking, remains to be seen.

Certainly the techniques of yield management correspond to a deregulated transport model in which operators compete on yield per unit. Imposing that model on the railways, however, has proved problematic. The *Cour des Comptes* Report found that the optimisation part of *Socrate* was introduced without a reliable way of analysing passenger data or of measuring the impact of the commercial changes involved. It criticised SNCF for "playing" with its new computer system, paying too much for it and becoming too dependent upon its provider, *American Airlines.*[48] In general, however, it would seem that SNCF, having tried to link a complex pricing strategy to high yields on TGV routes, learnt the lessons of *Socrate's* implementation and went back to basic principles. Instead of deregulation there is the notion that differentiated charging of train operators by rail infrastructure owners, i.e. higher fees for using busy and modernised tracks, will act as a market regulator. It is not clear how this will affect passenger pricing. Using yield management techniques also supports the new logic of separating infrastructures and operations, which leads to accounting for the profitability of each route, thereby transforming routes into individual and potentially competitive products. Karel van Miert, European competition commissioner, articulated the same logic when he said that SNCF, with its "high tech" TGVs and CRS, was in a position to attack other European rail markets.[49]

## IX.

How does the concept of "translation" help us understand the evidence presented so far? Figure 1 shows a series of "translations."

Starting at the organisational level, the reasons SNCF management gave for the purchase of *Sabre* were firstly technical – the need to increase capacity since the

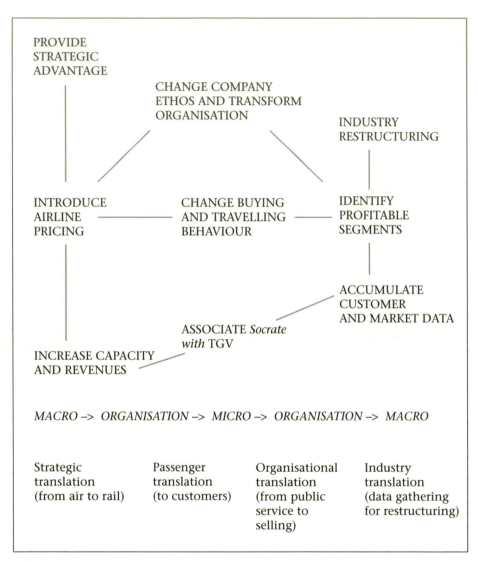

*Figure 1: A series of translations.*

existing system was reaching saturation. *Sabre* was the only technology available at the time that could cope with such large numbers of reservations. However, the belief that this system provided a strategic advantage to *American Airlines* greatly influenced SNCF's top management. In the general business literature, computerised reservation systems, and specifically *Sabre,* were seen as models of how information could provide strategic advantage. In 1991, with 85,000 terminals in travel agencies in 47 countries providing access to fares and schedules for 665 airlines, *Sabre* accounted for about 85 per cent of *American Airlines'* earnings. One crucial element of this advantage was electronic control over global distribution channels; emulating *American Airlines'* competitive positioning through the ownership of a CRS was very attractive to SNCF.[50]

This relates to macro issues, which link socio-economic conditions to organisational analysis and individual and group action. The *Socrate* project team was able to convince SNCF that this type of strategic advantage should be a priority since it could increase revenues on profitable lines, and SNCF was suffering from serious budget deficits. Other broader macro-perspectives which were called upon to justify introducing *Socrate* were how the French rail industry was evolving from a public monopoly to a situation of increased intermodal competition, deregulation of European transport and the introduction of high-speed trans-European networks.

However, the necessary modifications to turn *Sabre* into a French rail CRS and the controversial use of yield management and optimisation techniques exposed the difficulties in translating strategy from air to rail. Differences between American airlines and European rail transport deregulation highlight the social and economic conflicts between competition, co-operation and "complementarity" in intermodal and intramodal transport. The claimed effect of CRS in the restructuring of the American airline market began to be seen as a threat in the context of French railways. The strategic translation from air to rail therefore reflects a certain *political* reading of environmental changes and interprets the technology as an independent agent capable of intervening in this environment.

Returning to the *organisational level* of analysis, new commercial techniques to manage passenger travel and differentiated pricing were made possible by *Socrate* and its yield management software. From an economic and financial perspective, not only does the use of yield management techniques increase revenues, it can also become a management tool for maximising profitability through market segmentation. This reduces cross-subsidisation between profitable and unprofitable lines, and affects equality of access to transport and pricing. The CRS therefore became associated with a contentious effort to change the SNCF company into something more accountable, business-like and marketing-driven.

At the *level of the micro-social interactions* between management, staff, passengers and the computer system, *Socrate* came to symbolise the maximisation of profits, the drive for productivity gains, the reduction of over-capacity and the "streamlining" of unprofitable lines. The technology was seen as representative of a change in the organisational culture and an abandonment of the public service ethos, leading to tensions and conflict.[51] In terms of skills and human capital within the organisation, the transformation of certain jobs introduced different rationalities. For example, a "yield management expert" straddles the lines between marketing, operations and distribution. Sales jobs became standardised and monitored through a complex computer interface encapsulating an intricate pricing knowledge, making it inaccessible to sales counter staff, who became, if not exactly redundant, then merely the conduit of information and decisions from machine to customer. Many resisted their new selling and marketing role, having previously been proud of their knowledge of fares and their public service role, i.e. finding the cheapest route at the best time, and providing advice rather than selling the most profitable product.

At a *micro-social level* for passengers, *Socrate* was associated with a new marketing culture and an unwelcome change in buying and travelling patterns; the basic unit of "francs per kilometre" was replaced by more obscure pricing. This represents another failed "translation" for passengers: technology facilitated demand control and price discrimination, and *Socrate* aimed to make money out of the TGVs to the detriment of traditional and regional routes. Passengers became "clients" who were expected to behave rationally and adapt their choice of route, time of travel and type of train to whatever the system had to offer. They also had to alter their buying behaviour by booking as *early* as possible, thus the burden and responsibility of the commercial transaction was shifted onto the passengers, albeit mediated through the use of technology. Finally, at the *organisational and macro levels* again, CRS are intertwined with organisational, industrial and market changes in terms of infrastructure, operations and planning. At an organisational level, the traditionally *engineering-orientated* SNCF began to give prominence to computer specialists, accountants and marketing people. The marketability of specific routes was supported by information systems and different organisational forms emerged within SNCF and in the wider European rail transport industry. With infrastructure costs and train operations separately accounted for, it became possible to link profit and cost information much more precisely and accurately for each route and each individual train, through the accumulation of customer and market data in CRS.

However, as we have seen, even when supported by high technology, the transformation and restructuring of this market may not be a smooth exercise.

## X.

The above has explored and analysed the troubled introduction of *Socrate* within the context of a social, economic, cultural, political and technical *actor-network*. This removes managerialist and technicist assumptions about success and failure which are usually associated with technology implementation case studies. The analysis used the sociological notion of "translation" of technology to follow how the project succeeded or failed to enrol actors, from one position to another, between micro-, organisational and macro-levels as follows:

– Increase rail reservation capacity.
– Borrow airline pricing.

- Gain strategic advantage.
- Change passengers' buying and travelling behaviour.
- Transform the professional ethos of sales staff.
- Associate *Socrate* to the high-speed train TGV.
- Accumulate customer data.
- Identify profitable market segments.
- Restructure the French Railways organisation and the rail network.
- Exploit global electronic reservation markets.

It shows that the sociology of "translation" is useful as a descriptive language and for detailing relations between actors in socio-technical networks; but it may not be so effective in providing explanations.[52] Instead social explanations are necessary, in this case by pointing to changing social orders as embodied in the notion of public service, the role of the state and the nature of national identity.[53]

Applying airline reservation pricing systems and yield management techniques to SNCF also meant implanting the U.S. air deregulation model to French railways. This was not problem-free although it would now seem that SNCF has re-established its legitimacy as a national public service enterprise, despite the use of a global computer technology with the potential to undermine that concept. Many people argue that pricing policies should not set transport modal priorities.[54] Complex pricing policies have to be supported by computer technology, which in turn enables pricing to be envisaged and managed on a global scale. Whether this resistance to *cultural homogenisation through technology* will persist at SNCF is as yet unclear.

So far as the logic of *yield management software* is concerned, it clearly maximises revenue on profitable lines. This contributes to transport deregulation and to intramodal and intermodal competition, i.e. TGVs competing with normal intercity trains, and trains themselves competing with cars and planes. It has implications for transport planning through the separate accountability of identifiable and marketable transport segments; and it is associated with the split between rail operations and infrastructure. Yield management was important to established U.S. airlines since it enabled them to compete with potential new entrants in a liberalised market. Whatever role yield management plays in Europe, it is clear that the use of CRS and optimisation software cannot be isolated from the debate on European transport deregulation. It is particularly relevant to the conflict between the notion of *public* service in some European countries and that of *universal* service in Anglo-Saxon society.[55] The former regards the state as "above the market," integrating people as citizens, and providing equality of access to all. By contrast, the Anglo-Saxon *universal* service sees the market as king. Whether national transport institutions will be able to transform economic progress into citizens' welfare, remains to be seen, although this level of decision-making disappear, as the boundaries of national rail systems become less meaningful in global markets.

The use of American yield management techniques in France is also a good example of the increased *mobility of knowledge* in the form of information, technologies and management concepts. The discourse on managerial strategy in the international business press of the late 1980s contributed to the appeal of *Sabre*. Its choice shows that the railways wanted to copy the air transport industry. In the words of Metzler (Director of the *Socrate* project) and Lemaître (*Socrate* team member):

> rail must reach the level of its competitors, particularly air companies. The answer to this challenge is information systems, in the form of modern reservation systems (...). International sales must be facilitated through global distribution systems such as the ones found in air companies.[56]

This reflects the strange fascination of rail companies for aerospace, something which is also visible in models, pictures and posters displayed in SNCF offices.

Another important turning point in the air-rail "relationship" in France was the opening of railway stations in the second Paris *Charles de Gaulle* airport terminal and at *Satolas* airport near Lyon in 1994. The *CDG2* rail station benefits both air and rail travel and illustrates the "complementarity" between these two transport modes.[57] Although this seems to contradict the aim of *Socrate* to renew competition between air and rail, it can be argued that *Socrate* and yield management in fact increased competition between SNCF's own trains, particularly between the TGVs and traditional intercity trains. Regardless of the economics of multi-modal and intramodal transport, it now seems clear that high-speed trains are a *new transport mode,* a hybrid which is neither train nor airplane.

Technical systems such as CRS are increasingly transnational. CRS has accompanied the globalisation of air transport as CRS owners set up schemes whereby smaller airlines pay to have their flights appear on the computer screen, use the system and rent the hardware. Moreover global distribution systems (GDS) have become concentrated in a few systems, which dominate distribution channels. GDS clearly play an important role in the battles being fought over world air transport markets and it illustrates the point that the thrust of technology can undermine the nation state. However, it is difficult to predict whether the French and European rail transport network will be affected in the same manner by global computerised distribution systems and what shape it will take. SNCF intended that *Socrate* would give it a similar position of domination in the European rail distribution market as *American Airlines* had gained with *Sabre* amongst international airlines; SNCF would become an organiser, distributor and seller of transport.[58]

CRS constitute a market in themselves. They earn fees from other companies and *Socrate* had the potential to offer services to other railways, providing and charging for reservation access through the SNCF network and selling software licensing arrangements (in partnership with *American Airlines*). *American Airlines* capitalised on their cultural and technological superiority not only to sell *Sabre* to SNCF but also to try and penetrate other markets; although the evidence presented above suggests that they were premature in this endeavour. In organising multimodal freight transport in Europe, the most intractable problems are the determination of each transport segment's profitability, the co-ordination of bookings and the allocation of costs between partners across many countries. Perhaps computerised reservation and yield management expertise will become appropriate in what may only be a transitional period towards liberalised free markets in European freight and passenger transport.

While SNCF wanted to emulate *American Airlines* in the globalisation of European rail transport, they paradoxically revived elements of *techno-nationalism*. SNCF sought to preserve its reputation for technological innovation as a source of national strength, by buying into new concepts such as yield management and computerised distribution networks, and adapting them to rail. Among European transport enterprises, SNCF is the only railway with high expertise in CRS and yield management.[59] In other areas of the tourism industry, hotel chains, cruise lines and car rental companies use yield management technology and the biggest threat to the sector is *online* information systems supporting direct sales run by tour operators, hotels and airlines. Interestingly, *Socrate* is connected to Air France's global distribution system, *Amadeus*, giving it a position of strength in the European combined air/rail CRS market. Moreover *techno-nationalism* is evident in the relationship of *Socrate* to the TGV, a major French technical achievement which turns 19th century trains into 20th century planes. It was natural to want to repeat the success of the TGV by fusing this "train-plane technology" with computer technology. Indeed an objective of dominating European GDS with *Socrate* may have been to help launch French high-speed trains onto the European market. While the TGV reflects the enthusiasm of executives and engineers at SNCF for advanced rail technology and for stopping the decline of rail, it also shows their fascination with parallels between the TGV and planes, a fascination which provided fertile ground for adoption of an airline CRS. The same engineers seemed also to have been captivated with the complex mathematics and statistics of yield management techniques – as Archibugi and Michie remark, both technology-specific and nation-specific factors shape the innovative process.[60]

Technology makes social relations stable. Information technologies and electronic markets are intervening in the management of transport activities. Information is being used as a surrogate for free, contestable and global electronic markets.

And technology is, if not a causal explanation, at least a condition of global market restructuring. What remains unknown is the effect that global electronic travel markets will have on European transport industries. In a political context of conflicting market and non-market principles, will national policymaking be replaced with technology-supported free global markets?

## Notes

1  Steven Flowers, *Software failures, management failures: amazing stories and cautionary tales* (Chichester: J. Wiley and Sons, 1996).

2  Wiebe E. Bijker, Thomas P. Hughes and Trevor Pinch, eds., *The social construction of technological systems: new directions in the sociology and history of technology* (Cambridge, Mass.: MIT-Press, 1987), 11.

3  Madeleine Akrich, "Les objets techniques et leurs utilisateurs," in *Les objets dans l'action* (Paris: Editions de l'Ecole des Hautes Etudes en Sciences Sociales, 1993), 35-57, on 36f., author's translation.

4  Bijker, Hughes and Pinch, eds., *Social construction*, 14.

5  Michel Callon, "Society in the making: the study of technology as a tool for sociological analysis," in Bijker, Hughes and Pinch, eds., *Social construction*, 83-105, at 84.

6  Bijker, Hughes and Pinch, eds., *Social construction*, 14.

7  Michel Callon, "Techno-economic networks and irreversibility," in John Law, ed., *A sociology of monsters: essays on power, technology and domination* (London and New York: Routledge, 1991), 132-164; Bruno Latour, *Science in action: how to follow scientists and engineers through society* (Cambridge, Mass.: Harvard University Press, 1987).

8  In some cases interviews were only given in exchange for a guarantee of anonymity.

9  ("With SNCF everything is possible"); Daniel Naulleau, "Avec Socrate, tout est possible à la SNCF," *Terminal* 61 (Autumn 1993), 13-24.

10  Interview, Directeur Projet Socrate.

11  Herv Bentegeat, "Une autre culture pour la SNCF," *L'Expansion* (19 Sept.-2 Oct. 1991), 72-81.

12  Interview, Responsable Informatique Socrate; see also Laurent Bromberger, "Avec Socrate, le système de réservation de la SNCF, découvrez la nouvelle façon de prendre le train," *La Vie du Rail* (21-27 Jan. 1993), 10-17.

13  Max. D. Hopper, "Rattling Sabre: new ways to compete on information," *Harvard Business Review* 68:3 (1990), 118-125.

14  Interview, Gestionnaire de Projet Socrate.

15  See, with further literature, Natalie Mitev, "More than a failure? The computerised reservation systems at French Railways," *Information Technology and People* 9:4 (1996), 8-19.

16  Interviews, Gestionnaire de Projet Socrate, Manager de la Formation Socrate, Délégués aux Missions Extérieures.

17  Valerie Devillechabrolle, "La grève à la SNCF et la journée d'action CGT: le trafic ferroviaire a été fortement perturbé," *Le Monde* (29 May 1993), 18; Alain Faujas, "Dix-neuf associations de consommateurs mettent fin au dialogue avec la SNCF," *Le Monde* (13 March 1993).

18  Bernard Bouché et al., "Table ronde sur le projet Socrate," *Technologies Idéologies Pratiques* 11:3-4 (1993), 9-28.

19  SNCF, *La commercialisation des voyages SNCF dans les années 1990-2000* (Paris: SNCF, 1992).

20  Interview, Responsable Informatique Socrate.

21  Sylvain Daudel and G. Vialle, *Le yield management: la face encore cachée du marketing des services* (Paris: InterEditions, 1989); Ian Yeoman and Anthony Ingold, eds., *Yield management: strategies for the service industries* (London: Cassell, 1997).

22  Interview, Marketing Manager.

23  Daniel Faïta, "Socrate à l'heure de vérité: un bouleversement de la culture SNCF," *Technologies Idéologies Pratiques* 11:3-4 (1993), 5-8.

24  Interviews, Secrétaire Général, Secrétaire Adjoint, Membre, CGT Cheminots Paris Montparnasse.

25  The date of 1st April 1993 as the launch of *Socrate* was seen as crucial by SNCF management as it coincided with the opening of the new Paris-Lille TGV Nord high-speed connection. SNCF wanted to launch Socrate at the same time at TGV Nord as a publicity exercise. It also wanted to accumulate information about travel patterns on that new line as soon as it was opened, since it was considered a highly strategic line leading to the North of Europe and to the opening of the Channel Tunnel rail link in 1994. Monitoring demand and influencing travelling patterns as soon as the line was open was considered a top priority (Interview, Responsable Informatique Socrate). It was argued by many people afterwards that this strategic imperative caused rushed decisions, which had dramatic consequences. Many SNCF managers agreed that they should have started Socrate on that line only in April 1993, instead of launching it on the whole SNCF intercity network (Interview, Manager Audit de Gestion Socrate).

26  Jean-Pierre Adine and F. Lewino, "SNCF: à la recherche du client perdu. Après les ennuis de Socrate, la grogne et la perte de clientèle, la SNCF veut reconquérir le terrain perdu," *Le Point* 1094 (4 Sept 1993), 54-55.

27  Interview, Département du Personnel.

28  Interviews, Vendeurs Guichet, Inspecteurs Trains, Manager de la Formation Socrate.

29  Robin Foot, "Les automates et la vente de billets: un voyage à la carte?" *Terminal* 28 (Spring 1993), 7-17.

30  Interviews, Secrétaire Générale, Secrétaire Adjoint FNAUT.

31  Interview, Chef d'Equipe de Ventes.

32  Natalie Mitev, "The problematic transfer from American Airlines to French Railways: the role of global computerised reservation systems in the European transport industry," *Failure & Lessons Learned in Information Technology Management* 1 (1997), 259-271.

33  George Williams, *The airline industry and the impact of deregulation* (Aldershot: Avebury Aviation Ashgate, 1994), 49; also Hans-Liudger Dienel and Peter Lyth, eds., *Flying the flag. European commercial air transport since 1945* (Basingstoke: Macmillan, 1998).

34  Kenneth Button and Dennis Swann, "European aviation: the growing pains of a slowly liberalising market," in Kenneth Button and David Pitfield, eds., *Transport deregulation. An international movement* (London: Macmillan, 1991), 93-118, on 104-105.

35  Pat Hanlon, *Global airlines: competition in a transnational industry* (Oxford: Butterworth-Heinemann, 1996); Michel Caniaux, *Rail-route: la clé de l'avenir. Vers une nouvelle politique de transport en Europe* (Paris: L'Harmattan, 1995).

36  Dürr provoked some anxiety in France when he declared that he wanted the German high-speed train, the ICE, to reach Paris; see Christophe Jakubyszyn, "Le train à grande vitesse allemand doit arriver jusqu'à Paris: entretien avec Heinz Dürr, président du directoire de la Deutsche Bahn," *Le Monde* (16 October 1996); Christophe Jakubyszyn, "La coopération SNCF-Deutsche Bahn contredit le libéralisme de Bruxelles," *Le Monde* (30 Nov.-1 Dec. 1997).

37  Ulrich Blum, Haluk Gercek and Jos Veigas, "High-speed railway and the European peripheries: opportunities and challenges," *Transportation Research Part A (Policy & Practice)* 26A (1992), 211-221.

38  European Commission, *Europe 2000+. Cooperation for European territorial development* (Luxembourg: Office for Official Publications of the European Communities, 1994).

39  Christophe Jakubyszyn and Eric Le Boucher, "Louis Gallois souhaite que la SNCF baisse ses prix: entretien avec Louis Gallois, président de la SNCF," *Le Monde* (11 Oct. 1996).

40  Virginie Malingre, "Le rapport Martinand met en cause la politique commerciale de la SNCF," *Le Monde* (2 Mar. 1996).

41  Francois Grosrichard and Christophe Jakubyszyn, "Le rapport de la Cour des comptes critique sévèrement les entreprises publiques SNCF et EDF," *Le Monde* (6-7 Oct. 1996); Christophe Jakubyszyn, "La SNCF penche pour la technologie italienne du train pendulaire," ibid. For the following see various articles of Jakubyszyn in *Le Monde* 1996/97.

42  For instance, the Rapport de la Cour des Comptes (the French national audit office) mentioned above, examined Electricité de France (EDF) as well as SNCF.

43  Jean.-Marc Offner, "Les 'effets structurants' du transport: mythe politique, mystification scientifique," *L'Espace Géographique* 22 (1993), 233-242.

44  See Georges Ribeill, *Les cheminots. Que reste-t-il de la grande famille?* (Paris: Syros, 1993).

45  The emphasis was on building TGV lines and motorways, i.e. "All TGVs" and "All motorways."

46  Jean-Francois Bénard, "SNCF tackles the big issues. SNCF campaigns for road transport to play by the same rules, " *Railway Gazette International* 149:3 (1993), 143-146; Christophe Jakubyszyn, "Les syndicats de la SNCF s'inquiètent des projets de libéralisation de Bruxelles," *Le Monde* (27 Aug. 1996).

47  Christophe Jakubyszyn, "Le déficit de la SNCF a été inférieur à 1 milliard de francs en 1997," *Le Monde* (9 Jan. 1998), also for the following.

48  Grosrichard and Jakubyszyn, "Le rapport de la Cour des comptes."

49  Christophe Jakubyszyn, "Le Réseau Ferré de France veut conduire la SNCF à la sagesse financière," *Le Monde* (26 Feb. 1997).

50  Duncan G. Copeland, "So you want to build the next Sabre system?" *Business Quarterly* (Winter 1991), 56-60; William C. Schulz, "The emergence of the real-time computer reservation systems as a competitive weapon in the US airline industry," *Technovation* 12:2 (1992), 65-74.

51  See also Gilles Dumont, *Innovation organisationelle et résistance au changement. L'introduction du système Socrate à la SNCF* (Paris: Université Panthéon-Assas, Paris II, 1996).

52  Harry M. Collins and Steven Yearley, "Journey into space," in Andrew Pickering, ed., *Science as practice and culture* (Chicago: The University of Chicago Press, 1992), 369-389.

53  See Ezra Suleiman and Guillaume Courty, *L'âge d'or de l'état. Une métamorphose annoncée* (Paris: Editions du Seuil, 1997).

54  E.g. John F. L. Ross, *Linking Europe: transport policies and politics in the European Union* (Westport, Conn.: Praeger Publishers, 1998), 232.

55  Christian Barrère, "Gestion publique et gestion marchande du transport ferroviaire," *Sciences de la Société* 43:2 (1998), 25-46.

56  Jean-Marie Metzler and Andre Lemaitre, Vers un système de distribution ferroviaire inter-
    national avec RESARAIL 2000, *Revue Générale des Chemins de Fer* 109 (Dec. 1990), 21-24;
    author's translation.

57  Jean-Francois Troin, *Rail et aménagement du territoire: des héritages aux nouveaux défis*
    (Aix-en-Provence: Edisud, 1995), 107.

58  Interview, Gestionnaire de Projet *Socrate*.

59  Arthur Andersen, *Yield management in small and medium-sized enterprises in the tourism in-
    dustry* (Luxembourg: Office for Official Publications of the European Communities, 1997).

60  Daniele Archibugi and Jonathan Michie, "Technological globalisation and national sys-
    tems of innovation: an introduction," in ibid., eds., *Technology, globalisation and economic
    performance* (Cambridge: Cambridge University Press, 1997), 1-23.

# "Boardwalks across the Tar"

## Software Engineering and the Problems of Safety and Security

*Donald MacKenzie*

## Where is Khrushchev?

It was only 20 minutes, but it seemed like an eternity. On October 5, 1960, the President of IBM, Thomas J. Watson Jr., and two other business leaders were being shown round the North American Air Defense headquarters at Colorado Springs. They were in the War Room, where officers sat at their desks facing huge plastic display boards depicting Eurasia and North America. Above the map of Eurasia was an alarm level indicator directly connected to the radars and computer system of the missile warning station at Thule, Greenland. One of the visitors later recalled that "we were told that if No. 1 flashed, it meant only routine objects in the air. If two flashed, it meant there were a few more unidentified objects, but nothing suspicious. And so on. If five flashed, it was highly probable that objects in the air were moving toward America. In other words, an attack was likely." As they watched, the numbers started to rise. When they reached "4," senior officers started to run into the room. As "5" flashed, the visitors were hussled out of the War Room into an office. There, they could do nothing but wait. "Our first thoughts were of our families. ... They weren't with us and we couldn't reach them. It was a rather hopeless feeling."[1]

18,000 feet over South Dakota, General Laurence S. Kuter, commander-in-chief of NORAD, the North American Air Defense Command, was returning to Colorado Springs in his C-118. It was his command airplane, and his deputy, Canadian Air Marshal C. Roy Slemon, was able to reach him quickly. "Chief," said Slemon, "this is a hot one. We have a lot of signals on BMEWS," the Ballistic Missile Early Warning System. Recalled Kuter: "I listened ... as BMEWS recorded multiple missile launches from a general area in Siberia, and this was pretty hair raising. ... The indicators were all over the BMEWS scope. This could be a major missile launch against North America from Siberia. ... Roy [Slemon] had the Joint Chiefs on an open telephone line." Kuter listened, his staff sergeant working frantically to keep him in contact with Colorado Springs, as Slemon talked on the telephone hot lines to the duty officers in the war rooms in Washington, D.C., in Ottawa and in Omaha, Nebraska, headquarters of the Strategic Air Command, which had the responsibility of launching nuclear retaliation against the kind of attack that BMEWS was reporting.

"Everything was exceedingly tense for a matter of many minutes, perhaps 20 minutes, beyond the time of impact of what might have been those first missiles."[2]

On the ground at Colorado Springs, the NORAD Battle Staff faced a puzzling conflict of information. Alarm level 5 meant 99.9% certainty that a ballistic missile attack had been launched. If that were true, ellipses should be forming on the War Room's display map of North America, and should start to shrink, indicating the targets of the attack. Yet no ellipses were forming, and the "minutes-to-go" indicator showed nothing. Slemon turned to NORAD's Chief of Intelligence, Harris Hull, and asked him, "Where is Khrushchev?" To which Hull answered "In New York City." Slemon decided that the Soviet Union was unlikely to attack the United States with its leader in New York. It was characteristically human reasoning: it might have been fallible, but it helped reassure Slemon. Hull told him that the intelligence services had no reason to think an attack was imminent. Slemon also knew that BMEWS had been operational for only four days and was still being "run-in."[3]

Later that day, those involved gradually pieced together what had happened. What the radars in Greenland had detected was the moon rising over Norway. Apparently, no-one involved in BMEWS's development had realised that its powerful radars, designed to detect objects up to 3,000 miles distant, would receive echoes from one nearly a quarter of a million miles away. The BMEWS system software, designed to track fast-rising missiles, was thoroughly fooled by the slow-rising, far distant, moon. As radar echoes bounced back again and again, the BMEWS software interpreted them as sightings of multiple objects, not multiple sightings of the same object, and the consequent impression of a massive, continually growing missile attack was reinforced by the reflections from the moon of the radar beam's sidelobes.[4]

The October 1960 nuclear false alarm is indicative of what is potentially one of the most serious problems that are generated by the spread of computers and information technology over the past half century. The economic and technological benefits of computing mean an irresistible impulse to subject more and more systems to computer control. Yet, if those computers and the software that runs on them are subject to error, the obverse of the benefits of this aspect of the wiring of Prometheus is growing risk. Precisely because the wiring of Prometheus is global, the risk is globalised.

I shall begin by sketching the emerging perception (which I have also discussed elsewhere)[5] that the development of large software-control systems was problematic, and potentially the source of disaster. This perception can be traced to problems in the development in the 1950s of the first genuinely large-scale such system, the American SAGE air defence network. It intensified in the 1960s, for example as a result of the problem faced by IBM in developing the operating system for its System/360 series computers, and crystallised with the diagnosis in 1968 of a "software crisis." The paper will then review the attempts subsequent to 1968 to alleviate this crisis, in particular the effort to develop software that could be proven mathematically to conform to its specification. I shall examine how regulators in the key areas of safety-critical and security-critical software have generally "muddled through," with few truly radical departures from traditional procedures for the development and assessment of software, and, as yet, no resulting catastrophe. The paper will end by warning that the absence of catastrophe, to date, should not be taken as indicating that it will not happen as the (software-controlled and global) wiring of Prometheus becomes ever more intensive, ever more complex, and ever more critical to safety and security.

## The Tar Pit

The problems of the development of computer software, especially for large-scale real-time systems, first came into focus in the mid-1950s. Undergoing development then was the first truly large-scale software system, the SAGE (Semi Automatic Ground Environment) air defence network.[6] As early as April 1951, a combination of MIT's pioneering digital computer, Whirlwind, and the Missile Early Warning Radar at Hanscom Air Force Base, Massachusetts, demonstrated the capacity to track an incoming aircraft and to guide an interceptor towards interception. However, scaling up from this early success to a large-scale network proved immensely troublesome. At a time "when there were only about a thousand programmers in the world" the person-years of programming effort needed was "underestimated by six thousand."[7] In consequence, "Street-car conductors, undertakers ... school teachers, curtain cleaners," and many others with only rudimentary backgrounds in mathematics were frantically recruited, given a few weeks training, and set to work on a suite of programs that eventually totalled over a million lines.[8] Robert Everett, who headed the division of the MIT Lincoln Laboratory responsible for the overall system design and testing of SAGE, summed up the experience:

> When we all began to work on SAGE, we believed our own myths about software – that one can do anything with software on a general-purpose computer; that software is easy to write, test, and maintain; that it is easily replicated, doesn't wear out, and is not subject to transient errors. We had a lot to learn.[9]

Even the mighty IBM experienced trauma, especially with the development of the operating system, OS/360, for the more powerful machines in its famous System/360 series. System 360 revolutionised the computing industry in the 1960s by replacing IBM's previous range of different, incompatible computers with a single

*Figure 1: Rancho la Brea tar pits. Detail of drawing by David P. Willoughby from mural by Charles R. Knight, Courtesy George C. Page Museum.*

series of machines whose common architecture made it possible to run a program written for one machine on any other, subject only to the constraints of memory and input-output capability. This ambitious endeavor called for great sophistication in operating systems, the suites of programs that control a computer and its peripheral devices. Like SAGE, OS/360 was to grow to comprise over a million lines of code.[10] At the time of peak effort, over 1,000 people worked on OS/360, and in total IBM spent half a billion dollars (an enormous sum in the 1960s) on System/360 software. That was four times the original budget, and OS/360 was an embarrassing full year late in delivery. It was error-ridden, and though corrections were made in subsequent releases, these modifications themselves introduced new errors: "Each new release of OS/360 contains roughly 1,000 new software errors."[11]

As pressure mounted, leading figures in the OS/360 effort succumbed to stress-related illness. Three IBM insiders write:

> The cost to IBM of the System/360 programming support is, in fact, best reckoned in terms of the toll it took of people: managers who struggled to make and keep commitments to top management and to customers, and the programmers who worked long hours over a period of years, against obstacles of every sort, to deliver working programs of unprecedented complexity. Many in both groups left, victims of a variety of stresses ranging from technological to physical.[12]

Frederick P. Brooks, Jr., manager of OS/360 during its design phase, warned that a "tar pit" (see Figure 1) lay in wait for the developers of large software systems: "No

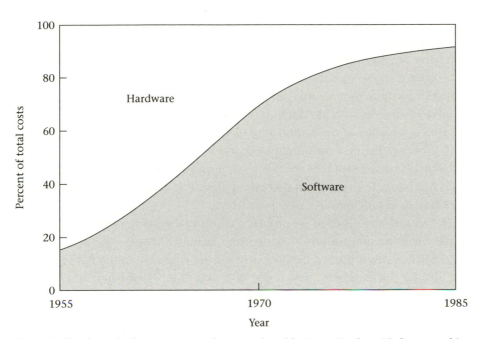

*Figure 2: Hardware/software cost trends, as analysed by Barry Boehm, "Software and its Impact: A Quantitative Assessment,"* Datamation *19 (5) (May 1973), 48-59, on p. 49.*

scene from pre-history is quite so vivid as that of the mortal struggles of great beasts in the tar pits. In the mind's eye one sees dinosaurs, mammoths and saber-toothed tigers struggling against the grip of the tar. The fiercer the struggle, the more entangling the tar, and no beast is so strong or so skillful but that he ultimately sinks. Large-system programming has over the past decade been such a tar pit."[13] For example, when a project began to slip behind schedule, extra personnel would typically be devoted to it. "Like dousing a fire with gasoline, this makes matters worse, much worse." Experienced people had to take time off to train the new ones; work had to be repartioned, with some being lost; more time had to be devoted to system testing.[14]

In the early days of computing, hardware had been expensive and software, relatively, cheap. When programmer Barry Boehm joined General Dynamics in 1955, his boss took him to the computer room and pointed out that while he was being paid $2 an hour, the corporation was paying $600 an hour for the machine.[15] By 1966, however, the cost to IBM of software development for System/360 was roughly equivalent to that of hardware development.[16] By the late 1960s, the U.S. Air Force was beginning to spend more on software than on computer hardware, and it began to be argued that the trend would intensify, a claim summarised in 1973 by Barry Boehm in a famous graph extrapolating the Air Force data (see Figure 2).

Certainly, programming as an occupation had expanded remarkably. There are no reliable figures for the number of programmers in the early 1950s (most people who wrote programs did so as part of jobs with quite different titles), but the estimate, quoted above, of a thousand worldwide is plausible. By 1970, there were a quarter of a million programmers and computer systems analysts in the U.S. alone: an increase of several hundred-fold in less than twenty years.[17] At one level, this was simply a marker of the astonishing success of the digital computer and of its rapid incorporation into the military, economic, and organisational infrastructure of the industrialised world. At another level, however, some computer-industry insiders had begun to suspect that there were pervasive, deep flaws in much of what these legions of programmers were producing.

The breadth and depth of the problems of software development were the focus of a key meeting on "Software Engineering," held in October 1968 at Garmisch-Partenkirchen, a resort town nestling beneath the Zugspitze in the Bavarian Alps. The idea for the conference had come originally from Friedrich L. Bauer of the Technische Hochschule München, a leading German computer scientist. Bauer was not the only one to coin the term software engineering – for example, Douglas Ross of the MIT Servomechanisms Laboratory, started teaching a course on the subject in Spring 1968[18] – but the choice of the term as the conference's title greatly increased the salience of the idea that, in Bauer's words:

> The time has arrived to switch from home-made software to manufactured software, from tinkering to engineering – twelve years after a similar transition has taken place in the computer hardware field. … It is high time to take this step. The use of computers has reached the stage that software production … has become a bottleneck for further expansion.[19]

In 1967, the NATO Science Committee established a Study Group on Computer Science, and it was that Study Group that organised the Garmisch conference. It was an invitation-only meeting, with invitees drawn from universities, computer manufacturers, the emerging "software houses," and a small number of important computer users. British computer scientist, John Buxton, recalled:

> The invitation list was carefully contrived. You know, we invited 50 or 60 people and it was done by the organizing committee specifically trying to pick the leading figures in their country. … They were all the top names.[20]

The keynote speech opening the conference was given by Alan Perlis, Chair of the Department of Computer Science at Carnegie-Mellon University in Pittsburgh. "Our goal this week," Perlis told participants, "is the conversion of mushyware to firmware, to transmute our products from jello to crystals."[21] Buxton recalls the tone being set by frank admissions in an after-dinner talk on the first evening by Robert S. Barton, who had played a leading role in the development of Burroughs's innovative B-5000 computer. Barton told participants, "that we were all guilty, essentially, of concealing the fact that big pieces of software were increasingly disaster areas." The confessional atmosphere – "everybody else just chimed in and said: 'Yes!'"[22] – created an unusual degree of rapport and openness, remembered by those involved for many years afterwards. "We undoubtedly produce software by backward techniques," said Doug McIlroy of the Bell Telephone Laboratories. "We undoubtedly get the short end of the stick in confrontation with hardware people because they are the industrialists and we are the crofters."[23]

To some of those involved, the situation was bad enough to merit being called a "software crisis."[24] One of the most influential of the participants at Garmisch was the Dutch computer scientist Edsger W. Dijkstra, one of the rising stars of computer science. David Gries, himself to become a leading computer scientist, was particularly struck by Dijkstra's habit of "pacing up and down during his discussions, which were punctuated by audible silence."[25] Dijkstra had an emerging reputation both as a theorist and as the designer of elegant systems – the operating system he designed for the computer centre at his university, the Technische Hoogeschool Eindhoven, was celebrated for its simplicity and elegance.[26] To Dijkstra, the Garmisch conference was a liberating experience. The acknowledgment by such an influential group of deep problems in software development justified the rigorous mathematical approach to software development that Dijkstra embraced. For him, even the early autumn weather at Garmisch symbolised the step forward that had been made: "The meeting in Garmisch-Partenkirchen was very exciting. For me it was the end of the Middle Ages. It was very sunny."[27]

## After Garmisch

Garmisch's sunshine was a false dawn. The mathematical approach to software development that Dijkstra desired did not gain anything beyond a foothold in the software industry, the particular cases of safety-critical and security-critical systems aside. Nevertheless, there is some justice to Andrew Friedman's claim that in the years after 1968 the crisis "eased."[28] Individual and corporate experience grew: one's second operating system, or second airline reservation system, was not *quite* as hard a job as one's first. A variety of technical systems to support software development came into widespread use, and standard packaged solutions to a variety of problems, such as database management, became available. But in no sense was the software crisis *solved*. The variety of factors that eased it did not add up to a predictable way of producing reliable software.

There was general agreement at Garmisch that "software engineering" was needed. But what was it? As an analogy, an aspiration, a slogan, few would have disagreed, but it remained an empty box awaiting content. Consensus around the slogan largely evaporated when it came to deciding, more concretely, of *what* software engineering should consist. The report of the Garmisch meeting talked about the phrase "software engineering" being chosen because it was "provocative in implying the need for software manufacture to be based on the types of theoretical foundations and practical disciplines, that are traditional in the established branches of engineering."[29] That formulation, however, immediately indicated the potential for radically different emphases on the relative importance of "practical disciplines" and "theoretical foundations." It would be too simple to portray this as a split between industry and academia – if nothing else, there was too much movement between firms and universities for individuals to be fitted easily into that divide – but tensions lying behind Garmisch's apparent consensus quickly became evident.

At Garmisch, at least one industrial participant already felt that the notion of a "software crisis" was an exaggeration that theorists had constructed in order to justify their work.[30] When, a year after Garmisch, a second NATO Conference on Software Engineering was convened in Rome, divides became much more open. The Rome conference "just never clicked"; it "was a disaster"; it was "bad-tempered," with most participants leaving with "an enormous sensation of disillusionment."[31] The evident tensions and apparent lack of communication led to an extra session being devoted to the relations between theory and practice. Discussion was led by computer scientist Christopher Strachey of Oxford University, who referred openly to the complaints of participants from industry that they felt like "monkeys to be looked at by the theoreticians," while theoreticians felt "they were not being allowed to say anything."[32]

## The Critique of Testing

With software development methods fallible, it was of obvious importance to be able to tell whether the outcome of such methods was a system that worked satisfactorily. Like engineers in other disciplines, the developers of computer systems naturally turned to the testing of such systems to gain knowledge of them. Sample data would be input to systems, their output examined, programming and other errors detected, and such errors corrected: testing, in other words, was a vital part of the process of "debugging." As a part of the practical tool kit of the software developer, testing was, and is, invaluable.

But was it good enough, especially in the cases of systems upon which lives and national security depended? In such cases, one would surely want to have assurance that after the process of testing and debugging *no* errors remained. Yet here an intractable problem emerged. The input space for a program of any complexity is enormous, so big that even the most highly automated testing cannot in practice hope to cover the entirety of that space. If testing could not be exhaustive, could it be said to guarantee that systems were error-free? That question was answered in the negative by Edsger Dijkstra, in a paper to the 1969 Rome Conference: *"Program testing can be used to show the presence of bugs, but never to show their absence!"*[33] Quoted and re-quoted,[34] Dijkstra's maxim was conceded even by those who were sceptical of the mathematisation of computing that Dijkstra was advocating, and who sought to defend a continuing, essential role for program testing. Andrew S. Tanenbaum of the Vrije Universiteit, Amsterdam, wrote in a 1976 paper "In Defense of Program Testing" that "Dijkstra' [sic] remark ... to the effect that testing can only demonstrate the presence of errors and not their absence in [sic] unquestionably true."[35]

## Formal Methods and Program Proof

What Dijkstra, and like-minded "theoreticians," wanted, in place of testing, or at least supplementary to it, was mathematical proof. "[P]roof of program correctness," wrote Dijkstra, immediately after his celebrated remark on the limitations of testing, "should depend only upon the program text."[36] If one had a formal statement – a *specification* – of what a program was intended to do, then one could seek to prove mathematically the program was a correct implementation of its specification. A series of papers in the 1960s from academic computer scientists began to lay the theoretical basis of such an approach.[37] By the early 1970s, formal verification, as the approach became known, had become a hot topic in academic computer science in the United States. Crucially, it attracted the interest of, and very considerable financial support from, national security interests, especially the U.S. National Security Agency. The emergence of time-sharing computer systems in the 1960s had, in the American national security community, raised consciousness that such systems had dangerous security loopholes. If they were operated in "multi-level" mode (that is, with files of different levels of security classification, and users with different levels of security clearance) it was extremely hard to demonstrate that information could not flow to those not cleared to see it. "Tiger team" experiments in circumventing the security controls of existing time-sharing machines nearly always succeeded, and, even if they had failed, they might demonstrate only that the tiger team had not been imaginative enough in its search for security flaws. Those responsible for computer security, especially at the National Security Agency (whose cryptographic work meant that it was the largest employer of mathematics PhDs in the world) were strongly attracted by the idea of a mathematical proof that a computer system was secure even in the face of "all those clever attacks" that its designers "never contemplated."[38]

Support from the National Security Agency, and like-minded organisations, helped move formal verification from academic research to practical possibility. The early program proofs of the 1960s were hand proofs, conducted with the traditional mathematician's tools of pencil and paper. However, nearly all of those involved in formal verification agreed that progress would be limited if proofs could be conducted only manually. A program proof is typically quite unlike the kind of elegant proof that mathematicians value: program proofs are often intricate, tedious, and shallow (that is, typically not involving deep concepts). They were, therefore, seen as natural targets for computerisation, and during the 1970s and 1980s a variety of program verification systems were developed, typically with support from the U.S. Department of Defense, with, at their heart, automated theorem provers: programs for proving mathematical theorems.[39]

Though national security interests provided the main practical support for formal verification, its potential applications to safety-critical systems were clear to those involved. One of the approach's key theoreticians, the British computer scientist Tony Hoare, was sharply aware that "the cost of error in certain types of program may be almost incalculable – a lost spacecraft, a collapsed building, a crashed aeroplane, or a world war." So, for him, "the practice of program proving is not only a theoretical pursuit," but a potential way of solving some of the most important real-world problems of software development.[40] Amongst the "boardwalks across the tar" that Brooks called for,[41] formal verification seemed the most promising.

## Muddling Through: Safety

The case for the formal verification of crucial software was widely circulated and, at one level, well received. In 1986, for example, a working group of the UK Cabinet Office suggested that in the case of "Disaster Level" software, whose failure "could involve more than ten deaths" the "whole of the software must be checked by formal mathematical proof, which is itself checked by a competent mathematician."[42] Yet policy-makers in the field of safety-critical computing did not, in general, proceed to set regulations demanding such proof, and, even when it was demanded, it was typically not in a rigorous and universal way.[43] Radical regulatory reform was attempted, with only very partial success, in essentially only one case: a UK defence procurement standard governing safety-critical software promulgated in 1991.[44] In other cases, in the UK and elsewhere, regulators behaved as political scientists would expect them to: they "muddled through." To describe them as doing so is not to criticise. As political scientist Charles E. Lindblom famously observed in 1959, "incremental adjustments" to policy are far more common than "leaps and bounds," at least in democracies: policy-makers are typically more comfortable "continually building out from the current situation, step-by-step and by small degrees."[45] In civil aviation, for example, software has steadily moved from an adjunct role to full safety criticality, especially with the advent of "fly-by-wire" airliners such as the Airbus A320 and Boeing 777. The international regulatory standards (DO-178 and DO-178B, and their European equivalents) governing such software, have, however, evolved only gradually and require only systematic testing and review, not use of formal proof.[46]

Twin considerations have made muddling through both necessary and possible. First, despite the very considerable investments that have been made in theoretical research and in the automation of proof, program proof remains hard and expensive. Proof is very difficult to apply to large programs (say beyond 5,000 lines in length); despite its automation, proof still requires highly skilled staff of whom the available numbers are limited; and it takes time, a commodity often in short supply in the fast-moving software industry.[47] Second, there have as yet been no large-scale disasters caused by software error. Up to the end of 1992, there were, very roughly, a total of around 1,100 deaths in computer-related accidents worldwide, accidents that took place in a wide variety of national contexts (one of the worst was the 1979 crash of a sight-seeing jumbo jet in Antarctica).[48] In only two of those accidents, however (overdoses from a radiation therapy machine and a failure of the Patriot missile-defence system during the Gulf War) was software error a major cause, and the two incidents involved a total of only 30 deaths. Over 90% of the deaths in computer-related accidents, up to the end of 1992, primarily involved failures in human-computer interaction. These latter deaths should not be seen as the result simply of "human error": in many of the cases, there were clear deficiencies in the technical design of a system's human interface. Nevertheless, these (unlike the deaths resulting from software error) were deaths that the application of program verification could not plausibly have prevented. The pattern of deaths since 1992 remains similar. In particular, there has been a worrying series of fatal accidents involving highly automated airliners. Again, though, these seem to have involved mistakes in human-computer interaction, rather than software error. For example, the single worst such accident, the 1994 crash of a China Airlines Airbus A300-600 at Nagoya Airport in Japan, which killed 249 passengers and 15 crew, occurred because the airliner's pilots were "fighting" the autopilot, trying to force the aircraft to land when the autopilot remained switched on and in a mode in which it was attempting to abandon the landing.[49]

## Muddling Through: Security

Regulators in the sphere of defence security-critical computing have been prepared to make larger steps in policy than those made by their counterparts in safety-critical computing. In 1983, the U.S. Department of Defense issued its Trusted Computer System Evaluation Criteria (a document universally known from the colour of its covers as the Orange Book), which demanded formal proof in its highest category of assurance of security: A1. Britain and other NATO countries later followed suit, with similar demands.[50] Even here, though, the use of formal proof was much more restricted than might at first be thought. First, the form of proof involved was *not* program proof (that is, proof of correspondence between the text of a program and its specification) but proof that the detailed specification for a system correctly implemented a formal model of what "security" was; the correspondence between program and detailed specification was still established by conventional means. Second, very few A1 systems (or systems complying with the corresponding European standards) were ever produced. Even with the restricted meaning of "proof," formal verification remained slow and expensive. By the time A1 systems had been verified, and the regulators had approved them, they were typically outdated technologically: newer systems were available that could *do* more, even though the level of assurance of their security was much more limited. Many defence organisations opted for the newer, more capable systems, leaving the A1 systems occupying a very narrow market niche. The combination of slow and expensive development with a limited market in turn meant that A1 systems were very expensive, and that expense further limited the market for them. Strict export controls, furthermore, were placed on such systems. The result, therefore, was a vicious circle that thoroughly undermined in practice what the defence security regulators had sought to achieve.[51]

Even the crude quantitative measure of failure of safety-critical systems that I discussed in the previous section is impossible to achieve for security-critical systems. There have been a small number of widely-publicised instances of security failures, perhaps the most serious being the 1994 episode when two young British hackers gained control of the computer systems at the United States Air Force's Rome (N.Y.) laboratory, responsible for research and development of command and control systems. Moving from such incidents to quantitative estimates is, however, precarious. The most serious failures of computer security are, almost by definition, those that are not detected, and, therefore, cannot be counted. The only method we have for estimating the magnitude of the problem is experimental. Since 1992, the U.S. Defense Information Systems Agency has conducted a systematic program of efforts to circumvent the security controls on the Department of Defense's sprawling system of over two million computers. 65% of its "attacks" between 1992 and early 1996 succeeded, and only around 4% of the successful attacks were detected by the organisation attacked. On this basis, the Agency estimates that there may have been around 250,000 "real" attacks on defence systems in 1995, but that figure is, at best, only a rough guess, and how many of those attacks succeeded is quite unclear.[52]

The situation is even murkier in the case of the other major area of security concern: financial systems. In advanced industrial countries, money is now predominantly "virtual": for example, notes and coins in circulation now make up only 3% of the UK money supply, and the vast bulk of the transactions involving the remainder are computerised.[53] Although some technical measures to prevent fraud, notably the encryption of transactions, are widespread, as of September 1998 I was able to find only one case of the application of formal proof to a financial services computer system. Incrementalism predominates: financial services firms typically update long-standing "legacy systems," rather than implementing entirely new ones. Institutions' practical concern is normally preventing – by means of relatively low technology – opportunistic fraud by their own employees, rather than deploying high-technology, high-assurance barriers against external attack (the concern which led defence security policy-makers to their embrace of formal methods). There is a gradually growing consciousness of the technological vulnerability of financial services, but, there too, response to this has so far primarily taken the form of continued "muddling through" rather than radical change.[54]

## Conclusion

The tide of computerisation cannot, indeed probably should not, be resisted. Aside from its economic and technological benefits, important environmental benefits, for example, may follow. For the sake of both safety and security, however, a welcome for computerisation's benefits needs to be tempered with an awareness of its risks, an awareness that is calm, sustained and well-thought-out. Neither complacency nor hysteria forms a basis for the making of wise policy. In the mid-1990s, consciousness of computer security threats intensified sharply, particularly as dire prognostications of the U.S.'s vulnerability to "cyberwar" circulated in Washington D.C.[55] Yet "cyberwar" is but part of the problem – it is perfectly conceivable that potential disaster may lie in error and accident rather than in deliberate hostile action – and, in any case, a sense (however heightened) of the existence of a problem has yet to be translated into any systematic, practicable means of solving it.

As we struggle to come to terms with computerisation's risks, perhaps history has a modest role to play. As this paper has shown, problems and dangers resulting from the computerisation of crucial systems date back more than 40 years, and a clear sense of those risks amongst computer scientists is at least three decades old. The record of the attempts to tackle those problems (and, indeed, partial though it is, the record of the incidence of the problems themselves) is a valuable resource for those seeking to formulate policies to deal with these issues. For example, public acknowledgment of problems in computer security in the defence sphere dates from 1967, and, as we have seen, systematic attempts to tackle those problems were in place as early as 1983.[56] The way in which regulators' good intentions were largely defeated by processes outside their control should stand as a warning to those who expect any simple solution to current computer security concerns.

In one crucial respect, however, we must be wary of extrapolating from history. As emphasised above, a key reason that "muddling through" has seemed satisfactory to those concerned is that, as yet, the sky has not fallen. Nuclear false alarms have, so far, all been diagnosed as such before catastrophic, irrevocable action was taken.[57] Although highly automated aircraft have crashed, with many resulting fatalities, clear-cut software error has as yet in no case been the cause. Computerised trading systems played a part in the 1987 stock market crash, and in August 1998 trading conditions apparently not anticipated by computerised risk management models caused massive losses to the "quant funds" which specialise in the application to trading of sophisticated mathematics,[58] losses that culminated in the spectacular near failure in September 1998 of the best-known quant fund, Long-Term Capital Management. Again, the world-wide interactions of computerised financial markets mean that risks are global: the American fund's problems were sparked by Russia's August 1998 default on its debt. Though the fund had almost no investments in Russia, the indirect consequences of the default for Western markets were sufficient to defeat its sophisticated, computerised trading strategies. Again, though, software error in the narrow sense seems to have played no role in the fund's failure, nor in the catastrophic £800 million losses at the venerable UK bank, Baring's, in February 1995, losses incurred by trading in Singapore.[59] However, that catastrophes such as those that have happened have not been *directly* computer-caused, should not lead us to conclude that computer-induced disaster *will* not happen. Computerisation is expanding at a rate that, while perhaps not quite exponential, is certainly not linear, and the qualitative degree of the dependence of safety and security upon this computerisation is also growing. Disaster, alas, may only have been postponed, not averted; globalisation means that the geographical location of its trigger is quite unpredictable, and its consequences may ramify worldwide.

# Notes

1  Anon., "'Missile Attack' Terror Described," *Oakland Tribune* (11 December 1960), 15. I am grateful to Scott Sagan for a copy of this article. The empirical work upon which this paper is founded was supported by a variety of research projects funded by the UK Economic and Social Research Council (A35250006, WA35250006, R000234031, and R00029008), the UK Safety Critical Systems Research Programme (Science and Engineering Research Council grant GR/J58619), and Engineering and Physical Sciences Research Council (GR/L37953). I would like to thank the researchers on these projects, notably Eloína Peláez, Margaret Tierney, Garrel Pottinger, and Claudio Russo, for their invaluable work. This paper draws upon material that has appeared in my book *Mechanizing Proof: Computing, Risk, and Trust* (Cambridge, Mass.: MIT Press, 2001), chapter 2.

2  General Laurence S. Kuter, U.S. Air Force Oral History Interview (Maxwell Air Force Base, Alabama: Albert F. Simpson Historical Research Center, K239.0512-810). Again, I am grateful to Scott Sagan for a copy of this interview.

3  John Hubbell, "You are under Attack!" *Readers Digest* 78 (May 1961), 47-51.

4  Hubbell, "You are Under Attack!" Hubbell's article contains at least one clear error – the return time of a radar echo from the moon is around 2½ seconds, not the 75 seconds quoted by Hubbell – but it remains the best available account of the incident. An archival search kindly conducted for me by Barry Spink of the Air Force Historical Research Agency, Maxwell Air Force Base, Alabama, turned up no definitive analysis. I am grateful to Tony King of GEC Marconi, Edinburgh, and to colleagues of his at GEC, Chelmsford, for helpful technical discussions of Hubbell's account.

5  See Donald MacKenzie, "A Worm in the Bud? Computers, Systems, and the Safety-Case Problem," in Agatha C. Hughes and Thomas P. Hughes, eds., *Systems, Expert, and Computers: The Systems Approach in Management and Engineering, World War II and After* (Cambridge, Mass.: MIT Press, 2001), 161-190.

6  On the history of SAGE, see Paul N. Edwards, *The Closed World: Computers and the Politics of Discourse in Cold War America* (Cambridge Mass.: MIT Press, 1996), chapter 3, and Thomas P. Hughes, *Rescuing Prometheus* (New York: Pantheon, 1998), chapter 2.

7  J. C. R. Licklider, "Underestimates and Overexpectations," in Abram Chayes and Jerome B. Wiesner, eds., *ABM: An Evaluation of the Decision to Deploy an Antiballistic Missile System* (New York: Harper and Row, 1969), 118-129, on 121.

8  Jules I. Schwartz, transcription of talk, in John N. Buxton and Brian Randell, eds., *Software Engineering Techniques: Report on a Conference Sponsored by the NATO Science Committee, Rome, Italy, 27th – 31st October 1969* (Brussels: NATO Science Committee, 1970), 41-43, on 41; Martin Campbell-Kelly and William Aspray, *Computer: A History of the Information Machine* (New York: Basic Books, 1996), 197. For a history of the programming of SAGE, see Claude Baum, *The System Builders: The Story of SDC* (Santa Monica, Calif.: System Development Corporation, 1981).

9  Robert R. Everett, "Editor's note," *Annals of the History of Computing* 5 (1983), 350.

10  Campbell-Kelly and Aspray, *Computer*, 197.

11  Barry Boehm, "Software and its Impact: A Quantitative Assessment," *Datamation* 19:5 (May 1973), 48-59, on 57; Campbell-Kelly and Aspray, *Computer*, 199; Eloína Peláez, *A Gift from Pandora's Box: The Software Crisis* (PhD thesis, University of Edinburgh, 1988).

12  Emerson W. Pugh, Lyle R. Johnson and John H. Palmer, *IBM's 360 and Early 370 Systems* (Cambridge, Mass.: MIT Press, 1991), 344.

13  Frederick P. Brooks, Jr., *The Mythical Man-Month: Essays on Software Engineering* (Reading, Mass.: Addison-Wesley, 1975), 4.

14  Brooks, *Mythical Man-Month*, 20 and 24.

15  Barry Boehm, presentation to Conference on the History of Software Engineering, Schloss Dagstuhl, Germany, 26 August 1996.

16  Peláez, *Pandora's Box*, 101.

17  The figure (254,537) is from the 1970 U.S. Census, as quoted by Philip Kraft, *Programmers and Managers: The Routinization of Computer Programming in the United States* (New York: Springer, 1977), 15.

18  Peláez, *Pandora's Box*, 173.

19  Peláez, *Pandora's Box*, 173.

20  John Buxton, interviewed by Eloína Peláez, as quoted in Peláez, *Pandora's Box*, 174.

21  Naur and Randell, *Software Engineering*, 138.

22  John Buxton, interviewed by Eloína Peláez, as quoted in Peláez, *Pandora's Box*, 175.

23  Naur and Randell, *Software Engineering*, 17.

24  Naur and Randell, *Software Engineering*, 120.

25  David Gries, "Remarks at the Banquet celebrating Edsger W. Dijkstra's 60th Birthday," *Software Engineering Notes* 15:3 (July 1990), 21-24, on 22.

26  It is briefly described in Edsger W. Dijkstra, "The Structure of the 'THE' – Multi-Programming System," *Communications of the ACM* 11 (1968), 341-346.

27  Edsger Dijkstra, interviewed by Eloína Peláez, as quoted in Peláez *Pandora's Box*, 175.

28  Andrew L. Friedman with Dominic S. Cornford, *Computer Systems Development: History, Organization and Implementation* (Chichester, West Sussex: Wiley, 1989), 174.

29  Naur and Randell, *Software Engineering*, 13.

30  Albert Endres (in 1968 at the IBM Programming Center at Böblingen, Germany) in contribution to discussion at Conference on the History of Software Engineering, Schloss Dagstuhl, Germany, 26 August 1996.

31  Douglas Ross, Edsger Dijkstra, Brian Randell, and John Buxton, as interviewed by Eloína Peláez, quoted in Peláez, *Pandora's Box*, 184.

32  Peláez, *Pandora's Box*, 185; Buxton and Randell, *Software Engineering*, 9.

33  Edsger W. Dijkstra, "Structured Programming," in Buxton and Randell, *Software Engineering*, 84-88, on 85, emphasis in original.

34  Because it was published in a more accessible place, a later formulation of the point by Dijkstra is better known: "program testing can be a very effective way to show the presence of bugs, but it is hopelessly inadequate for showing their absence." Edsger W. Dijkstra, "The Humble Programmer," *Communications of the ACM* 15 (1972), 859-866, on 864.

35  Andrew S. Tanenbaum, "In Defense of Program Testing, or, Correctness Proofs Considered Harmful," *ACM SIGPLAN Notices* 11 (May 1976), 64-68, on 64. Tanenbaum is referring to Dijkstra's later, 1972, formulation.

36  Dijkstra, "Structured Programming," 85.

37  J. McCarthy, "Towards a Mathematical Science of Computation," in *Information Processing 1962: Proceedings of IFIP Congress 62*, edited by Cicely M. Popplewell (Amsterdam: North

Holland, 1963), 21-28, on 21-22; see also McCarthy, "A Basis for a Mathematical Theory of Computation, Preliminary Report," in *Proceedings of Western Joint Computer Conference,* 9-11 May 1991, Los Angeles, 225-238; Peter Naur, "Proof of Algorithms by General Snapshots," *BIT* 6 (1966), 310-316; Robert W. Floyd, "Assigning Meanings to Programs," in *Mathematical Aspects of Computer Science: Proceedings of Symposia in Applied Mathematics, Vol. 19* (Providence, Rhode Island: American Mathematical Society, 1967), 19-32; and C. A. R. Hoare, "An Axiomatic Basis for Computer Programming," *Communications of the ACM* 12 (1969), 576-583.

38  R. R. Schell, "Computer Security: the Achilles' Heel of the Electronic Airforce?" *Air University Review* 30 (January- February 1979): 16-33, at 29. For a more detailed discussion, see Donald MacKenzie and Garrel Pottinger, "Mathematics, Technology, and Trust: Formal Verification, Computer Security, and the US Military," *IEEE Annals of the History of Computing* 19:3 (1997), 41-59.

39  The first automated verifier, admittedly a rather limited prototype, is described in James Cornelius King, *A Program Verifier* (PhD thesis, Carnegie-Mellon University, 1969). The history of automated provers is described in Donald MacKenzie, "The Automation of Proof: A Historical and Sociological Exploration," *IEEE Annals of the History of Computing* 17:3 (1995), 7-29.

40  Hoare, "An Axiomatic Basis," 579-580.

41  Brooks, *Mythical Man-Month*, 9.

42  Cabinet Office, Advisory Council for Applied Research and Development, *Software: a Vital Key to UK Competitiveness* (London: HMSO, 1986), 83.

43  For a review of the regulatory status of formal methods in the mid-1990s in Britain, see Donald MacKenzie and Margaret Tierney, "Safety-Critical and Security-Critical Computing in Britain: an Exploration," *Technology Analysis & Strategic Management* 8 (1996), 355-379.

44  Margaret Tierney, "Software Engineering Standards: the Formal Methods Debate in the UK," *Technology Analysis & Strategic Management* 8 (1996), 245-278. As of 1999, only a limited number of development projects (typically parts of systems, not their entirety) have been subject to the full rigours of the standard, Def Stan 00-55.

45  Charles E. Lindblom, "The Science of 'Muddling Through,'" *Public Administration Review* 19 (1959), 79-88, on 81 and 84.

46  In a fly-by-wire aircraft, actions by pilots are inputs to a primary flight computer that issues instructions to other computer systems controlling engine state and the position of control surfaces. On the regulatory situation in civil aviation, see MacKenzie and Tierney, "Safety-Critical and Security-Critical Computing," 359-361.

47  See George Cleland and Donald MacKenzie, "The Industrial Uptake of Formal Methods in Computer Science: An Analysis and a Policy Proposal," *Science and Public Policy* 22 (1995), 369-382.

48  Donald MacKenzie, "Computer-Related Accidental Death: An Empirical Exploration," *Science and Public Policy* 21 (1994), 233-248.

49  Eiichiro Sekigawa and Michael Mecham, "Pilots, A300 Systems Cited in Nagoya Crash," *Aviation Week & Space Technology* (29 July 1996), 36-37.

50  MacKenzie and Pottinger, "Mathematics, Technology, and Trust"; MacKenzie and Tierney, "Safety-Critical and Security-Critical Computing."

51  MacKenzie and Pottinger, "Mathematics, Technology, and Trust."

52  United States General Accounting Office, *Information Security: Computer Attacks at Depart-ment of Defense Pose Increasing Risks* (Washington, D.C.: General Accounting Office, May 1996; GAO/AIMD-96-84).

53  V. Keegan, "Defying Pitfalls of a Cashless Society," *The Guardian* (30 May 1995), 15.

54  For the financial services sector, see MacKenzie and Tierney "Safety-Critical and Secu-rity-Critical Computing," 367-368. The one case of the application of formal proof is to an "electronic purse" developed by National Westminster, a UK bank. The software house Logica constructed, by hand rather than by machine, a proof that the detailed, concrete specification of the "purse" (a smart card) correctly implemented a formal security policy, the key requirement of which is that there be no illegitimate way of adding value to the purse. The proof was described by Susan Stepney, a key figure in its development, in "A Tale of Two Proofs," paper read to the Northern Formal Methods Workshop, Ilkley, York-shire, 14-15 September 1998. Note that the purse is a relatively simple system, and a new one, not part of a "legacy system." There are, very likely, other formal verification projects underway in the financial sector (which typically does not seek publicity for its security measures), but my impression is that these do not, as yet, add up to a substantial body of formally proven systems.

55  See, for example, William B. Scott, "Information Warfare Policies Called Critical to Na-tional Security," *Aviation Week & Space Technology* (28 October 1996), 60-64.

56  MacKenzie and Pottinger, "Mathematics, Technology, and Trust."

57  There have been a variety of false alarms following the one with which I began this paper. See Alan Borning, "Computer System Reliability and Nuclear War," *Communications of the ACM* 30 (1987), 112-131.

58  Salomon Smith Barney Holdings lost $300 million, Merrill Lynch lost $135 million; High Risk Opportunities Fund was placed in liquidation with losses of $850 million; Long-Term Capital Management lost 44% of its value. See Peter Coy and Suzanne Woolley, "Failed Wizards of Wall Street," *Business Week* (21 September 1998), 54-59.

59  See Nick Leeson with Edward Whitely, *Rogue Trader* (London: Warner, 1997). However, in 1994, Askin Capital Management collapsed with $600 million losses, an event reportedly triggered by incorrect inputs to a trading model: Gary Weiss, "When Computer Models Slip on the Runway," *Business Week* (21 September 1998), 59.

# Audio Cassette Culture and Globalisation

*Andre Millard*

Most of the discussion about globalisation occurs within the context of the diffusion of technology and the activities of the multinational business organisations who own the technology. This has certainly been the case with most of the articles in this volume, addressing issues of the development and diffusion of technology. Globalisation is seen as a technological or economic movement. Consequently the cultural aspects of globalisation are normally defined within this context in that the spread of technology by transnational corporations is expected to lead to a diffusion of the cultural elements contained in the hardware or the embodied values of the institutions that sell it.

In this way the McDonald's Corporation is viewed all over the world as an agent of American economic and cultural expansion. The Golden Arches (along with Disney's ubiquitous rodent) are globally recognised and often the focus of anti-American demonstrations, but rarely are these demonstrations just about the food. Opposing the import of Quarter-Pounders or Big Macs is often considered (by the demonstrators) to be opposing issues as complex and as diverse as materialism, ungodliness and genetic engineering.[1]

In the entertainment industry – the first stop in any study of the globalisation of culture – the power and reach of American based corporations, with their advanced technology and marketing resources, means that their products dominate the world market for entertainment. That is a fact. In 1993 some 88 out of the top 100 grossing movies worldwide were American. The first non-American movie in the Top 100 appeared at number 27 on the list. In the early 1990s the domination of American record companies over the popular music of the world was even more complete. Simply put, all the world listened to Michael Jackson and watched his dancing not necessarily because he was the world's first choice for entertainment but because Time Warner and MCA have made him a global presence by relentlessly marketing him worldwide and submerging the competition with his songs and videos. Ten years later all the world will be listening to Britney Spears or the Backstreet Boys. The music changes, the faces change, but the business enterprises remain.

The spread of American culture – music, film, television, visual arts, design, eating habits and sports – has been growing since the end of World War Two. In the

1960s the term "Cultural Imperialism" was coined out of the discourse about the pernicious effects of diffusion of culture. The German director Wim Wenders summed up the dangers of this diffusion succinctly and exactly: "The Americans colonised our subconscious." Beginning with the cultural critic Theodor Adorno, many writers have chronicled the homogenisation of culture that follows in the wake of global capitalism. These studies have argued that a "cultural synchronisation" has occurred because the choices made by communities worldwide have tended to converge.[2] Whether these choices have been made autonomously or have been manipulated by multinationals is a question that no one has answered yet – what is incontestable is that we are now experiencing a measure of shared global culture that is unprecedented in history. Hardly any observers have concluded that this is a good thing; on the contrary the globalisation of culture is sometimes reduced to the shorthand of the "McDonaldisation" of world culture, a term that carries with it all the negative aspects of capitalism, lowest common cultural denominators as well as unhealthy fast food.

What is the role of technology in this synchronisation of culture? Does the stream of cultural influence always run from the high ground to the low, from home-made traditional culture to the expertly diffused mass culture of the industrialised West? Is this a conflict between virtuous, indigenous cultures and crass capitalism that the less developed communities can never win? The argument that "Third World countries should defend the natural innocence of their traditional values against corrupting incursions by Western materialism" is a seductive concept that feeds on our guilty pleasures as ravenous consumers of popular culture.[3]

Judging by the tone of both popular and academic writers on this topic, the most pressing question is also the most easily framed: Is it inevitable that a homogenous Western (meaning American) popular culture will become a global culture? This paper looks at one specific technology involved in the diffusion of popular culture and illustrates how the process works. The final section draws some conclusions that shed light on these important questions.


## I Wish I Was a Cowboy

Sound recording technologies are at the roots of the globalisation of popular culture. Edison's phonograph of 1877 started the international business of recording music. For the first time the organised trade of cultural commodities crossed national and geographic boundaries and brought a new mechanised entertainment to millions. The introduction of Western Electric's synchronised electronic sound system turned the movies into the talkies during the 1920s and should have made Hollywood a regional center for film production, limiting its markets to the English-speaking world. Instead a technological fix (re-recording the sound in another language) made it the center of a global film industry, a lead that it has not relinquished since then.

It is significant that the mechanisation of American entertainment was the starting point of both the globalisation of popular culture and the downfall of elite European "high" culture – the classical music, art and aesthetic that was considered obsolete by the first decades of the 20th century. Cultural exports also put pressure at the bottom of the cultural hierarchy in the submersion (or extinction) of local folk cultures, which were also vulnerable to competition from more sophisticated and more marketable entertainment products.

In the ancient history of pre-internet diffusion, most cultural exports were the result of the physical movement of print media, recordings of music, film and television programming. Direct transmission of these entertainments has also played a part in the diffusion of culture, but only between stations in close proximity, such as between West and East Europe. Global transmission used to depend on the export and import of containers of culture: books, magazines, records, reels of film and video cassettes are mass-produced duplicates that are traded as commodities.

The 12 inch 78 rpm shellac sound recording was a global standard from the 1930s to the 1960s. It could be played anywhere that was furnished with a phonograph or a gramophone: complex machines which were manufactured in the industrial West and marketed all over the world. Explorers took spring-motor models to the two Poles and to the heart of Africa. A short history of one song shows the global reach of sound recording technology. "The Laughing Song" was first recorded by George W. Johnson on a cylinder in 1891. He was a freed slave who made a living singing on street corners in Washington, D.C. At this time recordings were made acoustically on soft wax cylinders and discs. Mr. Johnson allegedly made 40,000 recordings of this particular song – this was before electrochemical mass duplication of recordings. The song made its way to England on exported recordings and was re-recorded by Bert Sheppard, the first European cover of an American hit record. It was such a popular song that it was recorded several more times, including electrical recordings on 78 rpm discs, and these records were exported from the United Kingdom to all parts of the British empire. The record producer later wrote: "In the bazaars of India, I have seen dozens of natives seated on their haunches around a gramophone, rocking with laughter, playing [Bert] Sheppard's laughing record."[4]

The 78 rpm recording and its gramophone player was a technology perfectly suited to strategies of the large, multinational entertainment corporations such as EMI, RCA\Victor\HMV and Warner Brothers – business organisations which I have called The Empires of Sound. Electronic recording was expensive and complex enough to be beyond the capabilities of all but the largest players and constant patented innovation helped to maintain an oligarchy over recording, pressing and marketing discs. In this way the Empires of Sound could keep control of the recording of popular music and divide the world up into marketing territories.[5] If you wanted to compete with them you had to acquire rights to the Western Electric recording technology, build a studio and equip it with recording and mastering equipment, find the trained technicians who were the only people who understood the recording process, establish a pressing plant and devise an international marketing network. Even if you accomplished this task you would probably find that the artist you wanted to record was already signed to an exclusive contract!

The rapid development technology of sound recording between the two World Wars determined that export of popular culture would be one-way traffic, moving from the industrialised West to the rest of the world. Nobody else had the control of this technology and the major record companies dominated the trade in entertainment as completely as the great trading companies of the 17th and 18th century dominated the trade in spices. Their products were irresistible. American jazz and blues, for example, enjoyed global diffusion under this system, and the affluent elites who purchased the records also bought the clothes, learned the dances, walked the walk and talked the talk. That the elites of London, Paris and Sydney should all be enjoying the dance called the Cakewalk at the turn of the century is testament to the power of the Empires of Sound. (That this dance was made up by the slaves to mimic the silly walk of their masters was an irony that nobody realised at the time.)

In the 1920s and 1930s recorded sound in popular music and in film soundtracks were a major source of information about American culture to the rest of the world. These recordings travelled unimaginable distances and had a potent effect on the imagination of those who listened. This is easily understood in the context of Western industrialised nations, but it had an even greater impact on those societies outside the Transatlantic cultural nexus.

In Sierre Leone (in West Africa) the popular singer S. E. Rogie listened to records of Jimmie Rodgers, the "Singing Brakeman" who was a seminal figure in country music in the 1920s. Rodgers was one of the first country artists to be recorded. His participation in the historic 1927 Bristol recording sessions earned him the honor of being one of the pioneers of that genre, even though at that time the label "country music" had yet to be invented! His recordings were phenomenally popular and widely distributed in the United States. From the late 1920s through early 1930s it was hard to avoid his cheery voice and distinctive yodelling coming from record players and radios. One of his contemporaries, Luther Patrick, took issue with this media blitz:

> Oh this country' overrun with Rogers (sic) records
> An' I am a leaving, where I'm goin' I don' know
> But this country's overrun with Rogers records
> I can't stand it any longer, I must go.[6]

Such was the long arm of the RCA Victor Company that Patrick would not have avoided hearing Jimmie Rodgers songs in Africa! Inspired by Rodgers' yodelling S. E. Rogie wrote a song entitled "I Wish I was a Cowboy."[7] Rodgers was no cowboy. He was born in Meridian, Mississippi and rarely ventured west of the river. His yodelling was probably learned from the African-American laborers he worked with on the railroad in Mississippi and Alabama.[8] The significant link between yodelling and the cowboy was probably visual and dated from the 1930s, when "singing cowboy" movies were a staple in film theaters.

The cultural information that S. E. Rogie decoded in Africa was contained in a commercial recording. The 78 rpm shellac record was both the symbol and substance of the Empires of Sound. It took special expertise and equipment to produce and was play only; the user had no way of altering, recording over or any way manipulating the medium. Whatever cultural message was embedded in the grooves could not be changed, it could only be received.

## Tape Recording

There are points in the history of technology when historians step back and perceive a new technology having an immediate and measurable effect on culture. Magnetic tape recording is one such point. The introduction of tape recorders as a substitute for disc recorders in the late 1940s (and the subsequent replacement of the 78 rpm disc with a spool of tape) has been hailed as the most culturally significant change in the history of sound recording. This new machine was simpler, cheaper and much more accessible than the technology maintained by the Empires of Sound. Some historians saw the professional tape recording machines as an important tool for small, independent companies in their efforts to compete with the big studios. Once recording had required costly facilities and complicated disc cutting machines, but now anyone could do it with an inexpensive tape recorder. It has assumed some importance in the emergence of rock'n'roll which occurred shortly after tape recorders were adopted: "The ubiquitous tape recorder freed recording from its dependence on the arduous and complicated studio procedure ... and made the process considerably more flexible, mobile, and inexpensive." The skills of the recorder were no longer required because an amateur could operate one. In short, the technological monopoly of professional sound recording was broken, or so it seemed, and the field of popular music was opened to the smaller independent record companies.[9]

There can be no doubt that independent companies were the originators of this new popular music. As locally run concerns, they recorded for a local audience. They adopted the policy of recording "ethnic" music that was originated by the big companies in the 1920s and abandoned by them during the 1930s. Despite the fact that the studios that made the historic rock'n'roll recordings – Sun in Memphis, Chess in Chicago – remained firmly in the old technology of 78 rpm discs (albeit with older and inferior equipment than that used in the Empires of Sound) the legend arose that tape recorders were the vehicle for this new music. Whatever the source, popular music in the 1950s and 1960s remained on disc, 7 inch 45 rpm vinyl discs, which were still play only. This was the format for the export of rock'n'-roll. From Kingston, Jamaica to Liverpool, England and beyond to Africa and Asia, people discovered this major cultural movement on revolving disc. As the author Salman Rushdie explained, rock'n'roll crossed the world "at high speed" and even in Bombay "this music made by this truck driver from Memphis seemed to be coming from next door."[10]

Despite all the claims made for magnetic tape it did not become the dominant media for sound recording; it was hampered by a host of conflicting standards (the width of the tape, the speed that it moves across the recording heads or the conventions for stereo sound) and there were difficulties in consumers handling lengths of tape. Threading tape through the narrow gate of a recording head and attaching it to the pick-up reel was a task too complicated for many users. These were not minor considerations; consumer difficulties with handling Edison's cylinders had played an important part in their downfall, and wire recorders had succumbed to tape because of the same problem. Reel-to-reel tape was too cumbersome to be the format for pre-recorded music, which is why the revolving disc survived the challenge of magnetic tape and defended its place as the leading medium for recorded sound and its diffusion.

The problems that retarded the spread of tape recorders were solved by adopting measures used by other users of lengths of tape: film cameras and projectors had suffered from the same problems and designers of dictating machines had experience in overcoming the difficulties of loading tape in and out of a machine. The endless loop of plastic tape was one method of solving this problem. Another was the tape cartridge devised for film cameras, in which the film was enclosed in a plastic shell and ran around a single spool. Cartridges had also been developed for use in automobile sound systems, where portability and ease of operation were at a premium. The cassette had tape on two reels instead of one, which made it possible to rewind and fast forward with ease. Several European concerns had employed the tape cassette in small, personal dictating machines. In 1962 the Philips Company developed a cassette in which the tape was half as wide as the standard ¼-inch tape and ran between two reels in a small plastic case. The tape moved at $1^{7}/_{8}$ inches per second, compared with the 3¾ on eight-tracks and home tape recorders. Its very slow speed put more words on the tape but paid the price in limited fidelity.

The Philips compact audio cassette was introduced in 1963. During the first year on the market, only 9,000 units were sold. Philips did not protect its cassette as a proprietary technology but encouraged other companies to license its use. The company required that all users of its compact cassette adhere to its standards, which guaranteed that all cassettes would be compatible. An alliance with several Japanese manufacturers ensured that when the format was introduced for home use in the mid-1960s, there were several cassette players available. The first sold in the United States were made by Panasonic and Norelco, (a subsidiary of Philips). The Norelco Carry-Corder of 1964, the first cassette player on the American market, was powered by flashlight batteries and weighed in at 3 pounds. It could record and play back and came complete with built-in microphone and speaker.

They were quickly joined by other companies as the compact cassette took hold. By 1968 around eighty-five different manufacturers had sold over 2.4 million cassette players worldwide. In that year the cassette business was worth about $150 million.[11] The Philips compact cassette became the standard format for tape recording by the 1970s. Japanese manufacturers such as Sony, Matsushita, and Nakamichi led the way in incorporating the cassette into home stereos. The transistor and the cassette became complementary technologies; the cheap radio/phonograph combination soon came with a cassette player built in, which could record any output of the unit. The Walkman personal stereo was built around the compact cassette. The compact audio cassette was the perfect format for a consumer electronics market moving headlong into portability. The fact that cassette players were usually battery powered was of special importance to consumers in the less developed countries.

Soon the cassette tape began to challenge the disc format in total sales. The number of LPs sold gradually declined while the sales of cassettes increased rapidly. By the beginning of the 1980s, the ratio of vinyl to tape sales was on the order of 6:4 and rapidly approaching parity. Record companies were issuing their product on both disc and cassette, and some were getting uncomfortable with the term "record" to describe their business.[12]

Thomas Edison had hoped that the phonograph would enable the Victorian gentlemen to record the music made in his home, but now with professional quality cassette decks it was possible to turn any home into a recording studio. Dual cassette decks were introduced which gave the user the means to record from recordings and duplicated any tape he or she had made. The compact audio cassette became the worldwide standard in tape recording. It was used nearly everywhere and for every purpose: most prerecorded popular music was released in the cassette format, promotional and demonstration recordings were taped on them, and everyday recording used in the home and car was on the ubiquitous cassette. It had become as interchangeable and widely used as Emile Berliner had predicted for his disc record back in 1888. This was the key to its importance as a diffusor of culture.

## Tape Cassettes and New Music

The ease of taping music on cassette helped break the oligarchy of professional recording maintained by the major record companies. Although the sound quality of
cassette tapes was not as good as microgroove discs, this drawback was far out-
weighed by the low entry costs of establishing a home recording studio around a
cassette recorder and the ease of recording on cassettes. Instead of pressing discs
(which was usually carried out in a separate pressing plant) cassette tapes could be
easily duplicated by either direct dubbing or on high-speed tape duplicating machines.

Audio cassette technology made an immediate impact on two underground
musical movements of the late 1970s. The first was rap and hip-hop, which came
out of African American communities in and around the New York area. The roots
of this music are to be found in funk, disco and Jamaican "toasting," when a DJ
talks over a recording. Although it shared a common format with disco – the 12
inch extended play vinyl disc – it was recorded and distributed on cassette tape.

The first rap single to make any impact on popular music was "Rapper's Delight"
by a group called the Sugar Hill Gang on their own independent Sugar Hill label in
1979. Although dismissed by the major record companies as a fad and "too black"
by radio stations, the Sugar Hill records are now seen as the vanguard of the new
movement, in the same way that "Rock around the Clock" heralded rock'n'roll.[13]
Rap and hip-hop was underground music in that it was produced locally and not
immediately co-opted by the Empires of Sound and marketed on records. Although
the record was the source of the music, the music was not put on records because
that was the preserve of corporations with their recording studios and stamping
presses. The wide availability of double cassette decks made it even easier to re-
record and copy songs. The cassette was the ideal vehicle for a noncommercial
music made by teenagers. Hardly any rappers had access to a recording studio, but
everybody had a boom box, and the universal practice of home taping had diffused
the essential skills of recording. The recordings were made in apartments and in
houses in New York and the Bronx. A rap record company was any organisation
which had a room to record in and a "professional" tape recorder with equalisation
controls and a couple of microphone inputs.

Once the rap song had been recorded on a cheap, transistorised cassette deck,
there still remained the old problem of distributing it. Rap was ignored by black stations, who stayed in the more predictable arena of gospel, soul, and funk. It was also
avoided by all the major record companies. The rappers duplicated tapes on dual cassette recorders and marketed their own songs in the urban ghettos of the Northeast.
Instead of nationwide distribution networks, rap musicians and their friends and
relatives hawked their tapes in the neighborhoods. Despite the lack of radio play and

the primitive marketing system, rap recordings slowly attracted public attention. This form of popular music is now within the domain of the Empires of Sound – major record companies and MTV – but its rise showed that a technology could overcome the control of large business organisations and give local music a chance.

The other underground musical form to flourish on cassette tape was punk, which (after some evolution and commercial dilution) was called new wave or alternative. Punk was also seen as uncommercial by the recording industry and ignored by radio. The cassette tape appealed to punk bands because it was the cheapest sound medium available and it was also the easiest recording technology to manage. One of the guiding principles of the new wave was to remain as low tech as possible – some recordings proudly bore the labels "lo fi" – and the accessible, familiar audio cassette fitted this requirement exactly. With no money to finance a recording session, local home-grown punk bands stayed in the cassette format. The following quotes are extracts from oral histories of the punk movement: "We had cassettes, we never did vinyl. We never had the money." "We sort of did it ourselves. We all made arrangements to record ourselves. Like our first tape was recorded upstairs at the pad, miking it thru Jeff's box." "We never got a recording contract, but we sold our own cassettes and made more money than (a rival band with a recording contract) ever made."[14]

The cassette tape had the most dramatic cultural effects in countries where the Empires of Sound had the strongest hold on sound recording and popular music. In India and some sub-Saharan African nations the lack of economic and technological development meant that there were few independent recording studios to compete with the multinational companies who exported well-produced recordings aimed at a general, affluent audience. In India the mighty EMI company held sway. As one of the largest record companies in the world, EMI could call on its global resources to dominate the market for recorded sound in the sub-continent. While working through the EMI archive in West London, I was constantly distracted by the Indian music being recorded in an adjacent building. These recordings were to be mass produced at one of EMI's pressing plants and exported to India.

Peter Manuel has explained how the transition from vinyl record to cassette broke the monopoly of multinational companies on recorded sound in India, promoting the decentralisation of commercial music and bringing forth an amazing variety of regional music.[15] The first cassette recorders were brought back to India by workers returning from the Middle East. Soon cheap players and recorders were being imported from Asia. With the relaxation of protectionist policies in 1978 the Indian consumer electronics industry boomed, as did the sales of recorded music – $1.2 million in 1980 to over $21 million in 1990. Entrepreneurs opened dubbing shops to duplicate tapes and it was a small step to set up a tape recording studio and enter the business of commercial recording.[16]

The multinational entertainment companies that operated in India sought to homogenise the market as much as possible, issuing their products in English or in Hindi. It made no sense for a giant corporation based in London to cater to the twenty or more languages spoken in India. But decentralising the technology of sound recording and placing into the hands of local entrepreneurs meant that every ethnic or religious group could have their own music on tape. And soon they did. Cassettes brought forth the folk music of Rajasthan, Garwhal, Haryana, Braj, Orissa, Bihar and Himachal Pradesh. The compact cassette enriched the regional music of India by enabling new voices to be heard. It was also the vehicle to spread these sounds through their export to the various communities of expatriate Indians all over the world.

Up to the 1980s the main vehicle for the export of African and Indian music was the audio cassette. African music was rarely commercially recorded on disc for the benefit of the rest of the world. While Africans could listen to European and American popular music, the distinct sounds of the South African townships or West African cities were not available outside the continent. Musical influences came into Africa – notably the discs of Cuban rhumba music which played such an important part in the development of Zairian Soukous music – but rarely out of it.

The cassette provided the means for African music to enrich the jaded popular music of the West in the 1970s. African percussion, always a favorite of record producers, began the movement. This can be heard in the landmark Joni Mitchell album "The Hissing of Summer Lawns," (1975). Peter Gabriel and Paul Simon provided the vanguard for the incorporation of African rhythms into popular music in the 1980s. Paul Simon's album "Graceland" (1986) was the single most important facilitator of diffusion of African music. The liner notes for this album tell us that his interest in African music was aroused when a friend gave him a cassette of "Gumboots: Accordion Jive Hits" in 1984. "Graceland" was such a commercial success that it opened the way for several African artists to enter the mainstream of Western pop, with the help of the multinational record companies.

In the 21st century we now talk of "world music," in which influences and artists from all over the world contribute to commercial music in Europe and the United States. This is now a genre with a recognisable tag that is used in the marketing of recordings. "World Music" or "World Beat" is now a category in record stores, in the accounting of sales, and a recognised and popular topic for academic discourse. Many listeners have praised this form of sonic tourism: "It takes the listener to a place where the world's various cultures meet happily and in the spirit of festival. It is a force for understanding and goodwill in an increasingly dark world."[17]

The success of a select group of musicians from Africa and Asia indicates that the popular culture of the industrialised West has been opened up to some extent. This happened before, but in the 1960s the great crossover hits were novelty songs like

"My Boy Lollipop" or calypso ballads. In the 1990s African and Caribbean artists retained their own musical identities. In 1992 the Algerian singer Cheb Khaled had a European hit with "Didi", a song sung in arabic and the first arabic language song to top the charts in France.[18]

The influence of diffused culture is not always so spectacular; it can be subtle and its influence only emerges over time. Jamaican reggae music was built on the foundations of the R&B records played in the Caribbean in the 1950s. After establishing itself in the immigrant communities in the United Kingdom, it first made its mark in the American and European pop music scene in the late 1970s with the spectacular success of Bob Marley and the Wailers. Although no reggae performer has since achieved the international recognition given to Bob Marley, the beat of reggae infuses much of Western pop. Several genres of Jamaican music – ska and blue beat – have been rediscovered in the general wave of nostalgia that marked popular music in the 1980s and 1990s.[19]

## Into the Digital Future

In the ten years between 1993 and 2003 the technology of recording and diffusion of popular music has undergone a technological transformation that (for once) can be called revolutionary. Digital encoding of music and its global transfer through the internet has transformed the production and consumption of recordings. The attempts of the Empires of Sound to quash this challenge – the most potent threat that they have ever faced – have failed and now they are trying to co-opt rather than destroy this technology and the opportunities it offers to musicians and listeners.

This said it would be unwise to predict the demise of these business organisations and the global mass culture they espouse. While production of recordings has been transformed and the diffusion of music enhanced exponentially, there are no signs that the global marketing networks of the Empires of Sound have been significantly changed. Whatever the changes brought about by the introduction of MP3 and internet technology, the issues raised in this paper remain much the same.

In much of the academic discussion about globalisation, the multinational company has been cast in the role of the villain, a force for centralisation and monopoly. The audio cassette provided the vehicle for indigenous entrepreneurs to compete with multinationals for local markets, but the rules of capitalism still apply. Musicians recording for local companies have been manipulated and exploited; rarely receiving adequate payment for their work (sometimes getting nothing at all), and usually deprived of royalties and credit. The picture of a Third Word recording industry depicted in the film "The Harder They Come" is one of ruthless, callous exploitation. No wonder that the central figure, Ivan O. Martin, is forced into a life of crime. A cursory examination of the careers of the African musicians who have reached a wider audience reveals that they made literally hundreds of cassettes for different unscrupulous producers before they broke out of a vicious cycle of exploitation. They were forced to continually produce songs, to mass produce popular music, to satisfy the demands of local record producers. Their treatment at the hands of the major record companies has been much better.

The activities of the multinationals in the global marketplace for entertainment have not all been directed towards homogeneity. Most of them have undertaken programs to record indigenous music in Third World countries. They built the first record studios in Africa and Latin America, which are now in the hands of governments or local record producers. Most important they control the global marketing system that every aspiring young musician, from Liverpool to Lagos, wants to enter. This has been the vehicle to export the music from underdeveloped countries to the affluent markets in the industrialised West. Despite the ability to flood the internet with original or pirated music, an alternative to this global marketing system has not yet emerged and shows no sign of doing so in the immediate future.

The technology that takes control of the recording industry out of the hands of the giant transnational companies is not without drawbacks for local musicians and record producers. The ease of acquiring the technology to duplicate cassettes led to widespread piracy of recorded-sound products. In the United States the problem was hometaping. In the 1980s the record companies claimed that piracy of its products was costing them billions of dollars of revenue each year.[20] In the 21st century the ease of acquiring copyrighted recordings from the internet and copying them onto compact disc with a home computer has increased the amount of piracy.

In the third world, piracy still plays an important part in the business of sound recording. Cassettes illegally made in Hong Kong, Taiwan and Singapore were estimated to comprise 70-80% of the recorded music sold in Nigeria, Morocco, Zambia, Sierre Leone, Ghana, and Kenya. The results have been catastrophic for local musicians. As Big Fayia (a singer from Sierre Leone) said: "when you make a record they buy only one and start cassetting them. The record has only 3 or 4 songs, but the cassette has five (on each side). Then bands can't make record any more, because they can't sell."[21] In India the pirates have helped maintained sales of vinyl records because this is the preferred format for mastering their duplicates!

Piracy has had the same effect on the film industry in the third world, both in production and exhibition. The advent of mass duplication of VHS video cassettes has severely undermined the indigenous film industry and put of lot of cinemas, in the native countries and emigre communities, out of business.[22] The impact of the ubiquitous cassette format on popular culture has not been linear; it has opened doors for some while closing them for others. How much the rise of audio cassettes has stunted live performance is still being debated, but surely it has played a part in replacing live music with recorded sound, to the detriment of musicians and musicianship.

In the case of tape cassette technology it can be seen that within the globalisation of culture several examples of local culture have not only survived but have flourished. Here is a technology that has created a two way diffusion of culture from industrialised to third world and, most important, vice versa. The ubiquitous tape cassette brought local music into the great global marketplace of popular culture and allowed it to compete with the products of the Empires of Sound. Digital copies of sounds retrieved on the internet have achieved the same result.

In the case of the diffusion of non-recordable 78 and 45 rpm discs we can follow their passage overseas, but with limited evidence it is difficult to determine the cultural impact of these exports. In the age of lightning fast digital transfer there will doubtless be many more opportunities to discover how musical genres evolve within this global interchange. Accessing the web sites and chat rooms of musicians has already become a very effective way of gathering evidence, which places the musician at the center of the analysis rather than the academic observer.

The one thing that is clear from studies of diffused culture is that the people on the receiving end use it for their own ends and find different meanings for it within the context of their own culture. Thus Jimmie Rodgers can be seen as a cowboy in one country and a country singer in another. In his excellent book on the diffusion of American popular culture overseas, Richard Pells points out that these exports were not consumed at face value but were incorporated into broader discussions about other issues that were important to Europeans, such as who, in their own societies, were to be the cultural arbiters of the future. One of his conclusions is that America, and its popular culture, became a scapegoat for some of the "very traits the Europeans disliked in themselves."[23]

The arguments that a global culture will be a completely homogenous one are not supported by the experience of the recorded sound industry. All the world has stopped listening to Michael Jackson, and the songs that have taken his place are much more diverse than they were ten years ago. His influence is still there but it has been modified and to some extent transformed by local culture. It is easy to see the Jackson influence in Indian movies, for example, but the hit songs which emerge from these movies are not slavish clones of the American originals but Indian music that has been slightly changed by the sound of Michael Jackson. The result cannot be interpreted as American culture: it has become Indian culture. In the conclusion to his book on global pop, Timothy Taylor has this optimistic outlook: "Rather than cultural imperialism simply wiping out indigenous musicking and indigenous sounds, new popular musics are being made, old ones altered or maintained … ."[24] In the final analysis even the despised McDonald's that we see all around the globe are not identical copies of the McDonald's of Main Street, USA. As

Vincent says to Jules in Quentin Tarrantino's *Pulp Fiction*: "Its the little differences. A lotta the same shit we got here, they got there, but there they're a little different."[25]

## Notes

1 For example see James L. Watson, "China's Big Mac Attack," in Katie Sjursen, ed., *Globalization* (New York: H. H. Wilson, 2000), 52-65.

2 Simon Frith, *Sound Effects: Youth, Leisure and the Politics of Rock'n'Roll* (New York: Pantheon, 1981), 46; see also Cees J. Hamelink, *Cultural Autonomy in Global Communications* (New York: Longman, 1983).

3 John Sinclair, *Images Incorporated* (London: Croom Helm, 1987), cited in John Tomlinson, *Cultural Imperialism* (Baltimore: Johns Hopkins, 1991), 120.

4 Fred Gaisberg, *The Music Goes Round* (New York: MacMillan, 1942), 45.

5 See Andre J. Millard, *America On Record* (New York: Cambridge University Press, 1995), chapter 8.

6 The Luther Patrick papers, Birmingham Public Library Archives, Folder 230.10.1.2.31.

7 Gary Stewart, *Breakout: Profiles in African Rhythm* (Chicago: University of Chicago Press, 1992), 42.

8 Nicholas Davidoff, *In the Country of Country* (New York: Vantage, 1998), 3-7.

9 Jan H. Rieger, "Crisis in the Youth Music Market," *Popular Music & Society* 4 (1975), 21; Hugh Mooney, "Just Before Rock, Pop Music 1950-1953 Reconsidered," *Popular Music & Society* 3 (1974), 93-94.

10 *New York Times* (18 April 1999), Book Review Section, 8.

11 *Billboard* (6 Nov. 1982), wc3.

12 *Billboard* (3 April 1982), 1.

13 Jefferson Morley, "Introduction," in Lawrence A. Stanley, ed., *Rap: The Lyrics* (New York: Penguin, 1992), xvi. See also Havelock Ellis and Michael A. Gonzales, *Bring the Noise: A Guide to Rap Music and Hip Hop Culture* (New York: Harmony, 1991).

14 Beam Collection, University of Alabama at Birmingham, 1998.

15 Peter Manuel, *Cassette Culture: Popular Music and Technology in North India* (Chicago: University of Chicago Press, 1993).

16 A dubbing or "copy shop" is where you go in India to get your blank tape recorded with your choice of music. To "tape" in India often means to go to one of these shops to get a customised sound recording rather than to actually tape record music, via Madhu Bhodaparti, 1998.

17 Peter Spencer, *World Beat: A Listener's Guide* (Pennington, N.J.: A Cappella Books, 1992), 2-3.

18 Tony Mitchell, *Popular Music and Local Identity* (London: Leicester University Press, 1996), 71-73. Cheb Khaled has been very successful in France and N. Africa but is unable to return to his homeland Algeria because he is in fear of his life; Moslem fundamentalists feel his music is too westernised and corrupting, *New York Times* (30 April 1995).

19 See Dick Hebdige, *Cut'n'Mix: Culture, Identity and Caribbean Music* (London: Routledge, 1994.)

20 *Billboard* (6 November 1982), wc3.

21 Quoted in Stewart, *Breakout*, 60.

22 *Sight and Sound* 8 (1998), 21.

23 Richard Pells, *Not Like Us* (New York: Basic Books, 1997), 162.

24  Timothy D. Taylor, *Global Pop: World Music, World Markets* (London: Routledge, 1997), 197.

25  Quote from *Pulp Fiction* is taken from screenplay published by Miramax (1994), 8.

# Contributors

**W. Bernard Carlson** is Associate Professor of Technology, Culture, and Communication at the University of Virginia. He is lead author and general editor of *Technology in World History*, 7 volumes (Oxford University Press, forthcoming).

**Richard Coopey** lectures in history at the University of Wales, Aberystwyth. He is author of *3i: Fifty Years Investing in Industry* (Oxford University Press, 1996), and *Information Technology Policy: International Perspectives* (Oxford University Press, 2004).

**Rainer Fremdling** is Professor at the University of Groningen and editor of the *European Review of Economic History*. His book publications include: *Technologischer Wandel und internationaler Handel im 18. und 19. Jahrhundert. Die Eisenindustrien in Großbritannien, Belgien, Frankreich und Deutschland* (Berlin, 1986).

**Helge Kragh**, Professor of History of Science and Technology at the University of Aarhus, Denmark, has worked extensively in the history of modern physical science. Within history of technology, he has published on communications technology and chemical industry.

**Stephan H. Lindner** is Lecturer for the History of Technology and Economic History at the Technical University of Munich and currently Visiting Professor for the History of Science at the University of the Federal Armed Forces, Munich. His latest book is *Den Faden verloren. Die westdeutsche und die französische Textilindustrie auf dem Rückzug, 1930/45-1990* (Munich, 2001).

**Peter Lyth** is Research Fellow at the Nottingham University International Business History Institute, England, and editor of the *Journal of Transport History*. His latest book (with Philip Bagwell) is *Transport in Britain: From Canal Lock to Gridlock,* London, 2002.

**Donald MacKenzie** holds a Personal Chair in Sociology at Edinburgh University, where he has taught since 1975. His books include *Inventing Accuracy: A Historical Sociology of Nuclear Missile Guidance* (MIT Press, 1990); *Knowing Machines: Essays on Technical Change* (MIT Press, 1996); *Mechanizing Proof: Computing, Risk, and Trust* (MIT Press, 2001).

**Bruce Mazlish** is Professor of History at MIT. His latest book is *The Uncertain Sciences* (Oxford University Press, 1998).

**Andre Millard** is Professor of History and Director of American Studies at the University of Alabama, Birmingham. He is the author of *America on Record: A History of Recorded Sound* (New York, 1995) and editor of *The Electric Guitar* (Washington, 2004).

**Nathalie Mitev** is a Lecturer at the London School of Economics, Department of Information Systems, England. She has published extensively on the implementation aspects of information technology in small business organisations, the health sector, the construction industry, and in transport.

**Paul Rosen** is a Research Fellow in the Science and Technology Studies Unit, University of York, England, and also works on the UK's National Cycling Strategy. His latest book is *Framing Production: Technology, Culture and Change in the British Bicycle Indus*try (MIT Press, 2002).

**Wolf Schäfer** is Professor of History and Director of the Center for Global History at Stony Brook University. Having published on labor history, history of science and technology, and new global history, he is currently completing a book of theoretical essays on global history.

**Helmuth Trischler** is Director of Research at the Deutsches Museum, Munich, and Professor of History and History of Technology at the University of Munich. His latest books are (with Wilhelm Füßl) *Geschichte des Deutschen Museums: Akteure, Artefakte, Austellungen,* Munich, 2003, and (with Stefan Zeilinger), *Tackling Transport,* London, 2003.

# Index

Names in italics refer to contemporary historians and social scientists.